Codes,
Ciphers,
and Computers

An Introduction to Information Security

Codes, Ciphers, and Computers

An Introduction to Information Security

BRUCE BOSWORTH
St. John's University
New York

HAYDEN BOOK COMPANY, INC.
Rochelle Park, New Jersey

Library of Congress Cataloging in Publication Data

Bosworth, Bruce
  Codes, ciphers, and computers.

  Bibliography: p.
  Includes index.
  1. Cryptography. 2. Computers—Access control—
Passwords. 3. Data protection. I. Title.
Z103.B58   001.54'36   82-3068
ISBN 0-8104-5149-2   AACR2

Printed in the United States of America

2   3   4   5   6   7   8   9   PRINTING

82 83 84 85 86 87 88 89 90   YEAR

Preface

At one time or another, each of us has encountered the idea of codes and ciphers. As children we may have solved puzzles and deciphered secret messages in game books. We may have read Edgar Allan Poe's tale "The Gold Bug," where the unraveling of a secret message provided the directions for the unearthing of a pirate's treasure of gold, diamonds, and rubies. For many, the ideas of cryptography and cryptanalysis have been fascinating areas for study and recreation.

This book presents the fundamentals of secret communication by describing and illustrating the traditional cryptographic techniques designed before the computer age. Modern computer cryptographic techniques, which provide the highest levels of security for data and information, are also explained.

After a brief introduction to communications security, Chapters 2 through 6 describe the traditional methods of codes and ciphers, as well as the cryptanalytical techniques for breaking a code or cipher. Computer hobbyists and computer game players will find numerous programs to carry out the cryptographic process. These programs are in the BASIC language, which is widely used in microcomputers and minicomputer systems. An appendix for BASIC is included for those not familiar with it or for those wishing to gain additional knowledge of the language. Most of the text programs are accompanied by a flowchart to provide documentation, as well as to enable individuals to write programs in other computer languages. Those readers wishing to skip the programs in the earlier chapters can do so without losing the background required for the more recent cryptographic techniques presented in Chapters 7 through 9.

The recent fear of computer crime and the need for privacy of information have resulted in an increased interest in cryptography as a means of concealing and protecting confidential data. Cryptography can provide a high degree of security at a minimum cost. Since traditional cryptographic methods may not provide the degree of security required, new techniques have been developed that, when implemented in a computer system, provide high levels of security. These new techniques use the principles of traditional cryptographic methods and mathematical concepts applied with a computer. Chapter 7 describes one such cryptographic technique, the Data Encryption Standard of the National Bureau of Standards. Another new technique, the public-key cryptosystem, which incorporates a *trapdoor one-way function,* is described and illustrated in Chapter 8. The implementation and management of computer cryptographic systems are discussed in Chapter 9.

Each text chapter concludes with questions for review and solution. Answers to all questions are provided in the back of the book.

This book may be used as an introduction to the BASIC programming language. It can also serve as a supplement to enrich the student's knowledge of programming, computer communications, and computer security.

I am indebted to my colleague, Dr. Andrew Russakoff, for his assistance in helping me "decipher" the current literature on public-key cryptography. Special thanks to Patricia Kane, who typed the draft manuscript with zeal and a high degree of accuracy.

BRUCE BOSWORTH

Contents

Codes,
Ciphers,
and Computers

An Introduction to Information Security

1

An Introduction to Communications Security

A Brief History of Secret Communications

The use of secret communications by means of coded messages has been a practice throughout ancient and modern history. When sending messages to his general, Julius Ceasar used an alphabet cipher to ensure that the message would not be read if it fell into enemy hands. This type of cipher is still used today. Codes and ciphers were used throughout European history to help plot against kings, to plan battles, and to transmit important information.

During the American Revolution, George Washington established a spy system to report on the strength of the British forces and their movements. To send such important information, each spy had a code book that contained code numbers, each number representing a specific word. A written coded message consisting of a series of numbers would be used to transmit the intelligence gathered about the enemy.

In recent wars codes and cipher have been used to ensure that secret information was not transmitted to the enemy. Many books have been written about military intelligence in World War II and the breaking of codes to uncover the enemy's secret plans to attack. Each side tried to break the other side's code. Today, both the United States and the Soviet Union gather information by using spy ships, electronic eavesdropping, spy satellites, and espionage.

The value of code books is illustrated in the case of the Glomar Explorer. This recovery ship was secretly built for the U.S. Central Intelligence Agency (CIA) at a cost of about $130 million for the purpose of recovering a Soviet submarine that sank in the Pacific Ocean in 1968. When the submarine went down, it carried nuclear missiles and advanced electronic gear. In addition, Soviet code books and code machines were also on board. Such books and machines, if recovered, would

1

be of tremendous help to the U.S. National Security Agency. We can be sure that one of the reasons for the costly attempt to recover the submarine was the chance of obtaining these very valuable code books.

In 1977 there was the case of two young men who sold top secret information to the Soviet Union. One of the men had access to a code room that handled messages for the CIA, as well as for the Army, Navy, and Air Force. Such messages, along with actual codes or code books, are invaluable to the Soviets. The newspaper accounts of this story, of course, could not report exactly what was stolen and sold (something only the Soviets know). However, we do know that the culprits received sentences of 40 years in prison.

Secret Communications in Everyday Use

In addition to the use of codes and ciphers by various government security agencies, the military, and the diplomatic corps to transmit secret communications, there are other uses as well. Many business communications transmitted by cable are in a coded form to reduce the expense and size of the message. The next time you are in the supermarket or other food store, examine some of the canned goods. Most packaged items have coded packing dates on them. If you know the specific code system, you can interpret the meaning. In general, each code gives the month, day, and year the item was packed. Figure 1-1 shows such a coded packing date.

When we address mail, it is desirable to use a ZIP code. Such a code represents a specific geographic location. Use of the code helps speed the sorting and processing of mail. It is easier to sort mail based on a ZIP code number than on the location name.

Recently, product code numbers have been affixed to items sold in food stores. The new *Universal Product Code* is designed to speed up the check-out counter in supermarkets. The code bars are "read" by a device

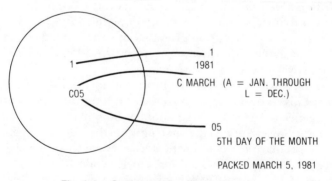

Fig. 1-1. Coded packing date on a can.

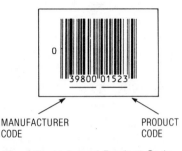

MANUFACTURER   PRODUCT
CODE   CODE

Fig. 1-2. Universal Product Code.

that translates the bars into useful information for the cash register as well as for the computer. Figure 1-2 shows an example of this code. The first set of numbers represents the product manufacturer. The second set of numbers indicates the product type.

The Need for Information Security

In most homes, offices, or businesses, confidential and/or private information is placed under lock and key. Money, valuable documents, jewelry, and so forth can be placed in a locked closet on premises or (for greater protection) in a safe deposit box at a bank. In all of these cases there is a multiple lock safety system; at least two keys for two locks are needed to get to the items. At home, entry must first be made through the front door, requiring a key. Then entry must be made into the locked room or security box, requiring another key. The safe deposit box at the bank is protected in a similar manner, as well as valuables at the office, where the building is locked, the office is locked, and filing cabinets are locked.

In the computer field there is much concern about information security. Although the computer itself can be locked beyond the physical reach and sight of individuals, there may be many "open doors" to the information it contains, some of which is confidential or secret. Today, time-sharing systems permit many users to have access to a single computer with many entry ports. To guard against illegal entry, we can give valid users identification numbers, which serve as keys. If the wrong number is given to the computer via a terminal, the computer will cause the terminal to be disconnected. However, an unauthorized individual with a valid number will be able to enter the system.

Programs can be protected by having passwords serve as keys to gaining access to the programs. Only people who know the correct password can gain access to a program or a data file. However, a password is not a physical object like a metal key. If you lose a key, sooner or later you will realize it. You can then change your lock and get a new key before any harm is done. If someone else obtains your computer password, either because they have looked over your shoulder or rummaged through your garbage or because you inadvertently scribbled it down, you may never know they have it. Thus any confidential information can be stolen without your knowledge.

Computer Communications

Recent developments in the computer field include the concepts of computer-based message systems and electronic mail. Here the computer is used as a clearing house for messages between points, both near and far. The device used to send the message is a time-sharing terminal. The message, properly addressed, is entered into the terminal and transmitted to the computer for storage. Transmission can be between locations within a building, from one in-town location to another, from one city to another (either by direct telephone line or microwave transmission), from one country to another via communications satellite, or from a land installation to a ship via satellite (as used by the U.S. Navy).

Once a message is sent, it is stored in the computer. The recipient queries the computer via his or her terminal to find out if any messages have arrived. If one or more are stored, the copy is outputted onto the terminal. Such computer message centers have their advantages, speed being the most significant. But as pointed out earlier, there may be some security problems if the information in the message(s) is of a confidential nature and for authorized eyes only.

How can we protect our most important and confidential information from prying and spying eyes? The solution is to use codes and ciphers. This book describes many of the traditional methods to encode and encipher messages and information as well as the most recent computer techniques. These methods provide added security for confidential information so that even is someone gains entry to the system and the information it contains, they will not be able to understand it readily.

Terminology

This book will explore both cryptographic methods and computer programming. *Cryptography* concerns the methods used to prepare messages that cannot be readily understood. Some common terms are the following:

Cryptography: From the Greek words *kryptos,* or "hidden," and *graphein,* or "to write," this is the science of secret communication. When doing cryptography, we start out with a *cleartext* or *plaintext* message and convert it into a scrambled message by either a *code* or *cipher.*

Plaintext: The original readable message. A plaintext is converted into a secret message or *cryptogram* by *encrypting* it. Converting the secret message back to plaintext is called *decrypting*.

Code: A method of putting messages into a secret form using words or symbols to represent the message words.

Cipher: A method of putting messages into a secret form using substitute characters for the original letters, or by transposing the characters of the original message.

Cryptogram: A message in code or cipher.

Encrypting: Encoding or enciphering a plaintext to produce a cryptogram.

Decrypting: Decoding or deciphering a cryptogram.

Figure 1-3 outlines the steps to be taken to convert an original message to a secret message, and vice versa.

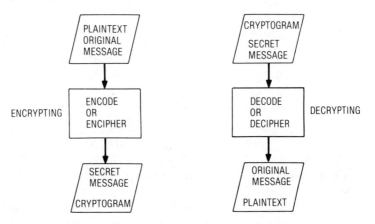

Fig. 1-3. The process of secret communications.

In the next few chapters we will examine the methods of encrypting and decrypting. In addition to seeing how these methods are normally done by hand, we will explore the use of computers to carry out the cryptographic methods. Another area we will explore is *cryptanalysis*. This is the science of deciphering or decoding cryptograms when we have no knowledge of the *key* or methods used to develop them.

Cryptanalysis: Solving or breaking codes and ciphers without a key.

Cryptology: The term that defines both cryptography and cryptanalysis; from the Greek words *kryptos* or "hidden" and *logos* or "word."

Key: The formula or device by which the code or cipher was employed.

In another sense, cryptology includes the areas of *signal security* and *signal intelligence*. Both of these relate to the communication of information and its protection, as well as to the gathering and distribution of information in ways that prevent unauthorized individuals from getting to it.

> *Signal security:* All the methods of protecting one's own signals (message and communications) from interception and reading or utilization.

In part, signal security is achieved by having physically secure facilities and procedures for safeguarding codes, ciphers, keys, and relevant equipment. In addition, the personnel using these codes and ciphers must be proven trustworthy.

> *Signal intelligence:* All the methods used to obtain information and intelligence by intercepting and solving someone else's cryptosignals.

Signal intelligence makes use of cryptanalysis to derive meaning from intercepted messages. Such interceptions are achieved by wiretapping, eavesdropping, theft of materials, and the like.

Cryptography and the Computer

The use of computers to convert messages and information into codes and ciphers is what modern signal security is all about. In this country the U.S. National Security Agency (NSA) has as one of its primary functions the development and breaking of codes and ciphers. To do this job the NSA makes use of all forms of computer equipment. Once you have completed this book, you will appreciate the fact that we have computers to perform cryptographic operations. Converting information into code or cipher and then reversing the operation are very time-consuming when done by hand. The computer reduces this time substantially and decreases the likelihood of error.

In Chapters 2 through 6, I have used many of the traditional encoding and enciphering methods and written computer programs for them in the BASIC language. Each computer program shown is a detailed set of instructions for the computer to follow to perform a specific task. Such programs will be used to illustrate how secret communications can be processed. A program itself is a code. For those not familiar with BASIC, it is explained in the Appendix. You should study this material before endeavoring to understand the programs.

Data Encryption Standard

Over the past few years there has been a growing concern about the protection of data stored within a computer system as well as messages transmitted between systems. Out of this concern came the development of a government-sponsored encryption or enciphering standard. Such a standard would be applied in the areas of electronic fund transfer, the Federal Privacy Act, and electronic security and commodity operations.

In July 1977 the National Bureau of Standards issued a *Data Encryption Standard* (DES). The purpose of the DES is to provide protection against possible theft or unauthorized access to information that is resident in the computer or stored on nonresident media such as magnetic tape or disk.

Many computer equipment manufacturers are expected to market products incorporating the DES in their hardware or software. The cryptographic methods and techniques discussed in subsequent chapters will be useful for a better understanding of both the implications of the DES and the new products resulting from it. The material in Chapter 7 describes the DES in detail.

Recent Computer Cryptographic Developments

Recent developments in computer security and the protection of information have brought forth the idea of a *public-key cryptosystem*. Such a system makes use of mathematics to produce cryptograms that can never be broken by unauthorized persons. The system is described and illustrated in Chapter 8.

Another recent development in computer security using cryptography is the implementation of computer cryptographic systems. A new area of management has evolved dealing with computer cryptographic systems and the problems associated with them. This material is covered in Chapter 9.

Summary

Secret communications in the form of codes and ciphers are found in everyday use. Codes and ciphers are part of the science known as *cryptography*. With computers playing an increasing role in communications, information transmission, and storage, it becomes necessary to secure such communications and information from unauthorized persons. By knowing and understanding the terminology and techniques of cryptography, within the framework of computer programming, the reader can better understand how computer data can be protected.

Questions

1. What was the relationship of the *Pueblo* incident to signal intelligence?
2. Would a traffic signal be a code or cipher system?
3. Cite several examples of code systems common to everyday life.

4. "Virtually all experts concerned with computer communications security agree that data encryption is a must." Comment on this statement.
5. What is the difference between *cryptography* and *cryptanalysis?*
6. Define these terms: *cleartext, code, cipher, cryptogram.*
7. What is *cryptology?*
8. Describe the essential steps in the process of secret communication.
9. Distinguish between *signal security* and *signal intelligence.*

References

"Blind Dates: How to Break the Codes on the Foods You Buy." Albany, New York: New York State Consumer Protection Board, 1977.

Burleson, Clyde W. *The Jennifer Project.* Englewood Cliffs, New Jersey: Prentice-Hall, 1977.

Burton, Anthony. "Sell-Out at the CIA Company Store." *The New York Daily News* (November 13, 1977): 88.

Callimahos, Lambros D. "Cryptology." *The New Encyclopedia Britannica,* 1974.

Calvocoressi, Peter. *Top Secret Ultra.* New York: Pantheon Books, 1981.

Denning, Dorothy E., and Denning, Peter J. "Data Security." *ACM Computing Surveys,* vol. 11, no. 3 (September 1979): 227–250.

Garliński, Józef. *Intercept, The Enigma War.* London: J. M. Dent & Sons, 1979.

Kahn, David. *The Codebreakers.* New York: MacMillan, 1967.

Masterman, John C. *The Double-Cross System.* New York: Avon Books, 1972.

Ranson, Harry H. "Intelligence and Counterintelligence." *The New Encyclopedia Britannica,* 1974.

Secrets & Spies, Pleasantville, New York: The Readers Digest Association, 1964.

Solomon, Richard J. "The Encryption Controversy." *Mini-Micro Systems,* vol. 11, no. 2 (February 1978): 22–26.

Sykes, David J. "Protecting Data by Encryption." *Datamation,* vol. 22, no. 8 (August 1976): 81–85.

Uhlig, Ronald P. "Human Factors in Computer Message Systems." *Datamation,* vol. 23, no. 5 (May 1977): 120–126.

2

Code Systems

Introduction

In general, a code system involves the substitution of code words for plaintext words. For example:

Code word	Meaning—plaintext
ABXYZ	RETREAT
ACWXY	ATTACK
ADVWX	DAWN
⋮	
BCMNO	PLAN
⋮	
XYKLM	BEGIN

To convey a message, we first write it out:

BEGIN   THE   ATTACK   AT   DAWN

Encoding this message, we have

XYKLM   ACWXY   ADVWX

The reader has to place the missing "the" and "at."

Codes can be constructed as either *one-part* or *two-part* code systems. The *one-part* code has both the plaintext words and the code words arranged in alphabetical order, for example:

One-part code	Plaintext
ABAB	A
ABAC	ABORT
ABAD	ACKNOWLEDGE
ABAE	ADVISE
ABAF	AMMUNITION
⋮	⋮
ZYZZ	ZERO

9

A one-part code system is easy to encode and decode. However, for greater security, the *two-part* code is useful. In this system the plaintext words are arranged in alphabetical sequence. The code words are assigned in a nonsystematic or random manner, for example:

Plaintext	Code word
ACKNOWLEDGE	XYZA
AMOUNT	KBCD
BANK	NMPQ
COLLECT	LXMC
DOLLAR	EDFG
FOUR	HLMO
⋮	⋮
THOUSAND	YTOA
⋮	⋮
ZERO	WSMF

The second part of this system requires that the code words be arranged alphabetically with the plaintext next to them. The first part of the code system is used for the encoding of a message, and the second part is used for decoding. Thus the second part of the two-part code looks like this:

Code word	Plaintext
EDFG	DOLLAR
HLMO	FOUR
KBCD	AMOUNT
LXMC	COLLECT
NMPG	BANK
⋮	⋮
WSMF	ZERO
⋮	⋮
YTOA	THOUSAND

Whether a one-part of two-part code system is used, a *code book* must be prepared and distributed to those individuals requiring it. A small book can only list a limited number of words or phrases and can be easily compiled by hand. A large code book can include many more words and phrases. However, if compiled by hand, it may require a long period of time to prepare. If the code book must be replaced, preparing a new one becomes a time-consuming task.

With appropriate computer programs and equipment, the creation of code systems becomes a rather easy task. The computer can be used to organize and alphabetize the words. The assignment of code words to plaintext can be done randomly, and the preparation of two-part code lists can be done without too much wasted time. Because printed output can be generated at rates of up to thousands of lines per minute, the computer can create code books in very short time spans.

Creating a Code Dictionary

The computer program shown in Fig. 2-1 generates three-letter code words. The words generated depend on the number of letters the user specifies as well as how the letters are entered in Line 110. For

```
5 DIM L$(30)
6 REM PROGRAM TO GENERATE 3 LETTER
7 REM CODE WORDS
8 PRINT "HOW MANY LETTERS DO YOU WISH TO USE";
9 INPUT N
10 FOR W=1 TO N
20      READ L$(W)
30 NEXT W
40 RESTORE
45 FOR W=1 TO N
50      READ L$(W)
60      FOR  I=1 TO N
65          IF W=I THEN 90
70          FOR J=1 TO N
75              IF W=J THEN 85
80              IF I=J THEN 85
81              PRINT L$(W);L$(I);L$(J)
85          NEXT J
90      NEXT I
100 NEXT W
110 DATA A,B,C
199 END

RUN

HOW MANY LETTERS DO YOU WISH TO USE ?3
ABC
ACB
BAC
BCA
CAB
CBA
```

Fig. 2-1. Program to generate three-letter code word dictionary.

example, if you need 24 code words, use four letters (four letters in groups of three can generate 24 code words).* Using five letters would give 60 code words in groups of three. A flowchart for this program is shown in Fig. 2-2.

The program uses the three letters A, B, and C entered as data in Line 110. This will provide six different code words:

| ABC | BAC | CAB |
| ACB | BCA | CBA |

* This is based on the *permutations* of n things taken r times, or $_nP_r = n!/(n - r)!$. Thus, $_4P_3 = 4!/(4 - 3)! = (4 \times 3 \times 2 \times 1)/1 = 24$.

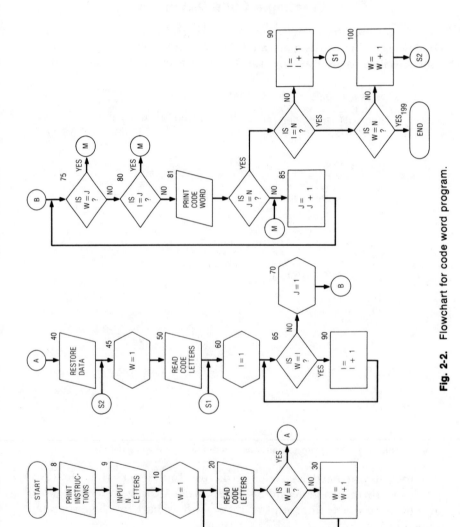

Fig. 2-2. Flowchart for code word program.

When creating code words, letters may be grouped as doubles or triples. For example, the doubles

AB, AC, AD

could be entered as data in the program shown in Fig. 2-1 and would yield these code words:

ABACAD
ABADAC
ACABAD
ACADAB
ADABAC
ADACAB

Duplicate codes should not be created since this would present problems when a message is deciphered. The decipherer may not know which plaintext word is correct. Thus a line of data such as

A, B, B

if used in the program in Fig. 2-1 would generate these code words:

ABB
ABB
BAB
BBA
BAB
BBA

Note that there are only three distinctly different code words. Each word has a duplicate.

A variation of a code word dictionary is a code number dictionary. This dictionary uses code numbers to correspond to plaintext words. For example:

One-part code	Plaintext
1011	A
1012	ABORT
1110	ACKNOWLEDGE
1112	ADVISE
1210	AMMUNITION
⋮	⋮

Such a dictionary can be generated by using the program in Fig. 2-1 and revising the data in Line 110. Rather than using letters as data, we have used the following values: 10, 11, and 12. Figure 2-3 shows this revised program, and it also shows the resulting code numbers as output.

```
5 DIM L$(30)
6 REM PROGRAM TO GENERATE 3 LETTER
7 REM CODE WORDS
8 PRINT "HOW MANY NUMBERS DO YOU WISH TO USE";
9 INPUT N
10 FOR W=1 TO N
20      READ L$(W)
30 NEXT W
40 RESTORE
45 FOR W=1 TO N
50      READ L$(W)
60      FOR  I=1 TO N
65          IF W=I THEN 90
70          FOR J=1 TO N
75              IF W=J THEN 85
80              IF I=J THEN 85
81              PRINT L$(W);L$(I);L$(J)
85          NEXT J
90      NEXT I
100 NEXT W
110 DATA "10","11","12"
199 END

RUN

HOW MANY NUMBERS DO YOU WISH TO USE ?3
101112
101211
111012
111210
121011
121110
```

Fig. 2-3.   Program to generate code number dictionary.

Creating a One-Part Code Dictionary

To generate a complete *one-part code dictionary* requires that the plaintext words be placed into the program as data. The following list of words is utilized.

AGREE	GET	NEED
AMOUNT	GOOD	OKAY
BUY	HURRY	OPPORTUNITY
CANCEL	INCLUDE	PLANS
DELAY	INVEST	RETHINK
DISCOUNT	LIKE	START
EXACT	MONEY	STOP
FINAL	MORE	TRANSMIT

Figure 2-4 shows a program (based on Fig. 2-1) to develop the desired output of code words and plaintext words. The flowchart for this program is given in Fig. 2-5. A program to produce a complete *one-part*

```
5 REM A ONE-PART CODE DICTIONARY OF 24 WORDS
10 DIM L$(30), P$(24)
15 PRINT "HOW MANY LETTERS DO YOU WISH TO USE";
20 INPUT N
25 FOR W=1 TO N
30      READ L$(W)
35 NEXT W
40 FOR X = 1 TO 24
45      READ P$(X)
50 NEXT X
55 PRINT "CODEWORD","PLAINTEXT WORD"
60 LET X=0
65 RESTORE
70 FOR W=1 TO N
75      READ L$(W)
80      FOR  I=1 TO N
85          IF W=I THEN 125
90          FOR J=1 TO N
95              IF W=J THEN 120
100                 IF I=J THEN 120
105                     PRINT L$(W);L$(I);L$(J),
110                     LET X = X+1
115                     PRINT P$(X)
120             NEXT J
125       NEXT I
130 NEXT W
135 DATA A,B,C,D
140 DATA AGREE,AMOUNT,BUY,CANCEL,DELAY,DISCOUNT,EXACT,FINAL
145 DATA GET,GOOD,HURRY,INCLUDE,INVEST,LIKE,MONEY,MORE
150 DATA NEED,OKAY,OPPORTUNITY,PLANS,RETHINK,START,STOP,TRANSMIT
160 END

RUN

HOW MANY LETTERS DO YOU WISH TO USE ?4
CODEWORD        PLAINTEXT WORD
ABC             AGREE
ABD             AMOUNT
ACB             BUY
ACD             CANCEL
ADB             DELAY
ADC             DISCOUNT
BAC             EXACT
BAD             FINAL
BCA             GET
BCD             GOOD
BDA             HURRY
BDC             INCLUDE
CAB             INVEST
CAD             LIKE
CBA             MONEY
CBD             MORE
CDA             NEED
CDB             OKAY
DAB             OPPORTUNITY
DAC             PLANS
DBA             RETHINK
DBC             START
DCA             STOP
DCB             TRANSMIT
```

Fig. 2-4. Program to generate a one-part code word dictionary.

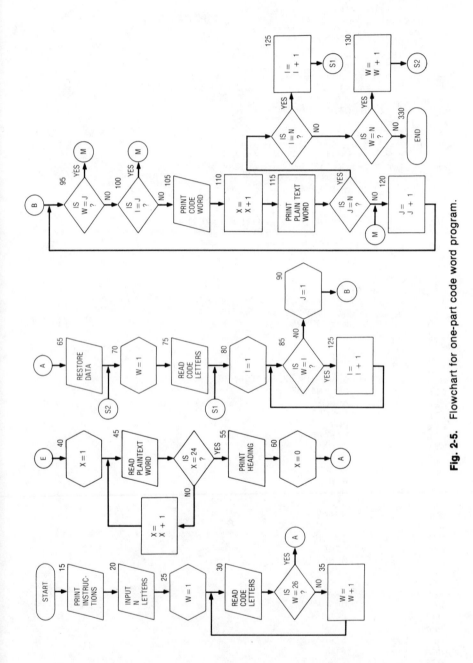

Fig. 2-5.   Flowchart for one-part code word program.

```
5 REM A ONE-PART CODE DICTIONARY OF 24 WORDS
10 DIM L$(30), P$(24)
15 PRINT "HOW MANY NUMBERS DO YOU WISH TO USE";
20 INPUT N
25 FOR W=1 TO N
30      READ L$(W)
35 NEXT W
40 FOR X = 1 TO 24
45      READ P$(X)
50 NEXT X
55 PRINT "CODENUMBER","PLAINTEXT WORD"
60 LET X=0
65 RESTORE
70 FOR W=1 TO N
75      READ L$(W)
80      FOR  I=1 TO N
85          IF W=I THEN 125
90          FOR J=1 TO N
95              IF W=J THEN 120
100                 IF I=J THEN 120
105                     PRINT L$(W);L$(I);L$(J),
110                     LET X = X+1
115                     PRINT P$(X)
120             NEXT J
125         NEXT I
130 NEXT W
135 DATA "10","11","12","13"
140 DATA AGREE,AMOUNT,BUY,CANCEL,DELAY,DISCOUNT,EXACT,FINAL
145 DATA GET,GOOD,HURRY,INCLUDE,INVEST,LIKE,MONEY,MORE
150 DATA NEED,OKAY,OPPORTUNITY,PLANS,RETHINK,START,STOP,TRANSMIT
160 END

RUN

HOW MANY NUMBERS DO YOU WISH TO USE ?4
CODENUMBER      PLAINTEXT WORD
101112          AGREE
101113          AMOUNT
101211          BUY
101213          CANCEL
101311          DELAY
101312          DISCOUNT
111012          EXACT
111013          FINAL
111210          GET
111213          GOOD
111310          HURRY
111312          INCLUDE
121011          INVEST
121013          LIKE
121110          MONEY
121113          MORE
121310          NEED
121311          OKAY
131011          OPPORTUNITY
131012          PLANS
131110          RETHINK
131112          START
131210          STOP
131211          TRANSMIT
```

Fig. 2-6. Program to generate a one-part code number dictionary.

number code dictionary is shown in Fig. 2-6. The same list of words is used in both programs. The output indicates each code word and its corresponding code number.

Security requirements may call for continual change in the code word dictionary. As long as both sender and receiver have the same program to generate a one-part code word dictionary, changes can be easily made. Only the starting letters in Line 135 of Fig. 2-4 need to be revised. Both parties can have prearranged revisions set to a specific calendar date, for example:

Date	Change Line 135 DATA to
March 5	D, C, B, A
May 10	X, Y, Z, A
June 30	K, L, M, N
July 4	M, B, S, R
September 24	I, S, A, B
December 1	R, A, E, L

Another approach would be to change the dictionary every time a message is transmitted. To make this work, the receiver must know the *key* used to generate the code word dictionary. In our example, the key is Line 135 in the program.

If the sender knows the key, how can this information be transmitted to the receiver? Again, some preplanned arrangements must be agreed upon. For example, the sender has decided that in any coded message he will plant the key as the fourth and fifth code words. The receiver, knowing this, will look for the key data characters in the fourth and fifth code words.

Assume the message to be sent is

FINAL   PLANS   OKAY.   INVEST   MORE   MONEY

Both sender and receiver have the program in Fig. 2-4. The sender wants to use Line 135 DATA A, B, C, D. He then creates a dictionary as shown in the figure. When encoding his message, the key must be incorporated in the prearranged manner. The coded message sent would be

BAD   DAC   CDB   <u>ABC</u>   <u>D</u>CA   CAB   CBD   CBA
key

The receiver would examine the coded message. Finding the key in the fourth and fifth code words, he would enter the letters A, B, C, D into his program to generate the required code word dictionary.

This method could be applied to senders and receivers using a code number dictionary as well.

CAD	AGREE	ABC	HURRY
CAB	AMOUNT	ABD	INCLUDE
CDA	BUY	ACB	FINAL
CDB	CANCEL	ACD	EXACT
CBA	DELAY	ADB	GOOD
CBD	DISCOUNT	ADC	GET
ACD	EXACT	BAC	RETHINK
ACB	FINAL	BAD	START
ADC	GET	BCA	OPPORTUNITY
ADB	GOOD	BCD	PLANS
ABC	HURRY	BDA	TRANSMIT
ABD	INCLUDE	BDC	STOP
DCA	INVEST	CAB	AMOUNT
DCB	LIKE	CAD	AGREE
DAC	MONEY	CBA	DELAY
DAB	MORE	CBD	DISCOUNT
DBC	NEED	CDA	BUY
DBA	OKAY	CDB	CANCEL
BCA	OPPORTUNITY	DAB	MORE
BCD	PLANS	DAC	MONEY
BAC	RETHINK	DBA	OKAY
BAD	START	DBC	NEED
BDC	STOP	DCA	INVEST
BDA	TRANSMIT	DCB	LIKE
(a)		(b)	

Fig. 2-7. **(a)** First part of a two-part code dictionary, **(b)** Second part of a two-part code dictionary.

Creating a Two-Part Code Dictionary

In general, a *two-part code word dictionary* has the code words in a nonsystematic sequence. The program in Fig. 2-4 generated a one-part code word dictionary with Line 135 DATA A, B, C, D in alphabetic sequence. By revising this sequence to C, A, D, B, for example, the first part of a two-part code word dictionary can be generated, as shown in Fig. 2-7a. You will note that the code words are no longer in alphabetic sequence, although the plaintext words are. To complete the two-part code word dictionary, the second part requires that the first part code words be alphabetized. This alphabetic sequence is shown in Fig. 2-7b.

Randomized Code Systems

The one-part codes shown here follow a systematic order. Code words and code numbers are developed sequentially. The code words are created in an alphabetic sequence. The code numbers are also developed in sequence.

What is desired is the assignment of a code word to a plaintext word in a nonsystematic or random manner as shown earlier in the two-part code system. A computer program can be created to select letters and

```
5 RANDOMIZE
10 DIM A$(26),L$(30)
20 REM PROGRAM TO GENERATE CODE
30 REM WORDS RANDOMLY
40 PRINT "HOW MANY LETTERS DO YOU WISH TO USE";
50 INPUT N
60 FOR W =1 TO 26
70      READ A$(W)
80 NEXT W
90 DATA A,B,C,D,E,F,G,H,I,J,K,L,M
100 DATA N,O,P,Q,R,S,T,U,V,W,X,Y,Z
110 PRINT "RANDOM CODE LETTERS ARE:"
120 FOR W = 1 TO N
130      LET R(W)= INT(26*RND(B)+1)
140      PRINT A$(R(W));" ";
150      LET A$(W)=A$(R(W))
160      LET L$(W)=A$(W)
170 NEXT W
180 PRINT
190 PRINT "ARE ALL THE LETTERS DIFFERENT(YES OR NO)";
200 INPUT Y$
210 IF Y$="NO" THEN 120
220 PRINT "CODE WORDS ARE:"
230 FOR W=1 TO N
240      FOR I=1 TO N
250      IF W=I THEN 310
260          FOR J=1 TO N
270              IF W=J THEN 300
280              IF I=J THEN 300
290                  PRINT L$(W);L$(I);L$(J)
300              NEXT J
310      NEXT I
320 NEXT W
330 END

RUN

HOW MANY LETTERS DO YOU WISH TO USE ?3
RANDOM CODE LETTERS ARE:
L T H
ARE ALL THE LETTERS DIFFERENT(YES OR NO) ?YES
CODE WORDS ARE:
LTH
LHT
TLH
THL
HLT
HTL
```

Fig. 2-8.   Program to generate code words randomly.

develop code words that are paired with plaintext words randomly. Such a program to create randomly generated code words is shown in Fig. 2-8 with a flowchart in Fig. 2-9. A complete program to develop a random code word dictionary is shown in Fig. 2-10.

In randomly selecting letters, the last two programs both utilize the statement

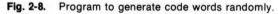

LET R(W)   =   INT(26*RND(B)+1)

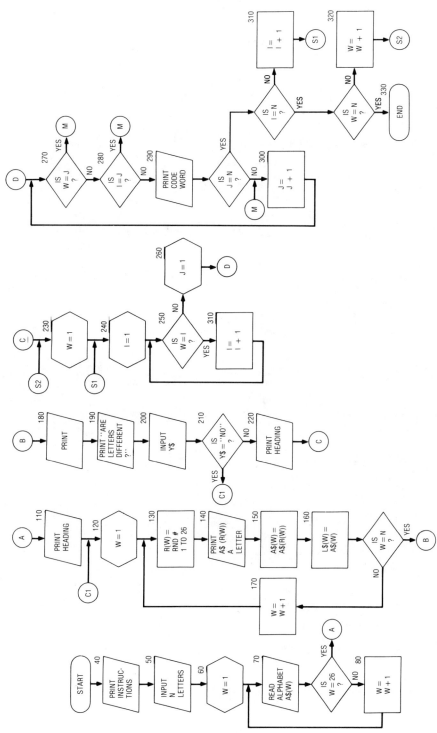

Fig. 2-9. Flowchart for random code word program.

```
10 RANDOMIZE
20 DIM A$(26),L$(30)
30 REM PROGRAM TO GENERATE
40 REM A RANDOM CODEWORD DICTIONARY
50 PRINT "HOW MANY LETTERS DO YOU WISH TO USE";
60 INPUT N
70 FOR W =1 TO 26
80     READ A$(W)
90 NEXT W
100 DATA A,B,C,D,E,F,G,H,I,J,K,L,M
110 DATA N,O,P,Q,R,S,T,U,V,W,X,Y,Z
120 PRINT "RANDOM CODE LETTERS ARE:"
130 FOR W = 1 TO N
140     LET R(W)= INT(26*RND(B)+1)
150     PRINT A$(R(W));" ";
160     LET A$(W)=A$(R(W))
170     LET L$(W)=A$(W)
180 NEXT W
190 PRINT
200 PRINT "ARE ALL THE LETTERS DIFFERENT(YES OR NO)";
210 INPUT Y$
220 IF Y$="NO" THEN 130
230 PRINT "CODEWORD","PLAINTEXT WORD"
240 FOR W=1 TO N
250     FOR I=1 TO N
260     IF W=I THEN 330
270         FOR J=1 TO N
280             IF W=J THEN 320
290             IF I=J THEN 320
300                 READ P$
310                 PRINT L$(W);L$(I);L$(J),P$
320         NEXT J
330     NEXT I
340 NEXT W
350 DATA FREEDOM,LAND,LET
360 DATA RING,THE,THROUGHOUT
370 END

RUN

HOW MANY LETTERS DO YOU WISH TO USE ?3
RANDOM CODE LETTERS ARE:
I B I
ARE ALL THE LETTERS DIFFERENT(YES OR NO) ?NO
J D N
ARE ALL THE LETTERS DIFFERENT(YES OR NO) ?YES
CODEWORD        PLAINTEXT WORD
JDN             FREEDOM
JND             LAND
DJN             LET
DNJ             RING
NJD             THE
NDJ             THROUGHOUT
```

Fig. 2-10. Program to generate a random code word dictionary.

to generate a random number from 1 to 26, inclusive. Numbers generated by computer using this type of random number function are often called *pseudorandom numbers* to indicate that the source is a computer implemented method and not a table of random numbers.

```
10 REM PROGRAM TO CREATE A RANDOM
20 REM CODENUMBER DICTIONARY
30 DIM W$(10)
40 PRINT "CODENUMBER","PLAINTEXT WORD"
50 FOR I= 1 TO 6
60     READ W$(I)
70     PRINT INT(10000*RND(X)),W$(I)
80 NEXT I
90 DATA AMOUNT,BANK,COLLECT
100 DATA DEPOSIT,VERIFY, WAIT
110 END

RUN

CODENUMBER      PLAINTEXT WORD
  4995            AMOUNT
  5278            BANK
  6704            COLLECT
  2727            DEPOSIT
  6019            VERIFY
  1571            WAIT
```

Fig. 2-11. Program to generate a random code number dictionary.

Code numbers can also be computer-generated in a random manner, and a random code number dictionary is thus created. Figure 2-11 shows the generation of four-digit random code numbers ranging from 0 to 9999. The program also creates a random code number dictionary. A flowchart for this program is shown in Fig. 2-12.

One drawback when using the program in Fig. 2-11 is that there is no guarantee a duplicate random code number will not be assigned to a plaintext word. This might occur if a very large dictionary is to be generated. Question 12 at the end of this chapter suggests one approach to ensure nonduplication of code numbers.

A major advantage of randomly generated code dictionaries is that the selection of key letters or numbers is a nonsubjective computer operation. Thus the computer would not use its initials or month, day, and year of birth as keys. Such keys are typically used by people and result in less secure code systems. If an unauthorized person wished to break your code, a logical guess for your key is your initials, birthdate, anniversary, and so forth. Using computer-generated random dictionaries makes breaking the code a very difficult task and thus provides greater security.

Encoding and Decoding by Computer

The previous discussion shows how messages can be encoded by using a code dictionary. To decode a message, a code dictionary must be physically present to reverse the process.

Since computers have sufficient internal storage capability with off-line storage available in various forms (magnetic tape, disks, and so on),

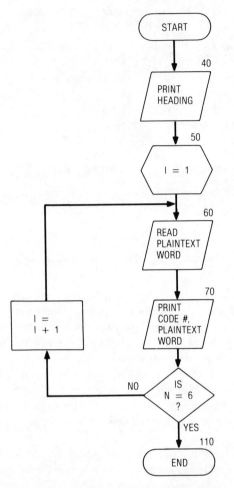

Fig. 2-12. Flowchart for random code number dictionary program.

the dictionaries can be placed in nonbook form. The actual code diction-ary does not have to be seen by the person wishing to transmit a message.

Consider a situation where confidential information must be stored. Since others may have easy access to the system, it may be useful to encode the confidential information. Using a program previously devel-oped, the user types the plaintext information into a computer terminal. The message is then encoded and stored for further use by authorized individuals.

Using the computer as a message center for *electronic mail,* a code system can provide security for confidential information transmitted or stored. When this information is retrieved by the authorized recipient, it can be decoded by using a decoding program.

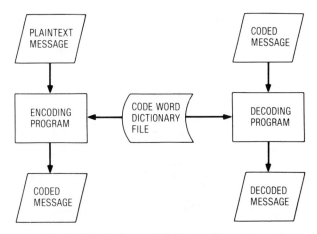

Fig. 2-13. Code word dictionary file system.

```
5 REM CREATING A CODEBOOK FILE
10 DIM L$(30), P$(24)
15 PRINT "HOW MANY LETTERS DO YOU WISH TO USE";
20 INPUT N
25 FOR W=1 TO N
30     READ L$(W)
35 NEXT W
40 FOR X = 1 TO 24
45     READ P$(X)
50 NEXT X
60 LET X=0
65 RESTORE
70 FOR W=1 TO N
75     READ L$(W)
80     FOR  I=1 TO N
85         IF W=I THEN 125
90         FOR J=1 TO N
95             IF W=J THEN 120
100            IF I=J THEN 120
105            LET X=X+1
110            PRINT:CDBOOK:LNM(10);L$(W);L$(I);L$(J);",";P$(X)
120        NEXT J
125    NEXT I
130 NEXT W
135 DATA A,B,C,D
140 DATA AGREE,AMOUNT,BUY,CANCEL,DELAY,DISCOUNT,EXACT,FINAL
145 DATA GET,GOOD,HURRY,INCLUDE,INVEST,LIKE,MONEY,MORE
150 DATA NEED,OKAY,OPPORTUNITY,PLANS,RETHINK,START,STOP,TRANSMIT
160 END
RUN
HOW MANY LETTERS DO YOU WISH TO USE ?4
```

Fig. 2-14. Program to generate a code word dictionary file.

An example of an encoding and decoding system using a code word dictionary is shown in Fig. 2-13. A code word dictionary file has been created by a program similar to the one shown in Fig. 2-14.* You will note that Line 110 places the desired dictionary into a file named CDBOOK. A listing of this file is seen in Fig. 2-15.

* This program is a modification of the program in Fig. 2-4.

```
LIST

10 ABC,AGREE
11 ABD,AMOUNT
12 ACB,BUY
13 ACD,CANCEL
14 ADB,DELAY
15 ADC,DISCOUNT
16 BAC,EXACT
17 BAD,FINAL
18 BCA,GET
19 BCD,GOOD
20 BDA,HURRY
21 BDC,INCLUDE
22 CAB,INVEST
23 CAD,LIKE
24 CBA,MONEY
25 CBD,MORE
26 CDA,NEED
27 CDB,OKAY
28 DAB,OPPORTUNITY
29 DAC,PLANS
30 DBA,RETHINK
31 DBC,START
32 DCA,STOP
33 DCB,TRANSMIT
```

Fig. 2-15.   Listing of the CDBOOK file.

To encode a plaintext message, an appropriate program such as that shown in Fig. 2-16 is needed. The message entered in Lines 120–140,

GOOD   OPPORTUNITY   GET   EXACT   AMOUNT   TRANSMIT   MONEY   HURRY

is matched against the CDBOOK dictionary file, with the resulting coded message as output:

BCD   DAB   BCA   BAC   ABD   DCB   CBA   BDA

To complete the code word dictionary file system requires a decoding program to reverse the encoding process. The program in Fig. 2-17 is a decoding program that makes use of the CDBOOK dictionary file. Into Line 120 is placed the following coded message:

ABC   ABD   CDB   CAD   DAC   BCA   BAC   ADC

When matched against the dictionary file by the computer program, it produces the decoded message:

AGREE   AMOUNT   OKAY   LIKE   PLANS   GET   EXACT   DISCOUNT

Computer Code System Security

Any system involving confidential or classified information requires specific management procedures to ensure that the system is not com-

```
5 REM PROGRAM TO ENCODE A MESSAGE
10 DIM C$(24),P$(24)
15 REM PROGRAM USES A FILE "CDBOOK"
20 FOR I= 1 TO 24
30     INPUT:CDBOOK:C$(I),P$(I)
40 NEXT I
45 PRINT
50 READ P$
60 IF P$="LAST ENTRY" THEN 160
70 FOR I= 1 TO 24
80     IF P$=P$(I) THEN 100
90 NEXT I
100 PRINT C$(I);" ";
110     GO TO 50
120 DATA GOOD, OPPORTUNITY, GET, EXACT
130 DATA AMOUNT, TRANSMIT
140 DATA MONEY, HURRY
150 DATA LAST ENTRY
160 END

RUN

BCD DAB BCA BAC ABD DCB CBA BDA
```

Fig. 2-16. Program to encode a message using a dictionary file.

```
5 REM PROGRAM TO DECODE A MESSAGE
10 DIM C$(24),P$(24)
15 REM PROGRAM USES A FILE "CDBOOK"
20 FOR I= 1 TO 24
30     INPUT:CDBOOK:C$(I),P$(I)
40 NEXT I
45 PRINT
50 READ C$
60 IF C$= "LAST ENTRY" THEN 160
70 FOR I= 1 TO 24
80     IF C$=C$(I) THEN 100
90 NEXT I
100 PRINT P$(I);" ";
110     GO TO 50
120 DATA ABC,ABD,CDB,CAD,DAC,BCA,BAC,ADC
150 DATA LAST ENTRY
160 END

RUN

AGREE AMOUNT OKAY LIKE PLANS GET EXACT DISCOUNT
```

Fig. 2-17. Program to decode a message using a dictionary file.

promised. That is, the system should not be open to unauthorized individuals, nor should it permit information to be used without permission.

In a code system it is important that the dictionary be secured. Physical copies of the dictionary must not be left unsecured. The same is true for magnetic tapes that contain the dictionary. These items should be locked up when not used. Access to them must be limited to authorized users only. Copies of coded output should not be left around or casually tossed into the wastebasket. Such trash may be useful to others desiring to gain illegal access to information about the way the code system works.

It is wise to revise the dictionary periodically by changing the code words or code numbers. Since we are using a computer, such changes can be easily made.

Summary

A code system substitutes code words for plaintext words. These systems may have a one-part code or a more secure two-part code. Computers provide the capability for easily developing code dictionaries. Dictionaries generated by computer programs can contain code words or code numbers, either of which can have one or two parts.

Appropriate computer programs create code systems based on random selection of code words or code numbers. Random codes are more difficult to break.

A complete code system can consist of a code dictionary file that is accessed by an encoding and decoding program. This system enables plaintext messages to be easily encoded, and coded messages to be easily decoded.

Procedures should always be taken to ensure that all code system materials—dictionaries, programs, keys, and so forth—are secured from unauthorized persons.

Questions

1. How does a *two-part* code differ from a *one-part* code?
2. What security measures should be taken with regard to code books?
3. How many different code words can be derived from six letters if groups of four are desired?
4. Why should different letters be used when creating code words?
5. What code words would result from the program in Fig. 2-1 if Line 110 were changed to 110 DATA M, B, B?
6. If Line 110 in the Fig. 2-1 program were changed to 110 DATA A, BC, DE, what code words would result?
7. In creating a complete one-part code dictionary using the program in Fig. 2-4, what problems would arise if Line 135 were written as 135 DATA AB, AC, AC, AD?
8. Using the one-part code word dictionary shown in Fig. 2-4, do the following:
   (a) Encode the message: HURRY NEED MORE MONEY GOOD OPPORTUNITY
   (b) Decode the message: DCA   DBA   DAC   BCA   BAD   ABD

9. Using the one-part code number dictionary shown in Fig. 2-4, do the following:
   (a) Encode the message: AGREE FINAL AMOUNT IS OKAY. TRANSMIT MORE MONEY.
   (b) Decode the message: 121310   121113   121110
                            101311   131012   131110
10. Create a two-part code number dictionary by revising the data in Fig. 2-6 as follows: 135 DATA "12", "10", "13", "11".
11. Any grouping of individual letters can be used to create a two-part code word dictionary as long as there are no duplicates. Revise the data in Fig. 2-6 as follows to create a two-part code word dictionary: 135 DATA S, R, M, B.
12. Revise the program in Fig.2-10to generate a random code number dictionary without duplicate code numbers. Use the 12 values of "10", "11", . . . , "21" for the data in Lines 100 and 110. Be sure to revise Line 140.
13. In a computer code system, must the code dictionary be physically present?
14. In what way is the program in Fig. 2-14 different from the program in Fig. 2-4?
15. A computer code system needs essentially three programs. What are they?
16. In some situations it would be wise to burn or shred any wastepaper from a computer code system. Why?

References

Bosworth, B., and Nagel, H. L. *Programming in BASIC for Business*. 2d ed. Chicago, Ill.: Science Research Associates, 1981.

Honess, C. B. "Three Types of Pseudorandom Sequences." *BYTE* (June 1979): 234–246.

Laffin, John. *Codes and Ciphers*. New York: Abelard-Schuman, 1964.

Lien, David. *The BASIC Handbook: An Encyclopedia of the BASIC Language*. San Diego, Cal.: Compusoft Publishing, 1978.

Zim, Herbert S. *Codes and Secret Writing*. New York: William Morrow and Co., 1948.

3

Cipher Systems—I

Introduction

Code systems transform plaintext *words* into code words, whereas cipher systems concentrate on *each character* of the word. There are two main classes of ciphers: *transposition ciphers* and *substitution ciphers*. Transposition ciphers will be described in this chapter.

Transposition Ciphers

Transposition ciphers involve an encryption procedure that changes the normal pattern of the characters in the original plaintext message. The characters in the plaintext will be scrambled following a specific procedure. Such procedures include message reversal, geometrical patterns, route transposition, and columnar transposition. Each of these encryption procedures will be examined.

Message Reversal

Enciphering a message using *message reversal* requires that the plaintext be written backwards to produce a ciphertext. If the plaintext reads

MEET ME MONDAY MORNING

it is reversed to form the encrypted message, or ciphertext,

GNINROM YADNOM EM TEEM

The encryption procedure is straightforward and easy. To decipher a message, simply reverse it. A program to carry out this procedure requires that the plaintext be read into the computer and then printed out in reversed sequence. Such a program is shown in Fig. 3-1, with a flowchart in Fig. 3-2. The FOR/NEXT loop in Lines 20–50 causes the message in Line 100 to be read into the computer and stored. Line 65 provides the index (R) of the last plaintext character read in. This index is used in the next FOR/NEXT loop (Lines 70–90) to print out the ciphertext starting with the M$(R) th character (the last plaintext charac-

```
5 REM MESSAGE REVERSAL PROGRAM
10 DIM M$(100)
15 REM READ IN PLAINTEXT MESSAGE
20 FOR I= 1 TO 100
30     READ M$(I)
40         IF M$(I) ="ZZ" THEN 65
50 NEXT I
60 REM PRINT OUT CIPHERTEXT
65 LET R=I-1
70 FOR I= R TO 1 STEP -1
80     PRINT M$(I);
90 NEXT I
100 DATA M,E,E,T,M,E,M,O,N,D,A,Y
110 DATA M,O,R,N,I,N,G
120 DATA ZZ
130 END

RUN

GNINROMYADNOMEMTEEM
```

Fig. 3-1. Program for message reversal encryption.

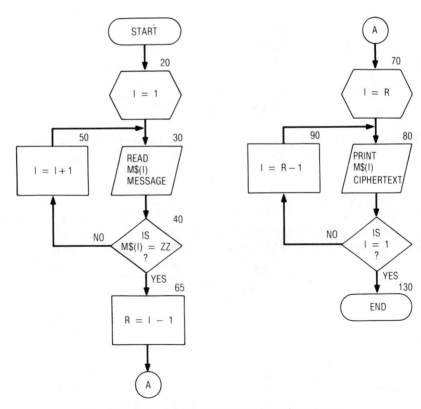

Fig. 3-2. Flowchart for message reversal programs.

ter) and continuing to the M$(1) st character. The printed output does not have blank spaces.

To decipher a ciphertext based on message reversal, we do not require another program. The program in Fig. 3-1 will be sufficient since it does not know if the message is in plaintext or in a ciphertext.

Geometrical Patterns

The normal writing of a message follows a pattern from left to right, one line at a time. Messages then form a *geometrical pattern* in the shape of a rectangle. Each shape can be read and understood because the geometrical pattern is a standard one for the transmission of printed information. Any other geometrical pattern would disguise the message, unless the reader knew the key to unscramble it.

The message, CONCEAL ALL MESSAGES, forms a single horizontal line. It can be transposed into rectangular shapes of (1) two columns of equal length, by writing the plaintext vertically

```
CL
OM
NE
CS
ES
AA
LG
AE
LS
```

or (2) two rows of equal length, by writing the plaintext horizontally

```
CONCEALAL
LMESSAGES
```

The number of different rectangular patterns depends on the number of characters in the message as well as the page size. In the previous message, there were 18 characters that could be transposed into four rectangles: 9 × 2, 2 × 9, or those shown below, 6 × 3 and 3 × 6:

```
CON        CONCEA
CEA        LALLME
LAL        SSAGES
LME
SSA
GES
```

Transposing a plaintext using an encryption procedure based only on geometrical shapes produces a very limited degree of message security. However, geometrical patterns are useful as an intermediate step for another encryption procedure, *route transposition*, which will be described next.

Route Transposition

Route transposition procedures provide a way of further scrambling geometrically shaped messages. When creating a geometric shape, a left-to-right pattern is followed. The message SEND HELP SOON is 12 characters in length. As a geometric ciphertext we can put it into a 6 × 2 rectangle following a left to right route and taking two characters at a time.

Plaintext:	SEND HELP SOON
Ciphertext:	SE
	ND
	HE
	LP
	SO
	ON

Since the route is left to right, the message is easily understood. Therefore, the procedure provides very little security. An increase in scrambling can be derived if the 6 × 2 shape is used as an intermediate step. The first column is written horizontally from left to right, and the next column is written under it. The result is a route transposition shown in this ciphertext:

Plaintext:	SEND HELP SOON
Ciphertext:	SNHLSO
	EDEPON

This encryption procedure produces a *zig-zag* transposition or a *rail fence* cipher. The plaintext gets divided into fixed lengths. One length contains every odd-positioned letter of the message. The other length contains every even-positioned letter of the message. The transposing process follows this type of pattern, thus the name *zig-zag:*

A program to encipher messages by zig-zag route transposition is shown in Fig. 3-3. The program is set for a message length of 12 characters. For longer messages the dimension statement (Line 15) and the FOR statements (Lines 25 and 60) must be revised. The message length cannot exceed twice the width of the output paper used. A flowchart for the program is provided in Fig. 3-4.

To reverse the encryption process requires another program. This decryption program is shown in Fig. 3-5. The ciphertext is read into the computer and stored. The zig-zag process is reversed and the deciphered plaintext message is printed out.

```
10 REM PROGRAM TO DO A TRANSPOSITION CIPHER
15 DIM L$(20)
20 PRINT "ORIGINAL MESSAGE IS:"
25 FOR I= 1 TO 12
30    READ L$(I)
35    PRINT L$(I);
40 NEXT I
45 PRINT
50 PRINT
55 PRINT"TRANSPOSED CIPHER MESSAGE IS:"
58 FOR J= 0 TO 1
60    FOR I= 1 TO 12 STEP 2
65       PRINT L$(I+J);
70    NEXT I
75    PRINT
80 NEXT J
95 DATA S,E,N,D,H,E,L,P,S,O,O,N
100 END

RUN

ORIGINAL MESSAGE IS:
SENDHELPSOON

TRANSPOSED CIPHER MESSAGE IS:
SNHLSO
EDEPON
```

Fig. 3-3. Program for zig-zag transposition cipher.

A variation of the zig-zag process is a *reversed zig-zag* route transposition. Here the enciphering starts with the last letter of the plaintext and continues back to the beginning of the message. First the odd-positioned letters are taken and then the even-positioned ones. Compare the following ciphertext with the one shown earlier using a direct zig-zag process:

Plaintext:	SEND HELP SOON
Ciphertext:	NOPEDE
	OSLHNS

To program this reverse zig-zag process, the program in Fig. 3-3 was modified. The changes appear in Lines 60 and 65:

```
60    FOR 1 = 12 TO 1 STEP -2
65    PRINT L$(I-J)  ;
```

These modifications result in the reversal of the ciphertext, as can be seen by comparing the output of Fig. 3-3 with the output of Fig. 3-6.

The person receiving the ciphertext must know that it was enciphered using a zig-zag route transposition; otherwise, the message cannot be deciphered. To decipher a zig-zag message requires that the process for enciphering be reversed. By rewriting the ciphertext into columns and then transcribing it in a left-to-right pattern, the plaintext appears. Using the previous message:

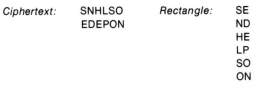

Ciphertext: SNHLSO   Rectangle: SE
             EDEPON   ND
                                       HE
                                       LP
                                       SO
                                       ON

Plaintext: SENDHELPSOON

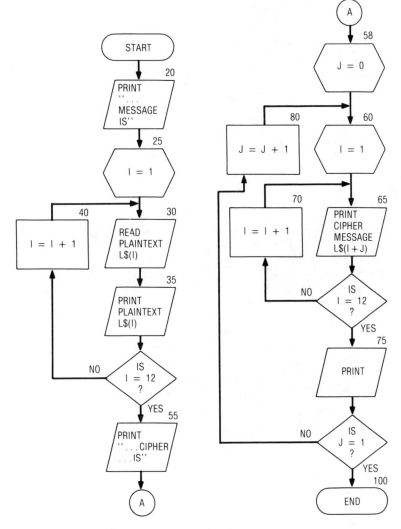

Fig. 3-4. Flowchart for zig-zag program.

```
10 REM DECIPHERING PROGRAM FOR ZIG-ZAG CIPHERTEXT
20 DIM L$(20)
30 PRINT "ZIG-ZAG CIPHER MESSAGE IS:"
40 FOR J= 0 TO 1
50     FOR I= 1 TO 12 STEP 2
60          READ L$(I+J)
70          PRINT L$(I+J);
80     NEXT I
90     PRINT
100 NEXT J
110 PRINT
120 PRINT "DECIPHERED-PLAINTEXT MESSAGE IS:"
130 FOR I= 1 TO 12
140     PRINT L$(I);
150 NEXT I
160 DATA S,N,H,L,S,O,E,D,E,P,O,N
170 END

RUN

ZIG-ZAG CIPHER MESSAGE IS:
SNHLSO
EDEPON

DECIPHERED-PLAINTEXT MESSAGE IS:
SENDHELPSOON
```

Fig. 3-5. Program to decipher a zig-zag ciphertext.

```
10 REM PROGRAM TO DO A ZIGZAG TRANSPOSITION
11 REM   CIPHER AND REVERSE THE CIPHER MESSAGE
15 DIM L$(20)
20 PRINT "ORIGINAL MESSAGE IS:"
25 FOR I= 1 TO 12
30     READ L$(I)
35     PRINT L$(I);
40 NEXT I
45 PRINT
50 PRINT
55 PRINT"TRANSPOSED CIPHER MESSAGE IS:"
58 FOR J = 0 TO 1
60     FOR I = 12 TO 1 STEP -2
65          PRINT L$(I-J);
70     NEXT I
75     PRINT
80 NEXT J
95 DATA S,E,N,D,H,E,L,P,S,O,O,N
100 END

RUN

ORIGINAL MESSAGE IS:
SENDHELPSOON

TRANSPOSED CIPHER MESSAGE IS:
NOPEDE
OSLHNS
```

Fig. 3-6. Program for reversed zig-zag transposition cipher.

Route Variations

Route transpositions can go in many different directions: *horizontal, vertical, diagonal, clockwise,* or *counterclockwise.* If we use the message SEND HELP SOON in a 3 × 4 geometric shape, several of these route transpositions can be illustrated, as follows:

Horizontal routes

(1) SEND
HELP
SOON

(2) NOOS
PLEH
DNES

Vertical routes

(1) SDLO
EHPO
NESN

(2) NSEN
OPHE
OLDS

Diagonal routes

(1) SEDL
NHPO
ESON

(2) NOSE
OPHN
LDES

Clockwise (spiral) routes

(1) SEND
OONH
SPLE

(2) ELPS
HNOO
DNES

Counterclockwise routes

(1) SOSP
EONL
NDHE

(2) EHDN
LNOE
PSOS

```
5 REM HORIZONTAL ROUTE TRANSPOSITION
10 DIM M$(100)
15 REM READ IN PLAINTEXT MESSAGE
20 FOR I= 1 TO 100
30     READ M$(I)
40     IF M$(I) ="ZZ" THEN 65
50 NEXT I
60 REM PRINT OUT CIPHERTEXT
65 LET R=I-1
70 FOR I=R TO 1 STEP -4
80     PRINT M$(I);M$(I-1);M$(I-2);M$(I-3)
90 NEXT I
100 DATA I,F,O,N,E,L,I,G,H,T,E,N,E,M,Y
110 DATA C,O,M,E,S,B,Y,L,A,N,D,T,W,O
120 DATA L,I,G,H,T,S,B,Y,S,E,A
130 DATA ZZ
140 END


RUN

AESY
BSTH
GILO
WTDN
ALYB
SEMO
CYME
NETH
GILE
NOFI
```

Fig. 3-7. Program for a horizontal route transposition cipher.

Programs can be written to produce transposition ciphers that follow these routes. The program in Fig. 3-1 that produces messages in a reverse sequence follows horizontal route (2).

The following lines have been added to the message reversal program in Fig. 3-1:

```
70    FOR I = R TO 1 STEP -4
80    PRINT  M$(I);  M$(I-1);  M$(I-2);  M$(I-3)
```

These changes will cause the ciphertext to form a rectangle of four columns by ten rows. The revised program for a horizontal route transposition is shown in Fig. 3-7. A flowchart is shown in Fig. 3-8. The message to be enciphered by this program is as follows:

IF ONE LIGHT ENEMY COMES BY LAND TWO LIGHTS BY SEA

The ciphertext shown in the output of Fig. 3-7 follows horizontal route (2).

The output produced by the zig-zag program in Fig. 3-3 is a ciphertext that follows vertical route (1). To encipher a larger message of 40 characters by this route transposition program, the following changes were made in Fig. 3-3:

```
15    DIM  L$(40)
25    FOR I = 1 TO 40
58    FOR J = 0 TO 3
60    FOR I = 1 TO 40 STEP 4
```

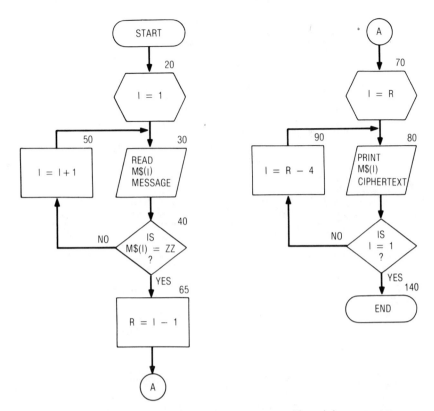

Fig. 3-8. Flowchart for horizontal route transposition cipher program.

Fig. 3-9 shows the revised program and the output that results for the plaintext message, IF ONE LIGHT . . . SEA. The ciphertext is a four-line vertical route transposition.

Columnar Transposition

Encryption by *columnar transposition* requires the shifting of the columns of a plaintext message already in the geometrical form of a rectangle. Generally, the plaintext is placed in rectangular form following vertical route (1). Begin with the message

SHIP EQUIPMENT ON THE FOURTH OF JULY

A decision must be made concerning the size (rows and columns) of the rectangle to be used. The previous message has 30 characters and can be shaped 2 × 15, 3 × 10, 5 × 6, 6 × 5, 10 × 3, and 15 × 2. If the message consisted of an uneven or unformable number of characters, say 29, a dummy or *null* character such as the letter X could be added to the plaintext.

If we want to write the plaintext in the form of six rows by five columns, we produce this ciphertext:

```
10 REM VERTICAL ROUTE TRANSPOSITION
15 DIM L$(40)
20 PRINT "ORIGINAL MESSAGE IS:"
25 FOR I= 1 TO 40
30     READ L$(I)
35     PRINT L$(I);
40 NEXT I
45 PRINT
50 PRINT
55 PRINT"TRANSPOSED CIPHER MESSAGE IS:"
58 FOR J= 0 TO 3
60     FOR I= 1 TO 40 STEP 4
65         PRINT L$(I+J);
70     NEXT I
75     PRINT
80 NEXT J
85 DATA I,F,O,N,E,L,I,G,H,T,E,N,E,M,Y
90 DATA C,O,M,E,S,B,Y,L,A,N,D,T,W,O
95 DATA L,I,G,H,T,S,B,Y,S,E,A
100 END

RUN

ORIGINAL MESSAGE IS:
IFONELIGHTENEMYCOMESBYLANDTWOLIGHTSBYSEA

TRANSPOSED CIPHER MESSAGE IS:
IEHEOBNOHY
FLTMMYDLTS
OIEYELTISE
NGNCSAWGBA
```

Fig. 3-9. Program for a vertical route transposition cipher.

Column numbers:	1	2	3	4	5
Ciphertext:	S	U	T	F	O
	H	I	O	O	F
	I	P	N	U	J
	P	M	T	R	U
	E	E	H	T	L
	Q	N	E	H	Y

In the shape of a vertical transposition, the preceding ciphertext is easily read and affords no security at all. To further secure the plaintext, the columns of the 6 × 5 rectangle can be shifted, resulting in a *columnar transposition.* For example, the column positions 1 2 3 4 5 may be arbitrarily shifted to positions 3 4 5 2 1, one of 120 possible arrangements.* The columnar transposition produced is as follows:

Column numbers:	3	5	4	2	1
Ciphertext:	T	O	F	U	S
	O	F	O	I	H
	N	J	U	P	I
	T	U	R	M	P
	H	L	T	E	E
	E	Y	H	N	Q

* There are C factorial (C!) columnar transpositions possible for C=5 columns; that is, 5! = 5 × 4 × 3 × 2 × 1 = 120 arrangements.

The security of the plaintext is further improved when the columnar transposed message is transcribed in blocks of five characters taken off horizontally from the rectangle to produce a final ciphertext:

Plaintext: SHIP EQUIPMENT ON THE FOURTH OF JULY
Ciphertext: TOFUS OFOIH NJUPI TURMP HLTEE EYHNQ

An alternative approach would be to take the characters off the rectangle in a vertical route. This produces the following ciphertext, transcribed in blocks of five characters:

Plaintext: SHIP EQUIPMENT ON THE FOURTH OF JULY
Ciphertext: TONTH EOFJU LYFOU RTHUI PMENS HIPEQ

Columnar ciphertexts cannot be read easily without the reader knowing something about the encryption procedure used. The recipient of the ciphertext must have certain information:

1. He must know that the ciphertext was taken off a geometric shape either horizontally, vertically, diagonally, or whatever.
2. He must know the number of rows and columns of the rectangle.
3. He must know the key. That is, the columns of the rectangle were rearranged by a *number key,* for example: 3 5 4 2 1. Both sender and receiver must know this key.

Figure 3-10 is a program that will take a plaintext in the form of a rectangular transposition, transpose the columns, and produce a final

```
10 REM PROGRAM COLUMNAR ROUTE TRANSPOSITION
20 DIM A$(250)
30 PRINT "HOW MANY ROWS AND COLUMNS";
40 INPUT R,C
50 PRINT "WHAT IS THE KEY";
60 INPUT K1,K2,K3,K4,K5
70 FOR K=1 TO R
80      FOR I=1 TO C
90          READ A$(I)
100     NEXT I
110     PRINT A$(K1);A$(K2);A$(K3);A$(K4);A$(K5);" ";
120 NEXT K
130 DATA S,U,T,F,O
140 DATA H,I,O,O,F
150 DATA I,P,N,U,J
160 DATA P,M,T,R,U
170 DATA E,E,H,T,L
180 DATA Q,N,E,H,Y
190 END

RUN

HOW MANY ROWS AND COLUMNS ?6,5
WHAT IS THE KEY ?3,5,4,2,1
TOFUS OFOIH NJUPI TURMP HLTEE EYHNQ
```

Fig. 3-10. Program for a columnar route transposition cipher.

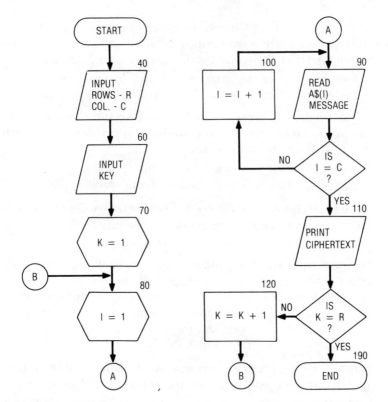

Fig. 3-11. Flowchart for columnar route transposition cipher program.

ciphertext horizontally. The program user must enter the number of rows and columns of the rectangle. The number of columns can be up to five, and the number of rows can be up to 50. A flowchart for the program is given in Fig. 3-11.

A program to decipher a columnar transposition message must reverse the enciphering process. The program must have the key and the ciphertext read into the computer. The key is essential for the cipher-text to be correctly sequenced when deciphered into the plaintext.

The program in Fig. 3-12 will cause a columnar transposition ciphertext to be deciphered. The key is entered as an INPUT (Line 70), the ciphertext is entered as a READ (Lines 100 to 120), and the PRINT (Line 130) causes the cleartext message to be produced.

So far the discussion of columnar transposition ciphers has been restricted to a key of up to five digits in length using the values 1, 2, 3, 4, or 5. As indicated earlier, these five digits will provide only 120 different key possibilities. To find the key by trial and error would be a time-consuming task, but not impossible to do. Using a computer would ena-ble the key to be found quite easily. To improve the key and its security

```
10 REM PROGRAM TO DECIPHER A
20 REM COLUMNAR TRANSPOSITION CIPHERTEXT
30 DIM A$(250)
40 PRINT "HOW MANY ROWS AND COLUMNS";
50 INPUT R,C
60 PRINT "WHAT IS THE KEY";
70 INPUT K(1),K(2),K(3),K(4),K(5)
80 PRINT
90 FOR K=1 TO R
100     FOR I=1 TO C
110         READ A$(K(I))
120     NEXT I
130     PRINT A$(1);A$(2);A$(3);A$(4);A$(5)
140 NEXT K
150 DATA T,O,F,U,S,O,F,O,I,H
160 DATA N,J,U,P,I,T,U,R,M,P
170 DATA H,L,T,E,E,E,Y,H,N,Q
180 END

RUN

HOW MANY ROWS AND COLUMNS ?6,5
WHAT IS THE KEY ?3,5,4,2,1

SUTFO
HIOOF
IPNUJ
PMTRU
EEHTL
QNEHY
```

Fig. 3-12. Program to decipher a columnar transposition ciphertext.

from discovery, we can expand the range of digits using the values 0, 1, 2, 3, 4, 5, 6, 7, 8, and 9. From these ten digits we can derive 30,240 different five digit keys.*

By using these digits the key can take on a specific meaning. A sender and receiver can agree to use a year, such as 1945, as a key. Or they may agree to use a month and a year, such as February 1970, which becomes the key 31970.

How is such a key used? Its use can be illustrated with the plaintext shown before: SHIP EQUIPMENT ON THE FOURTH OF JULY. This message was put into a columnar transposition as

Column numbers:	1	2	3	4	5
Ciphertext:	S	U	T	F	O
	H	I	O	O	F
	I	P	N	U	J
	P	M	T	R	U
	E	E	H	T	L
	Q	N	E	H	Y

The enciphering key is 3 1 9 7 0, and the columns are 1 2 3 4 5. To encrypt the plaintext, we must arrange the columns so that the

* $_{10}P_5 = n!/(n - r)! = 10!/5! = 10 \times 9 \times 8 \times 7 \times 6 = 30,240$ possible keys.

highest key value represents the last column, the lowest key value represents the first column, and so on. In this example, we have the following situation:

Plaintext key values:	3	1	9	7	0
Column positions:	1	2	3	4	5
Ciphertext positions:	3	2	5	4	1

The columnar transposition takes this form:

Key:	3	1	9	7	0
Route transposition columns:	3	2	5	4	1
Ciphertext:	T	U	O	F	S
	O	I	F	O	H
	N	P	J	U	I
	T	M	U	R	P
	H	E	L	T	E
	E	N	Y	H	Q

Transcribing the results horizontally in blocks of five produces the following ciphertext:

Plaintext:	SHIP EQUIPMENT ON THE FOURTH OF JULY
Ciphertext:	TUOFS OIFOH NPJUI TMURP HELTE ENYHQ

An encryption program using a five-digit key, drawn from the ten digits 0 to 9, requires a sorting operation to match the key digits with the low-to-high (1 to 5) column positions of the route transposition rectangle. A *sorting* routine, combined with a program such as the one presented in Fig. 3-10, can produce the desired results. The program is shown in Fig. 3-13. A generalized flowchart is shown in Fig. 3-14. The program uses the key 31970 and encrypts the . . . JULY FOURTH message.

An alternative approach to a number key is the concept of a *word key*. Both the sender and receiver must agree to use a specific word as a key. For example, they select the word FIGHT. To use such a word key, the relative alphabetic position of the key letters provides the sequence for transcribing the route transposition into a ciphertext.

Again, the . . . JULY FOURTH plaintext in columnar form had these column positions: 1 2 3 4 5. The key word shifts these positions as follows:

Column positions:	1	2	3	4	5
Key word:	F	I	G	H	T
Ciphertext positions:	1	4	2	3	5

The ciphertext positions are based on the *alphabetic order* of the key word FIGHT. Alphabetically, the key word is

```
10 REM COLUMNAR TRANSPOSITION-0 TO 9 DIGIT KEY
20 DIM A$(250)
30 PRINT "HOW MANY ROWS AND COLUMNS";
40 INPUT R,C
45 PRINT "THE KEY IS";
50 FOR M= 1 TO C
60      READ K(M)
70      PRINT K(M);
80 NEXT M
90 DATA 3,1,9,7,0
100 FOR I= 1 TO C-1
110     FOR J= 1 TO C-1
120     IF K(J+1)>K(J) THEN 160
130     LET A=K(J)
140         LET K(J)=K(J+1)
150         LET K(J+1)=A
160     NEXT J
170 NEXT I
180 PRINT
190 RESTORE
200 FOR L=1 TO C
210 READ B
220     FOR M=1 TO C
230         IF K(M)<>B THEN 250
240             LET X(L) =M
250     NEXT M
260 NEXT L
270 PRINT
300 PRINT
310 PRINT "CIPHERTEXT FOLLOWS:"
320 FOR K=1 TO R
330     FOR I= 1 TO C
340         READ A$(I)
350     NEXT I
360     PRINT A$(X(1));A$(X(2));A$(X(3));A$(X(4));A$(X(5));" ";
370 NEXT K
380 DATA S,U,T,F,O
390 DATA H,I,O,O,F
400 DATA I,P,N,U,J
410 DATA P,M,T,R,U
420 DATA E,E,H,T,L
430 DATA Q,N,E,H,Y
440 END

RUN

HOW MANY ROWS AND COLUMNS ?6,5
THE KEY IS 3   1   9   7   0

CIPHERTEXT FOLLOWS:
TUOFS OIFOH NPJUI TMURP HELTE ENYHQ
```

Fig. 3-13. Program for a columnar transposition using a key from ten digits.

	F	G	H	I	T
Position:	1	2	3	4	5
Key word:	F	I	G	H	T
Column positions:	1	4	2	3	5

Applying this key word produces the columnar transposition on the right below. The original transposition is on the left.

Column numbers:	1	2	3	4	5
Ciphertext:	S	U	T	F	O
	H	I	O	O	F
	I	P	N	U	J
	P	M	T	R	U
	E	E	H	T	L
	Q	N	E	H	Y

Column numbers:	1	4	2	3	5
Ciphertext:	S	F	U	T	O
	H	O	I	O	F
	I	U	P	W	J
	P	R	M	T	U
	E	T	E	H	L
	Q	H	N	E	Y

By taking off each row of the key word transposition, the complete ciphertext is

SFUTO HOIOF IUPWJ PRMTU ETEHL QHNEY

Key Words as ASCII Values

To program a columnar transposition encryption procedure using a key word requires some way of sorting the key word to obtain the

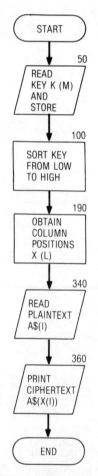

Fig. 3-14. Flowchart for ten-digit key columnar transposition program.

character positions for scrambling the columns. Instead of doing an alphabetic sort and repositioning the columns based on the results, it may be easier to use a CHANGE statement.*

By programming the key word as a single string character and using a CHANGE statement, each character in the key word is now assigned an ASCII number value. Figure 3-15 shows the ASCII number equivalent for the uppercase characters A through Z.

A	65	J	74	S	83
B	66	K	75	T	84
C	67	L	76	U	85
D	68	M	77	V	86
E	69	N	78	W	87
F	70	O	79	X	88
G	71	P	80	Y	89
H	72	Q	81	Z	90
I	73	R	82		

Fig. 3-15. ASCII alphabetic number equivalents.

The abbreviation ASCII stands for the American Standard Code for Information Interchange (or "askey"). The code is based on the fact that data in the computer is represented by the presence or absence of electrical signals in the circuitry of the machine. There are only two possible states: either there is a signal (1), or there isn't a signal (0). This two-state system is called the *binary system.*

The binary system uses 0's and 1's in different combinations to represent alphabetic and numeric characters. These 0's and 1's are called *bits* (an abbreviation for *bi*nary dig*its*).

As computer systems developed and needs changed, various *binary-coded decimal* (BCD) notations evolved to represent characters. For example, the uppercase letter A could be represented in a six-bit BCD, seven-bit BCD, or eight-bit BCD in the following way:

	Character A
6-bit BCD	110001
7-bit BCD	1000001
8-bit BCD	11000001

The seven-bit BCD is also known as ASCII-7 or the ASCII Transmission Code.† It was developed in 1967 by the American National Standards Institute (ANSI) to provide a standard code for computer devices and communications equipment. The coding scheme is also re-

---

* See Appendix.

† A complete set of characters and ASCII-7 values is shown in Chapter 7, Fig. 7-8.

ferred to as the United States of America Code for Information Interchange (USASCII).

In addition to the seven-bit BCD code for characters, there is also an ASCII code of integer values for the character set of the BASIC programming language. For example, with the upper-case alphabetic characters A through Z, the code sets A at a value of 65, B at 66, and so on (Fig. 3-15).

To illustrate the use of the ASCII values, the key word FIGHT is changed to a subscripted numeric array, as follows:

Key word:	F	I	G	H	T
Variable designation:	B(1)	B(2)	B(3)	(B4)	B(5)
ASCII:	70	73	71	72	84

A program to encipher a columnar transposition with a key word is provided in Fig. 3-16.

If a key word has duplicate letters, positions of the columnar transposition are still based on the relative alphabetic position of each key word character. Duplicate letters are assigned positions going from left (low) to right (high). Suppose the key word is PEACE, having a duplicate character E. To transpose five columns using this key word, the sequence would be

Key word letters:	A	C	E	E	P
Column assignment:	1	2	3	4	5
Transposed sequence:	5	3	1	2	4
Key word:	P	E	A	C	E

When selecting a key word, it is wise not to use words that can be easily guessed by unauthorized persons: for example, names associated with the sender and receiver, company names, and so forth. This same procedure is advised when selecting number keys. Addresses, phone numbers, and birth dates should not be used.

Generating Random Numeric Keys

One procedure to provide an objective method for key selection utilizes a computer program to generate random keys. Such a program is shown in Fig. 3-17. It will provide keys from two to ten characters in length that are drawn from the digits 0, 1, 2 . . . , 9. A flowchart is provided in Fig. 3-18.

Other Transpositions

In addition, there are other enciphering arrangements that can be used, such as a *double columnar transposition*. This method requires enciphering a ciphertext a second time with another key.

```
10 REM COLUMNAR TRANSPOSITION USING KEYWORD
20 DIM A$(250),K$(10),K(10),B(10)
30 PRINT "HOW MANY ROWS AND COLUMNS";
40 INPUT R,C
45 READ K$
50 DATA FIGHT
60 PRINT "THE KEY IS   ";K$
70 CHANGE K$ TO K
80 CHANGE K$ TO B
90 FOR I= 1 TO C-1
100      FOR J=1 TO C-1
110      IF K(J+1)>K(J) THEN 150
120           LET A=K(J)
130           LET K(J)=K(J+1)
140           LET K(J+1)=A
150      NEXT J
160 NEXT I
170 FOR L=1 TO C
180      FOR M=1 TO C
190      IF K(M)<>B(L) THEN 210
200           LET X(L) =M
210      NEXT M
220 NEXT L
230 PRINT
260 PRINT
270 PRINT "CIPHERTEXT FOLLOWS:"
280 FOR K=1 TO R
290      FOR I= 1 TO C
300           READ A$(I)
310      NEXT I
320      PRINT A$(X(1));A$(X(2));A$(X(3));A$(X(4));A$(X(5));"  ";
330 NEXT K
340 DATA S,U,T,F,O
350 DATA H,I,O,O,F
360 DATA I,P,N,U,J
370 DATA P,M,T,R,U
380 DATA E,E,H,T,L
390 DATA Q,N,E,H,Y
400 END

RUN

HOW MANY ROWS AND COLUMNS ?6,5
THE KEY IS  FIGHT


CIPHERTEXT FOLLOWS:
SFUTO HOIOF IUPNJ PRMTU ETEHL QHNEY
```

Fig. 3-16. Program for columnar transposition with a key word.

Instead of a single character transposition or *monoliteral transposition* as has been the approach so far, another method, *polyliteral transposition,* can be used. This transposition takes letters in groups of two, or three, or four, etc., to form a geometric pattern before transposing columns.

To further secure code messages, the plaintext can be processed into a geometric pattern and then transposed as though a ciphertext were being created.

```
10 REM PROGRAM TO GENERATE RANDOM KEYS
20 RANDOMIZE
30 FOR I= 0 TO 9
40     LET A(I) = I
50 NEXT I
60 PRINT "HOW MANY DIGITS IN THE KEY";
70 INPUT L
80 PRINT "THE KEY IS ";
90 FOR N= 1 TO L
100     LET R= INT(10*RND(X))
110     IF A(R) = -999 THEN 100
120         PRINT A(R);
130         LET A(R)=-999
140 NEXT N
150 END

RUN

HOW MANY DIGITS IN THE KEY ?5
THE KEY IS  3  8  2  1  7
```

Fig. 3-17. Program to generate random keys.

Each of these enciphering procedures is illustrated here, using the following plaintext message:

NEGOTIATIONS STALLED SEND INSTRUCTIONS TODAY

Double Columnar Transposition

The four-column plaintext is as follows:

N	N	E	T
E	S	N	I
G	S	D	O
O	T	I	N
T	A	N	S
I	L	S	T
A	L	T	O
T	E	R	D
I	D	U	A
O	S	C	Y

Using the first number key of 4213, the plaintext is transposed:

Column:	1	2	3	4
Key column positions:	4	2	1	3
	T	N	N	E
	I	S	E	N
	O	S	G	D
	N	T	O	I
	S	A	T	N
	T	L	I	S
	O	L	A	T
	D	E	T	R
	A	D	I	U
	Y	S	O	C

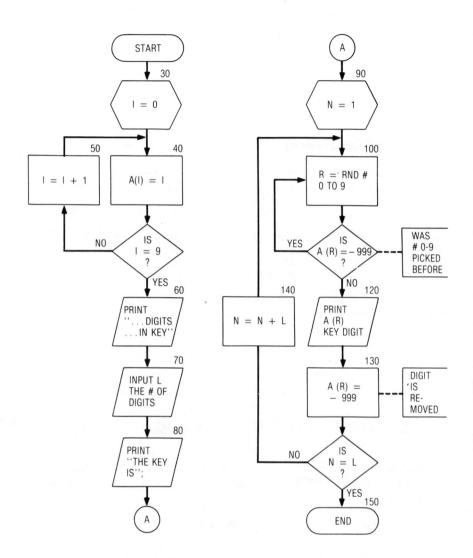

Fig. 3-18. Flowchart for random key generating program.

A second number key of 5926 produces a transposition of columns:

Key:	5	9	2	6
Column positions:	2	4	1	3
	N	E	T	N
	S	N	I	E
	S	D	O	G
	T	I	N	O
	A	N	S	T
	L	S	T	I
	L	T	O	A
	E	R	D	T
	D	U	A	I
	S	C	Y	O

Transcribed in blocks of four, taken off horizontally, the result is the ciphertext:

NETN SNIE SDOG TINO ANST LSTI LTOA ERDT DUAI SCYO

Polyliteral Transposition

Using two characters as a unit, a four-column pattern is formed from the plaintext NEGOTIATIONS STALLED . . ., as follows:

1	2	3	4
NE	NS	EN	TI
GO	ST	DI	ON
TI	AL	NS	ST
AT	LE	TR	OD
IO	DS	UC	AY

Using the key word LIFE, which converts the columns into a sequence of 4 3 2 1, the following transposition results:

4	3	2	1
TI	EN	NS	NE
ON	DI	ST	GO
ST	NS	AL	TI
OD	TR	LE	AT
AY	UC	DS	IO

Taken off horizontally in blocks of three units (six characters), the final ciphertext is

Plaintext: NEGOTIATIONS STALLED SEND INSTRUCTIONS TODAY
Ciphertext: TIENNS NEONDI STGOST NSALTI ODTRLE ATAYUC DSIOXY

Note that the last two characters, XY, were added as nulls to round out the six character groups of the ciphertext.

Code Word Transposition

Assume that the plaintext words have code word equivalents, as follows:

Plaintext	Code word
INSTRUCTION	JMXY
NEGOTIATIONS	KEWB
SEND	LSRB
STALLED	MLMA
TODAY	NMBB

The plaintext and code message are as follows:

Plaintext: NEGOTIATIONS STALLED SEND INSTRUCTIONS TODAY
Codetext: KEWB MLMA LSRB JMXY NMBB

Forming units of two characters in five columns produces

1	2	3	4	5
KE	ML	LS	JM	NM
WB	MA	RB	XY	BB

Transposing the columns with a numeric key of 81978, which gives the column positions of 3   1   5   2   4, the result is

Column positions:	3	1	5	2	4
	LS	KE	NM	ML	JM
	RB	WB	BB	MA	XY

Note that the number key has a duplicate 8. The first 8 is assigned to column position 3, and the second 8 to column position 4. That is, the key digits 17889 are equivalent to column positions 1   2   3   4 and 5. The final ciphertext in blocks of four horizontally transcribed is below:

LSKE   NMML   JMRB   WBBB   MAXY

Information Security and the Cipher System

Ciphers are simple and easy to use. Enciphering and deciphering by hand can be done rapidly, particularly for short messages. With computers, the length of the plaintext is not a problem, and the speed of operations permits easy encryption and decryption of messages.

Ideally, encrypted messages will not be intercepted by unauthorized individuals. If messages are intercepted, it is possible for a skilled expert to break the cipher.

Messages that will result in actions shortly after receipt are suitable for encryption. By the time the message may have been intercepted and analyzed, the action to be taken by the true recipient will have occurred.

Simple ciphers can be used for low-priority messages. More involved ciphers (polyliteral transposition, code word transposition) may be employed for messages of higher priority.

If a particular key type of cipher system is established for use, the key should be changed regularly. Key numbers and key words should not be carelessly left around, scribbled on pieces of paper, or pasted onto terminals.

In addition, if route transpositions are used, varying the direction (vertical, horizontal, and so forth) is a good practice to follow.

It is important to remember that a secure cipher system is no better than the security-minded people using it.

Summary

One class of cipher system is based on transposition or rearrangement of each character in the plaintext message to produce a ciphertext. Procedures for transposition encryption include a variety of rearrangements: reversal of the entire message, reforming the message into a geometrical shape, scrambling the plaintext by following a specific route (horizontal, vertical, clockwise, or counterclockwise), and rearranging the plaintext by scrambling the sequence of columns.

Each transposition cipher procedure can be programmed so that longer messages can be quickly processed. The computer permits rapid encryption and decryption that can effectively assist in the establishment of secure records and files.

Other transposition ciphers include double columnar transposition and polyliteral transposition.

Whatever cipher system is used, operational controls must be followed so that unauthorized persons do not defeat the purpose of the security system.

Questions

1. How do *code systems* differ from *cipher systems?*
2. Decipher the following messages:

    (a) TSAOC EHT NO DEDNAL SAH YMENE EHT
    (b) KCAT TAKC ATTA KCAT TA

3. Use the program in Fig. 3-1 to decipher this message:

NIAGRABDRAHAEVIRDSRALLODNOILLIMEERHTNAHTSSEL GNIHTYNATPECCA

4. How many different rectangular patterns can be formed from a message of 24 characters?
5. Place the following message into a square geometrical figure:

WE WILL NOT ACCEPT LATEST OFFER STOP TALKS

6. Using the message in question 5,
    (a) Develop a 2 × 18 zig-zag ciphertext.
    (b) Place it in the program in Fig. 3-3 using these revisions:

```
15  DIM  L$(36)
25  FOR  I  =  1  TO  36
60  FOR  I  =  1  TO  36  STEP  2
```

Run the program and verify your answer to part (a).
7. What route direction does the ciphertext output

```
NOPEDE
OSLHNS
```

of the program in Fig. 3-5 follow?
8. Decipher the messages shown. Encryption is based on different route transpositions.

(a) SNS	(b) YLRAL	(c) SEUMSETIOL	(d) ERMON
EAR	UGERS	CREAWHANRU	WANSD
TME	YEKRE	ESGIDGAOTE	SRTMA
UEH	HPICE		NATIY
OKP	GNAHC		
RAI			
YTC			

9. How many different columnar transpositions are possible with a six-column rectangle?

10. Decipher this ciphertext:

    ISMLE   FVHAL   NIEIR   ATFOP   CRWTN   MHRIH

    The message was taken off a rectangle horizontally using the key 728429.

11. Decipher this ciphertext:

    ENTWI   LLARR   IVEON   SHIPM   MEARCH   FIFTH

    The message was taken off a rectangle vertically using the key word BINARY.

12. Encipher a message of your own using the program in Fig. 3-10. The number key must be based on the digits 1, 2, 3, 4, or 5. Decipher the message using the program in Fig. 3-12.

13. Encipher a message of your own using the program in Fig. 3-13.

14. Using the key word BASIC in the program shown in Fig. 3-15, generate a new ciphertext.

15. Encipher this message:

    IMPORTANT   COMPUTER   INFORMATION   CAN   BE   SECURED   BY   CIPHER
    SYSTEMS

    Use the key word CANNONS, adding nulls of X as needed.

16. Revise the program shown in Fig. 3-17 so that random number keys will be generated for 12 months with a single program run.

References

Smith, Laurence D. *Cryptography*. New York: Dover Publications, 1955.

Wolf, James R. *Secret Writing*. New York: McGraw-Hill Book Company, 1970.

Zim, Herbert S. *Codes and Secret Writing*. New York: William Morrow and Company, 1948.

4

Cipher Systems—II

Introduction

Chapter 3 covered transposition ciphers, one class of cipher that involves changing the normal pattern of the characters in a plaintext to produce a ciphertext. This chapter will cover another class of cipher that involves substitution.

Substitution cipher systems require the replacement or substitution of each character in the plaintext by some other character. Typically, the plaintext consists of alphabetic characters. The position of the characters is not changed, only the characters themselves. Substitutions can be made with other letters, numbers, or symbols. Cipher systems illustrating these and other substitution procedures will be explored.

Morse Code As a Cipher

One cipher system that uses other symbols to replace alphabetic characters is the *Morse code*. The code looks like this:

A	·—	J	·———	S	···
B	—···	K	—·—	T	—
C	—·—·	L	·—··	U	··—
D	—··	M	——	V	···—
E	·	N	—·	W	·——
F	··—·	O	———	X	—··—
G	——·	P	·——·	Y	—·——
H	····	Q	——·—	Z	——··
I	··	R	·—·		

Each alphabetic character has a replacement consisting of dots and dashes. In the name Morse code the term *code* is a misnomer. A true code, as shown in Chapter 2, requires that plaintext words have corresponding code words.

To encipher a plaintext using Morse code, you simply replace characters. For example:

```
10 REM MORSE CODE ENCRYPTION PROGRAM
20 DIM A$(30),C$(100),M$(30)
30 FOR I= 1 TO 26
40     READ A$(I),M$(I)
50 NEXT I
60 DATA A,".-",B,"-...",C,"-.-.",D,"-.."
70 DATA E,".",F,"..-.",G,"--.",H,"...."
80 DATA I,"..",J,".---",K,"-.-",L,".-.."
90 DATA M,"--",N,"-.",O,"---",P,".--."
100 DATA Q,"--.-",R,".-.",S,"...",T,"-"
110 DATA U,"..-",V,"...-",W,".--",X,"-..-"
120 DATA Y,"-.--",Z,"--.."
130 PRINT "PLAINTEXT IS:"
140 FOR I = 1 TO 100
150     READ C$(I)
160     IF C$(I) = "ZZZ" THEN 210
170     PRINT C$(I);
180 NEXT I
190 DATA C,H,A,N,G,E,C,I,P,H,E,R,K,E,Y
200 DATA ZZZ
210 PRINT
220 PRINT
230 PRINT "MORSE CODE CIPHERTEXT IS:"
240 FOR A= 1 TO 100
250     IF C$(A) = "ZZZ" THEN 320
260     LET C$=C$(A)
270     FOR I = 1 TO 26
280         IF C$ = A$(I) THEN 300
290     NEXT I
300     PRINT M$(I);"   ";
310 NEXT A
320 END

RUN

PLAINTEXT IS:
CHANGECIPHERKEY

MORSE CODE CIPHERTEXT IS:
-.-.   ....   .-   -.   --.   .   -.-.   ..   .--.   ....   .   .-.   -.-   .   -.--
```

Fig. 4-1. Program for Morse code encryption.

Plaintext: CHANGE CIPHER KEY

Ciphertext: _._·   ····   ·_   _·   __·

             _·_   ··   ·_·   ····   ·   ·_·

             _·_   ·   _·_

With Morse code the ciphertext must have a space between characters for clarity.

A program to encipher messages requires that the normal alphabet be matched with the Morse code symbols. Such a program is provided in Fig. 4-1.

A Number Cipher

A simple, straightforward substitution cipher involves the numerical position of the 26 letters of the alphabet. That is, A is the first letter, B is the second, and so on. We then have a substitution system such as this:

A	1	J	10	S	19
B	2	K	11	T	20
C	3	L	12	U	21
D	4	M	13	V	22
E	5	N	14	W	23
F	6	O	15	X	24
G	7	P	16	Y	25
H	8	Q	17	Z	26
I	9	R	18		

To encipher a clear message requires that each plaintext character be replaced by its corresponding number. For example:

> *Plaintext:* THINK SECURITY
>
> *Ciphertext:* 20 8 9 14 11 19 5 3 21 18 9 20 25

```
10 REM NUMERIC CHARACTER ENCRYPTION PROGRAM
20 DIM A$(30),C$(100)
30 FOR I= 1 TO 26
40    READ A$(I)
50 NEXT I
60 DATA A,B,C,D,E,F,G,H,I,J,K,L,M
70 DATA N,O,P,Q,R,S,T,U,V,W,X,Y,Z
80 PRINT "PLAINTEXT IS:"
90 FOR I = 1 TO 100
100    READ C$(I)
110    IF C$(I) = "ZZZ" THEN 160
120    PRINT C$(I);
130 NEXT I
140 DATA T,H,I,N,K,S,E,C,U,R,I,T,Y,A,T,A,L,L,T,I,M,E,S
150 DATA ZZZ
160 PRINT
170 PRINT
180 PRINT "THE NUMERIC CIPHERTEXT IS:"
190 FOR A= 1 TO 100
200    IF C$(A) = "ZZZ" THEN 270
210    LET C$=C$(A)
220    FOR I = 1 TO 26
230       IF C$ = A$(I) THEN 250
240    NEXT I
250    PRINT I;
260 NEXT A
270 END

RUN

PLAINTEXT IS:
THINKSECURITYATALLTIMES

THE NUMERIC CIPHERTEXT IS:
 20   8   9  14  11  19   5   3  21  18   9  20  25   1  20   1  12  12  20
  9  13   5  19
```

Fig. 4-2. Program for numeric character encryption.

Spaces are needed between each ciphertext character to avoid confusion when deciphering. Otherwise, a ciphertext such as 25 could be taken for the letter Y, when in fact it may represent the word BE.

A program to encipher a clear message using numeric equivalents from A = 1 to Z = 26 is shown in Fig. 4-2. In this program a *normal alphabet* is read in and subscripted as A$(I), with I going from 1 to 26, thereby providing a numeric value for each letter. A flowchart for the program is provided in Fig. 4-3. The clear message to be enciphered is

THINK SECURITY AT ALL TIMES

Many of the encryption programs that follow in this chapter use a logic similar to the one shown in Fig. 4-2. That is, you first read and store the normal alphabet; you then read and store the clear plaintext message; finally, you match a clear character with its cipher replacement, printing out the cipher character.

The level of security that a number cipher gives is quite low. This is particularly true if unauthorized individuals have any knowledge of codes and ciphers. For very simple tasks such a cipher may be useful, but it is not appropriate for most security systems.

ASCII Cipher Systems

Another number cipher system to consider uses the ASCII code described in Chapter 3. This code sets A at a value of 65, B at 66, and so on. The code is as follows:

A	65	J	74	S	83
B	66	K	75	T	84
C	67	L	76	U	85
D	68	M	77	V	86
E	69	N	78	W	87
F	70	O	79	X	88
G	71	P	80	Y	89
H	72	Q	81	Z	90
I	73	R	82		

Such an integer code can be useful in developing cipher systems. As a substitution cipher, each character of a clear message is replaced by its equivalent ASCII value. The encryption of a plaintext and the resulting ciphertext using an ASCII substitution can be seen in this example:

Plaintext: SECRET COMMUNICATION

Ciphertext: 83 69 67 82 69 84
67 79 77 77 85 78 73 67 65 84 73 79 78

As with a number system using A = 1 through Z = 26, spaces are needed in the ciphertext to avoid confusion.

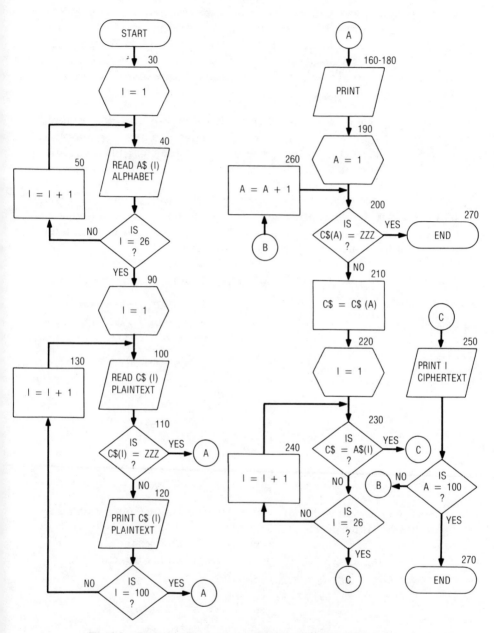

Fig. 4-3. Flowchart for numeric character encryption program.

```
10 REM ASCII CHARACTER ENCRYPTION
20 DIM B(100)
30 READ A$
40 PRINT "PLAINTEXT IS:"
50 PRINT A$
60 PRINT
70 DATA MESSAGE ENCRYPTION IS PART OF SECRET COMMUNICATION
80 CHANGE A$ TO B
90 PRINT "CIPHERTEXT IN ASCII CODE IS:"
100 FOR I= 1 TO B(0)
110     PRINT B(I);" ";
120 NEXT I
130 END

RUN

PLAINTEXT IS:
MESSAGE ENCRYPTION IS PART OF SECRET COMMUNICATION

CIPHERTEXT IN ASCII CODE IS:
 77  69  83  83  65  71  69  32  69  78  67  82  89  80
 84  73  79  78  32  73  83  32  80  65  82  84  32  79
 70  32  83  69  67  82  69  84  32  67  79  77  77  85
 78  73  67  65  84  73  79  78
```

Fig. 4-4. Program for ASCII character encryption.

Since the BASIC programming language has a CHANGE statement, a program can be written to substitute directly ASCII numbers for the alphabetic characters in a plaintext.* A program to encipher using the ASCII codes is shown in Fig. 4-4. Figure 4-5 is a flowchart for this program.

To decipher an ASCII code message requires a program that reverses the process taken in Fig. 4-5. If the following message was received as a ciphertext,

69 78 67 73 80 72 69 82 68 65 84 65

the plaintext, upon matching ASCII numbers to letters, becomes

ENCIPHER DATA

Figure 4-6 is a program that will take a numeric ciphertext like this one and convert it to a plaintext. One drawback to using the ASCII code as an encryption device is that anyone familiar with it can readily decipher a ciphertext based on it. Other encryption processes using this code and providing a higher degree of security will be described later in this chapter and in the following one.

The ASCII code is not limited to a numeric-alphabetic substitution. The code has a numeric value for almost every character, as can be seen in Fig. 4-7.

* Not every BASIC dialect has this statement. See Appendix for variations.

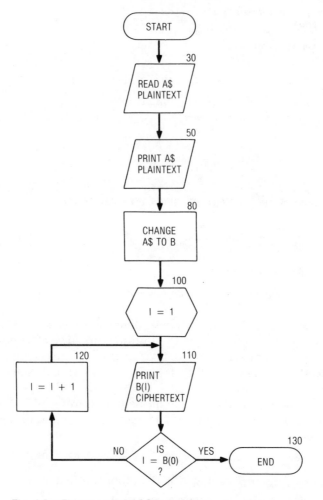

Fig. 4-5. Flowchart for ASCII character encryption program.

Using the complete ASCII code, a complex message can be enciphered. The program in Fig. 4-8 will do so. Look at data Lines 50–120 in Fig. 4-8.

Reciprocal Ciphers

It is possible to encipher a message by taking the alphabet used in the plaintext and reversing it to produce a ciphertext. This type of substitution is *reciprocal* in that Z replaces A, Y replaces B, and so on. Such a reciprocal alphabet used as a ciphertext follows:

Plaintext: ABCDEFGHIJKLMNOPQRSTUVWXYZ
Ciphertext: ZYXWVUTSRQPONMLKJIHGFEDCBA

```
10 REM DECRYPTION OF ASCII CIPHERTEXT
20 DIM B(50)
30 PRINT "CIPHERTEXT IS:"
40 FOR I= 1 TO 50
50     READ B(I)
60     IF B(I) = 32 THEN 110
70     PRINT B(I);
80 NEXT I
90 DATA 69,78,67,73,80,72,69,82,68,65,84,65
100 DATA 32
110 LET B(0) = I
120 PRINT
130 PRINT
140 PRINT "PLAINTEXT IS:"
150 CHANGE B TO A$
160 PRINT A$
170 END

RUN

CIPHERTEXT IS:
 69  78  67  73  80  72  69  82  68  65  84  65

PLAINTEXT IS:
ENCIPHERDATA
```

Fig. 4-6. Program for decryption of ASCII numeric message.

To use a reciprocal substitution, the plaintext character is replaced by the character in the ciphertext alphabet. For example, to encipher the message

SEND   GUNS   SOON

each S is replaced by the ciphertext letter H, E is replaced by V, N by M, D by W, and so forth. The complete ciphertext is then:

Plaintext: SEND   GUNS   SOON
Ciphertext: HVMW   TFMH   HLLM

The program in Fig. 4-9 follows the procedure described here. A single normal alphabet is used and reversed. The plaintext is then read in and the substitution completed.

To decipher a reversed alphabet ciphertext requires basically the same process as enciphering. The ciphertext characters must be replaced by their plaintext reciprocals. Figure 4-10 contains a program to decipher messages enciphered by the program in Fig. 4-9.

An alternate programming approach with a reciprocal cipher system uses the ASCII code. With this code, A is set at 65, B is set as 66, continuing through Z set at 90. The program shown in Fig. 4-11 changes the plaintext to ASCII values. Using a replacement algorithm in Line 90, the ASCII value of each plaintext character is converted into a new ASCII value equivalent and then into a reciprocal alphabet character.

CHARACTER	VALUE	CHARACTER	VALUE	CHARACTER	VALUE
	32	6	54	K	75
!	33	7	55	L	76
"	34	8	56	M	77
#	35	9	57	N	78
$	36	:	58	O	79
%	37	;	59	P	80
&	38	<	60	Q	81
'	39	=	61	R	82
(	40	>	62	S	83
)	41	?	63	T	84
*	42	@	64	U	85
+	43	A	65	V	86
,	44	B	66	W	87
-	45	C	67	X	88
.	46	D	68	Y	89
/	47	E	69	Z	90
0	48	F	70	[	91
1	49	G	71	\	92
2	50	H	72	]	93
3	51	I	73	^	94
4	52	J	74	_	95
5	53				

Fig. 4-7. ASCII characters.

This operation can be shown as follows:

Plaintext:	A	B	M	N	Y	Z
ASCII value:	65	66	77	78	89	90
Subtract ASCII value from 90:	25	24	13	12	1	0
Add 65 to result:	90	89	78	77	66	65
Ciphertext:	Z	Y	N	M	B	A

```
10 REM LARGE MESSAGE ENCRYPTION WITH ASCII CODE
20 DIM B(100)
30 READ A$
40    IF A$= "END OF MESSAGE" THEN 190
50    DATA DATE:3/5
60    DATA TO:JACK SMITH
70    DATA FROM:BILL JONES
80    DATA SUBJECT:CONTRACT NEGOTIATIONS
90    DATA BETTER HOLD OFF UNTIL NEXT WEEK THE FINAL
100   DATA ON THE XYZ CO. CONTRACT. WE EXPECT SOME NEW
110   DATA INFORMATION THIS WEEK. NO RESPONSE TO THIS
120   DATA MEMO IS NECESSARY.
130   DATA "END OF MESSAGE"
140   CHANGE A$ TO B
150    FOR I= 1 TO B(0)
160       PRINT B(I);
170    NEXT I
180 GO TO 30
190 END

RUN

68  65  84  69  58  51  47  53  84  79  58  74  65  67  75  32  83
77  73  84  72  70  82  79  77  58  66  73  76  76  32  74  79  78
69  83  83  85  66  74  69  67  84  58  67  79  78  84  82  65  67
84  32  78  69  71  79  84  73  65  84  73  79  78  83  66  69  84
84  69  82  32  72  79  76  68  32  79  70  70  32  85  78  84  73
76  32  78  69  88  84  32  87  69  69  75  32  84  72  69  32  70
73  78  65  76  79  78  32  84  72  69  32  88  89  90  32  67  79
46  32  67  79  78  84  82  65  67  84  46  32  87  69  32  69  88
80  69  67  84  32  83  79  77  69  32  78  69  87  73  78  70  79
82  77  65  84  73  79  78  32  84  72  73  83  32  87  69  69  75
46  32  78  79  32  82  69  83  80  79  78  83  69  32  84  79  32
84  72  73  83  77  69  77  79  32  73  83  32  78  69  67  69  83
83  65  82  89  46
```

Fig. 4-8. Program for large message encryption using ASCII code.

Program Line 90 (Fig. 4-11) shows this replacement operation as

$$\text{LET} \quad C(I) = (90 - B(I)) + 65$$

where $B(I)$ is the plaintext ASCII value and $C(I)$ is the new ASCII value.

Caesar Ciphers

A Caesar cipher is an alphabetic substitution encryption procedure that involves shifting of the normal alphabet. It was named after Julius Caesar, who first used it.

This cipher replaces a plaintext character with a character three positions further down in the alphabet. Here is a normal plaintext alphabet and a ciphertext alphabet shift of three characters:

Plaintext: A B C D E F G H I J K L M N O P Q R S T U V W X Y Z

Ciphertext: D E F G H I J K L M N O P Q R S T U V W X Y Z A B C

```
10 REM RECIPROCAL CIPHER ENCRYPTION
20 DIM A$(30),C$(100),R$(30)
30 FOR I = 26 TO 1 STEP -1
40     READ R$(I)
50 NEXT I
60 PRINT "RECIPROCAL ALPHABET:",
70 FOR I =1 TO 26
80     PRINT R$(I);
90 NEXT I
100 PRINT
110 DATA A,B,C,D,E,F,G,H,I,J,K,L,M
120 DATA N,O,P,Q,R,S,T,U,V,W,X,Y,Z
130 RESTORE
140 PRINT
150 PRINT "NORMAL ALPHABET:",
160 FOR I = 1 TO 26
170     READ A$(I)
180     PRINT A$(I);
190 NEXT I
200 PRINT
210 PRINT
220 PRINT "PLAINTEXT:",
230 FOR I = 1 TO 100
240     READ C$(I)
250     IF C$(I) = "ZZZ" THEN 300
260     PRINT C$(I);
270 NEXT I
280 DATA S,E,N,D,G,U,N,S,S,O,O,N
290 DATA ZZZ
300 PRINT
310 PRINT
320 PRINT "CIPHERTEXT:",
330 FOR A = 1 TO 100
340     IF C$(A) = "ZZZ" THEN 400
350     FOR I = 1 TO 26
360         IF C$(A) = A$(I) THEN 380
370     NEXT I
380     PRINT R$(I);
390 NEXT A
400 END

RUN




RECIPROCAL ALPHABET:          ZYXWVUTSRQPONMLKJIHGFEDCBA

NORMAL ALPHABET:              ABCDEFGHIJKLMNOPQRSTUVWXYZ


PLAINTEXT:        SENDGUNSSOON

CIPHERTEXT:       HVMWTFMHHLLM
```

Fig. 4-9. Program for reciprocal substitution encryption.

```
10 REM RECIPROCAL CIPHER DECRYPTION
20 DIM A$(30), E$(100), R$(30)
30 FOR I=26 TO 1 STEP -1
40    READ R$(I)
50 NEXT I
60 PRINT "RECIPROCAL ALPHABET:",
70 FOR I=1 TO 26
80    PRINT R$(I);
90 NEXT I
100 PRINT
110 DATA A,B,C,D,E,F,G,H,I,J,K,L,M
120 DATA N,O,P,Q,R,S,T,U,V,W,X,Y,Z
130 RESTORE
140 PRINT
150 PRINT "NORMAL ALPHABET:",
160 FOR I=1 TO 26
170    READ A$(I)
180    PRINT A$(I);
190 NEXT I
200 PRINT
210 PRINT
220 PRINT "CIPHERTEXT:",
230 FOR I=1 TO 100
240    READ E$(I)
250    IF E$(I)="ZZZ" THEN 300
260    PRINT E$(I);
270 NEXT I
280 DATA H,V,M,W,T,F,M,H,H,L,L,M
290 DATA ZZZ
300 PRINT
310 PRINT
320 PRINT "PLAINTEXT:",
330 FOR A=1 TO 100
340    IF E$(A)="ZZZ" THEN 400
350    FOR I=1 TO 26
360       IF E$(A)=R$(I) THEN 380
370    NEXT I
380    PRINT A$(I);
390 NEXT A
400 END

RUN


RECIPROCAL ALPHABET:        ZYXWVUTSRQPONMLKJIHGFEDCBA

NORMAL ALPHABET:            ABCDEFGHIJKLMNOPQRSTUVWXYZ


CIPHERTEXT:     HVMWTFMHHLLM

PLAINTEXT:      SENDGUNSSOON
```

Fig. 4-10. Program for reciprocal substitution decryption.

```
10 REM RECIPROCAL SUBSTITUTION WITH ASCII CODE
20 DIM B(50),C(50)
30 READ A$
40 DATA ALLIMPORTANTINFORMATIONSHOULDBEPROTECTED
50 PRINT "PLAINTEXT IS:"
60 PRINT A$
70 CHANGE A$ TO B
80 FOR I= 1 TO B(0)
90      LET C(I) =(90-B(I))+65
100 NEXT I
110 LET C(0)=B(0)
120 CHANGE C TO E$
130 PRINT
140 PRINT "RECIPROCAL CIPHERTEXT IS:"
150 PRINT E$
160 END

RUN

PLAINTEXT IS:
ALLIMPORTANTINFORMATIONSHOULDBEPROTECTED

RECIPROCAL CIPHERTEXT IS:
ZOORNKLIGZMGRMULINZGRLMHSLFOWYVKILGVXGVW
```

Fig. 4-11. Program for reciprocal substitution encryption using ASCII code.

To encipher a message each plaintext character is replaced by the equivalent ciphertext character, for example:

Plaintext:	SECURE	ALL	MESSAGES
Ciphertext:	VHFXUH	DOO	PHVVDJHV

In the plaintext, the word ALL was encrypted by replacing each character with the cipher letter three places further down in the alphabet. Thus, A was replaced by D, and L was replaced by O.

A program to carry out encryption with a Caesar-cipher shift is shown in Fig. 4-12. The program logic has the plaintext alphabet subscripted as a string variable A\$(I), with A\$(1) = A, A\$(2) = B, and so on through A\$(26) = Z. Using a *shift key* of K = 3 produces a ciphertext character of A\$(I+K). If the word NAME is to be enciphered, the process is

Plaintext:	N	A	M	E
I:	14	1	13	5
Shift K=3:	17	4	16	8
Ciphertext:	Q	D	P	H

The Caesar cipher uses a *cycle* process of A\$(1) to A\$(26). If the plaintext characters X, Y, and Z are enciphered by A\$(I+K) with K=3, we get:

Plaintext:	X	Y	Z
I:	24	25	26
I+K:	27	28	29
Ciphertext:	?	?	?

Because A\$(I+K) cannot go beyond A\$(26) to produce a ciphertext character, an additional programming device is needed for the cycle process to work. The following lines are used in Fig. 4-12:

```
270   IF I > 26-K THEN 300
300   PRINT A$(I+K-26)
```

The IF/THEN statement causes a branch to occur when the cycle reaches $26-K$, where K is the shift key. Above the point $26-K$, the program is instructed to PRINT A\$(I+K-26). Using K=3, we have

```
10 REM CAESAR CIPHER ENCRYPTION PROGRAM
20 DIM A$(30),C$(100)
30 FOR I= 1 TO 26
40     READ A$(I)
50 NEXT I
60 DATA A,B,C,D,E,F,G,H,I,J,K,L,M
70 DATA N,O,P,Q,R,S,T,U,V,W,X,Y,Z
80 READ K
90 DATA 3
100 PRINT "THE MESSAGE TO BE ENCIPHERED IS:"
110 FOR I = 1 TO 100
120     READ C$(I)
130     IF C$(I) = "ZZZ" THEN 180
140     PRINT C$(I);
150 NEXT I
160 DATA A,D,V,A,N,C,E,A,T,D,A,W,N
170 DATA ZZZ
180 PRINT
190 PRINT
200 PRINT "THE CAESAR CIPHERTEXT IS:"
210 FOR A= 1 TO 100
220     IF C$(A) = "ZZZ" THEN 320
230     LET C$=C$(A)
240     FOR I = 1 TO 26
250         IF C$ = A$(I) THEN 270
260     NEXT I
270     IF I>26-K THEN 300
280         PRINT A$(I+K);
290         GO TO 310
300             PRINT A$(I+K-26);
310 NEXT A
320 END

RUN

THE MESSAGE TO BE ENCIPHERED IS:
ADVANCEATDAWN

THE CAESAR CIPHERTEXT IS:
DGYDQFHDWGDZQ
```

Fig. 4-12. Program for Caesar cipher encryption.

```
10 REM CAESAR CIPHER ENCRYPTION WITH ASCII CODE
20 DIM B(100),C(100)
30 READ K
40 DATA 3
50 READ A$
60 DATA SECURE ALL MESSAGES USE CODES AND CIPHERS
70 PRINT "PLAINTEXT IS:"
80 PRINT A$
90 CHANGE A$ TO B
100 FOR I= 1 TO B(0)
110     IF B(I) > 90-K THEN 140
120         LET C(I) = B(I)+K
130         GO TO 150
140             LET C(I) = (B(I)+K-90) + 64
150 NEXT I
160 PRINT
170 LET C(0)=B(0)
180 CHANGE C TO E$
190 PRINT "CAESAR CIPHERTEXT IS:"
200 PRINT E$
210 END

RUN

PLAINTEXT IS:
SECURE ALL MESSAGES USE CODES AND CIPHERS

CAESAR CIPHERTEXT IS:
VHFXUH#DOO#PHVVDJHV#XVH#FRGHV#DQG#FLSKHUV
```

Fig. 4-13. Program for Caesar cipher encryption using ASCII code.

Plaintext:	X	Y	Z
I:	24	25	26
I+K−26:	1	2	3
Ciphertext:	A	B	C

Thus we get the correct substitution of A for X, B for Y, and C for Z.

A Caesar cipher program using this logic and ASCII code is provided in Fig. 4-13. The plaintext is found in data Line 60. The ciphertext should be checked to see if a shift key of K=3 produces the correct result. Figure 4-14 is a flowchart for this Caesar cipher program.

To decipher a Caesar cipher, both the sender and receiver must already know the encryption process and the key (K) being used. If the key is K=3, the receiver could set up both a plaintext and a ciphertext alphabet

Ciphertext:	DEFGHIJKLMNOPQRSTUVWXYZABC
Plaintext:	ABCDEFGHIJKLMNOPQRSTUVWXYZ

and replace ciphertext characters with plaintext characters. The following ciphertext was encrypted with a key of K=3. The preceding plaintext and ciphertext alphabets were used to decipher this message:

Ciphertext:	XVH	FRGHV	DQG	FLSKHUV
Plaintext:	USE	CODES	AND	CIPHERS

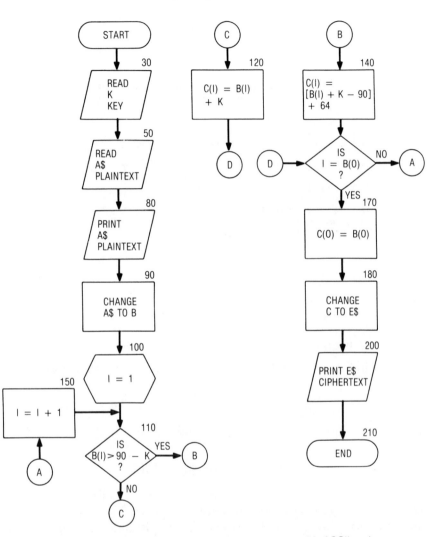

Fig. 4-14. Flowchart for Caesar cipher program with ASCII code.

A program for Caesar cipher decryption is shown in Fig. 4-15. The key is entered in Line 30 (READ K) and the ciphertext is found in data Line 70.

The program logic in Fig. 4-15 reverses the encryption process of the program in Fig. 4-13 by recognizing that a Caesar cipher follows a closed cycle starting with A=1 and continuing through Z=26. If there is a shift forward using a key K=3, where A=1 is replaced by D=4, then to get back to A we shift forward by 26−K or by 23 characters. This would take the cycle from D back to A. Thus in Fig. 4-15, the decryption program shows Line 50 as

```
10 REM CAESAR CIPHER DECRYPTION WITH ASCII CODE
20 DIM B(100),C(100)
30 READ K
40 DATA 3
50 LET K= 26-K
60 READ A$
70 DATA VHFXUH#DOO#PHVVDJHV#XVH#FRGHV#DQG#FLSKHUV
80 PRINT "CAESAR CIPHERTEXT IS:"
90 PRINT A$
100 CHANGE A$ TO B
110 FOR I= 1 TO B(0)
120     IF B(I) > 90-K THEN 150
130         LET C(I) = B(I)+K
140           GO TO 160
150             LET C(I) = (B(I)+K-90) + 64
160 NEXT I
170 PRINT
180 LET C(0)=B(0)
190 CHANGE C TO E$
200 PRINT "PLAINTEXT IS:"
210 PRINT E$
220 END

RUN

CAESAR CIPHERTEXT IS:
VHFXUH#DOO#PHVVDJHV#XVH#FRGHV#DQG#FLSKHUV

PLAINTEXT IS:
SECURE:ALL:MESSAGES:USE:CODES:AND:CIPHERS
```

Fig. 4-15. Program for Caesar cipher decryption using ASCII code.

50   LET K = 26 − K

which is the only change made to the encryption program in Fig. 4-13.

Monoalphabetic Substitution

When cipher systems use a single cipher alphabet for substitution, they are called *monoalphabetic* substitution ciphers. All of the alphabetic substitutions shown so far have been monoalphabetic; that is, only one cipher alphabet has been used.

The Caesar cipher encryption process can generate 25 monoalphabetic substitution alphabets. These alphabets are shown in Fig. 4-16 and are a result of the program in Fig. 4-17.

Caesar cipher substitution does not provide us with a very secure ciphertext, even though such ciphertexts are not readily decipherable upon reading them. However, once it is recognized that there has been a shift in character position, the key can be derived and the ciphertext read. The fact that there is a *fixed displacement* or shift of characters with the Caesar cipher is its major drawback in terms of security. Such a drawback can be overcome with some of the cipher systems that follow.

```
NORMAL ALPHABET FOLLOWED BY 25 CAESAR CIPHER ALPHABETS
ABCDEFGHIJKLMNOPQRSTUVWXYZ

BCDEFGHIJKLMNOPQRSTUVWXYZA

CDEFGHIJKLMNOPQRSTUVWXYZAB

DEFGHIJKLMNOPQRSTUVWXYZABC

EFGHIJKLMNOPQRSTUVWXYZABCD

FGHIJKLMNOPQRSTUVWXYZABCDE

GHIJKLMNOPQRSTUVWXYZABCDEF

HIJKLMNOPQRSTUVWXYZABCDEFG

IJKLMNOPQRSTUVWXYZABCDEFGH

JKLMNOPQRSTUVWXYZABCDEFGHI

KLMNOPQRSTUVWXYZABCDEFGHIJ

LMNOPQRSTUVWXYZABCDEFGHIJK

MNOPQRSTUVWXYZABCDEFGHIJKL

NOPQRSTUVWXYZABCDEFGHIJKLM

OPQRSTUVWXYZABCDEFGHIJKLMN

PQRSTUVWXYZABCDEFGHIJKLMNO

QRSTUVWXYZABCDEFGHIJKLMNOP

RSTUVWXYZABCDEFGHIJKLMNOPQ

STUVWXYZABCDEFGHIJKLMNOPQR

TUVWXYZABCDEFGHIJKLMNOPQRS

UVWXYZABCDEFGHIJKLMNOPQRST

VWXYZABCDEFGHIJKLMNOPQRSTU

WXYZABCDEFGHIJKLMNOPQRSTUV

XYZABCDEFGHIJKLMNOPQRSTUVW

YZABCDEFGHIJKLMNOPQRSTUVWX

ZABCDEFGHIJKLMNOPQRSTUVWXY
```

Fig. 4-16. Monoalphabetic Caesar ciphers.

```
10 REM PROGRAM TO PRODUCE 25 CAESAR CIPHER ALPHABETS
20 DIM B(100),C(100)
30 READ A$
40 DATA ABCDEFGHIJKLMNOPQRSTUVWXYZ
50 PRINT"NORMAL ALPHABET FOLLOWED BY 25 CAESAR CIPHER ALPHABETS"
60 PRINT A$
70 PRINT
80 CHANGE A$ TO B
90 FOR K= 1 TO 25
100     FOR I= 1 TO B(0)
110         IF B(I) > 90-K THEN 140
120             LET C(I) = B(I)+K
130             GO TO 150
140         LET C(I) = (B(I)+K-90) +64
150     NEXT I
160     LET C(0)=B(0)
170     CHANGE C TO E$
180     PRINT E$
190     PRINT
200 NEXT K
210 END
```

Fig. 4-17.   Program to produce monoalphabetic Caesar ciphers.

Decimated Alphabet Ciphers

A Caesar cipher alphabet has a fixed displacement based on a key, with letters in a consecutive sequence. What is needed is an alphabet using a key to provide a displacement but *not* having letters in a consecutive sequence. Such an alphabet is provided by a *decimated* cipher system.

With a Caesar cipher a single key value of 1 to 26 was added to the original alphabet to produce a shift and the resulting cipher alphabet. Rather than adding a key, a multiplier will be used to develop a *decimated alphabet*. To illustrate the process for developing a decimated cipher alphabet, a key number of K=3 will be used. The development of a consecutive sequence Caesar cipher and a nonconsecutive sequence decimated cipher is as follows:

1. Consecutive sequence—Caesar cipher, K=3

Plain:	A	B	C	D	E	F	. . .	U	V	W	X	Y	Z
(Number):	1	2	3	4	5	6	. . .	21	22	23	24	25	26
Cipher:	D	E	F	G	H	I	. . .	X	Y	Z	A	B	C
(Number):	4	5	6	7	8	9	. . .	24	25	26	1	2	3

The shift from letter to letter is a constant:

The letters DEF . . . follow consecutively.

2. Nonconsecutive sequence—decimated cipher, K=3

Plain:	A	B	C	D	E	F	. . .	U	V	W	X	Y	Z
(Number):	1	2	3	4	5	6	. . .	21	22	23	24	25	26
Cipher:	C	F	I	L	O	R	. . .	K	N	Q	T	W	Z
(Number):	3	6	9	12	15	18	. . .	11	14	17	20	23	26

The shift from letter to letter is *not* constant:

$$A \text{ to } C = 1 \text{ to } 3$$
$$B \text{ to } F = 2 \text{ to } 6$$
$$Y \text{ to } W = 25 \text{ to } 23$$

The letter pattern is not consecutive. The cipher alphabet consists of every third letter of the plain alphabet. All the plain alphabet letters are resequenced.

To produce a decimated alphabet, the following procedure is used:

1. Take each letter of the normal alphabet and replace it by the corresponding number value: $A=1$, $B=2$, . . ., $Z=26$.
2. Take each number value and multiply it by a key number (K). This key could be any *odd* number (*not* 13) or a multiple of 13 (26, 52, and so forth).
3. Divide the result of step 2 by 26.1. Take the integer part of the quotient (0, 1, or 2) and multiply it by 26. Subtract the value derived from the result of step 2.
4. Derive the cipher alphabet by using the letter equivalents for the numbers obtained in step 3.

To illustrate the process for developing a decimated cipher alphabet, let

a = a number value of the normal alphabet characters
K = key value
$b = Ka/26.1$
c = a number value of the decimated alphabet characters

Plain-text letter	Number value(a)	Ka (K=3)	b = (Ka)/26.1	c = Ka − b'(26)	Decimated letter
A	1	3	0.115	3 = 3 − 0 × 26	C
B	2	6	0.230	6 = 6 − 0 × 26	F
C	3	9	0.346	9 = 9 − 0 × 26	I
M	13	39	1.494	13 = 39 − 1 × 26	M
N	14	42	1.609	16 = 42 − 1 × 26	P
X	24	72	2.759	20 = 72 − 2 × 26	T
Y	25	75	2.874	23 = 75 − 2 × 26	W
Z	26	78	2.989	26 = 78 − 2 × 26	Z

Fig. 4-18. Partial decimated cipher alphabet, key of K = 3.

Normal alphabet	A	B	C	D	E	F	G	H	I	J	K	L	M	N	O	P	Q	R	S	T	U	V	W	X	Y	Z
Number value (a)	1	2	3	4	5	6	7	8	9	10	11	12	13	14	15	16	17	18	19	20	21	22	23	24	25	26
K=3, Ka	3	6	9	12	15	18	21	24	27	30	33	36	39	42	45	48	51	54	57	60	63	66	69	72	75	78
c	3	6	9	12	15	18	21	24	1	4	7	10	13	16	19	22	25	2	5	8	11	14	17	20	23	26
Cipher	C	F	I	L	O	R	U	X	A	D	G	J	M	P	S	V	Y	B	E	H	K	N	Q	T	W	Z
K=5, Ka	5	10	15	20	25	30	35	40	45	50	55	60	65	70	75	80	85	90	95	100	105	110	115	120	125	130
c	5	10	15	20	25	4	9	14	19	24	3	8	13	18	23	2	7	12	17	22	1	6	11	16	21	26
Cipher	E	J	O	T	Y	D	I	N	S	X	C	H	M	R	W	B	G	L	Q	V	A	F	K	P	U	Z
K=9, Ka	9	18	27	36	45	54	63	72	81	90	99	108	117	126	135	144	153	162	171	180	189	198	207	216	225	234
c	9	18	1	10	19	2	11	20	3	12	21	4	13	22	5	14	23	6	15	24	7	16	25	8	17	26
Cipher	I	R	A	J	S	B	K	T	C	L	U	D	M	V	E	N	W	F	O	X	G	P	Y	H	Q	Z

Fig. 4-19. Decimated cipher alphabets, keys of K = 3, 5, and 9.

```
10 REM DECIMATED ALPHABET PROGRAM
20 DIM A(30),C(30),X(30)
30 READ K
40 DATA 3
50 READ A$
60 DATA ABCDEFGHIJKLMNOPQRSTUVWXYZ
70 PRINT "NORMAL ALPHABET:"
80 PRINT A$
90 CHANGE A$ TO X
100 FOR I= 1 TO X(0)
110     LET A(I) =X(I)-64
120     LET B1 = (K*A(I))/26.1
130     LET B=INT(B1)
140     LET C(0) =26
150     LET C(I) =(K*A(I) - B*26) +64
160 NEXT I
170 PRINT
180 CHANGE C TO C$
190 PRINT "DECIMATED ALPHABET   K=";K
200 PRINT C$
210 END

RUN

NORMAL ALPHABET:
ABCDEFGHIJKLMNOPQRSTUVWXYZ

DECIMATED ALPHABET   K= 3
CFILORUXADGJMPSVYBEHKNQTWZ
```

Fig. 4-20. Program for decimated cipher alphabet.

Then,

$$c = Ka - b'(26)$$

where b' is the integer part of b (that is, 0, 1, or 2).

With a key of $K=3$ and plaintext letters A, B, C, M, N, X, Y, and Z, the result will be that shown in Fig. 4-18.

Figure 4-19 shows three complete decimated alphabets based on this process, using keys $K=3$, 5, and 9. The program in Fig. 4-20 also uses the decimation process. A key is read in followed by a normal alphabet, A$. The alphabet is changed to the subscripted array X in Line 90:

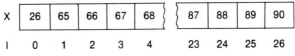

A new array A(I) is created by using Line 110, where

$$A(I) = X(I) - 64$$

so that

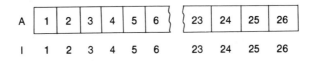

Note that X(0) equals 26, which is the length of the array. This length is not revised into the array A(I).

Using a key of K=3 with normal alphabet letters A, H, O, and W, the program process is as follows:

Line					
40	A$ Letter	A	H	O	W
90	X(I)	65	72	79	87
110	A(I)	1	8	15	23
120	B1=(K*A(I))/26.1	0.115	0.920	1.724	2.644
130	B=INT(B1)	0	0	1	2
150	C(I)=(K*A(I)−B*26)+64	67	88	83	81
200	C$ Letter	C	X	S	Q

By revising the program in Fig. 4-20 with this loop

```
90      FOR K = 1 TO 15 STEP 2
210     NEXT K
```

and with one or two other changes, we come up with the program in Fig. 4-21. This program produces eight different decimated alphabets using keys of K=1, 3, 5, 7, 9, 11, 13, and 15. All of these alphabets can be seen as the output in Fig. 4-21. Note how the alphabet for K=13 produces a repeating cycle MZMZ . . . MZMZ, and therefore an alphabet that is not completely decimated. This result is a caution not to use a key of K=13 or a multiple of thirteen.

Using a decimated alphabet is no different than using any of the alphabet substitutions described so far. A plaintext character must be replaced by a ciphertext character. For example, using a decimated alphabet from Fig. 4-19 with a key K=5 converts the following plaintext to the ciphertext shown. Each plaintext character is replaced by its substitution character. Thus for K=5, N is replaced by R, E is replaced by Y, D is replaced by T, and so on.

> Plaintext: NEED ADVICE ON ACTION TO TAKE
> Ciphertext: RYYT ETFSOY WR EOVSWR VW VECY

The program in Fig. 4-20 can be used to encipher a plaintext by the decimation process. If the alphabet in Line 60 is replaced by a plaintext, upon running the program the result will be a ciphertext in decimated form (see questions 18 and 19).

Polyalphabetic Substitution

A cipher system that uses two or more cipher alphabets in a substitution process is called a *multiple* or *polyalphabetic* substitution system.

Multiple alphabets have already been covered in the material on Caesar ciphers and decimated alphabets. Figure 4-22 is a complete set of

```
10 REM DECIMATED ALPHABETS WITH MANY KEYS
20 DIM A(30),C(30),X(30)
30 READ A$
40 DATA ABCDEFGHIJKLMNOPQRSTUVWXYZ
50 PRINT "NORMAL ALPHABET:"
60 PRINT A$
70 PRINT
80 PRINT "KEY","DECIMATED ALPHABET"
90 FOR K= 1 TO 15 STEP 2
100      CHANGE A$ TO X
110      FOR I= 1 TO X(0)
120          LET A(I) =X(I)-64
130          LET B1 = (K*A(I))/26.1
140          LET B=INT(B1)
150          LET C(0) =26
160          LET C(I) =(K*A(I) - B*26) +64
170      NEXT I
180      PRINT
190      CHANGE C TO C$
200      PRINT K,C$
210 NEXT K
220 END

RUN

NORMAL ALPHABET:
ABCDEFGHIJKLMNOPQRSTUVWXYZ

KEY               DECIMATED ALPHABET

1                 ABCDEFGHIJKLMNOPQRSTUVWXYZ

3                 CFILORUXADGJMPSVYBEHKNQTWZ

5                 EJOTYDINSXCHMRWBGLQVAFKPUZ

7                 GNUBIPWDKRYFMTAHOVCJQXELSZ

9                 IRAJSBKTCLUDMVENWFOXGPYHQZ

11                KVGRCNYJUFQBMXITEPALWHSDOZ

13                MZMZMZMZMZMZMZMZMZMZMZMZMZ

15                ODSHWLAPETIXMBQFUJYNCRGVKZ
```

Fig. 4-21. Eight decimated alphabets and program.

Caesar alphabets called a *Vigenère table*. It is named after the sixteenth century French cryptographer Blaise de Vigenère, who first described it and popularized its use.

To carry out encryptions using a Vigenère table, the top line of letters represents plaintext and the column on the left indicates the key letters. Suppose the plaintext to encipher is

CARRYOUT PLAN B WEDNESDAY

and the key is the word END. It is the key that tells which alphabet to use. In this case, we will use alphabets E, N, and D. The key word is repeated under the plaintext and a character is substituted from the indicated alphabet. For our example we have the following:

Plaintext:	CARRYOUT	PLAN	B	WEDNESDAY
Key:	ENDENDEN	DEND	E	NDENDENDE
Ciphertext:	GNUVLRYG	SPNQ	F	JHHAHWQDC

Each substitution character is found by going down the column of the plaintext letter until the key letter is reached. The substitution letter is found at the intersection of the plaintext letter and the key letter:

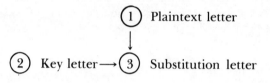

(1) Plaintext letter

(2) Key letter ⟶ (3) Substitution letter

    An easier way of using the Vigenère table is to write the key word first with the plaintext transposed next to it. For the previous message then,

```
               VIGENERE TABLE

          ABCDEFGHIJKLMNOPQRSTUVWXYZ

     0  A  ABCDEFGHIJKLMNOPQRSTUVWXYZ
     1  B  BCDEFGHIJKLMNOPQRSTUVWXYZA
     2  C  CDEFGHIJKLMNOPQRSTUVWXYZAB
     3  D  DEFGHIJKLMNOPQRSTUVWXYZABC
     4  E  EFGHIJKLMNOPQRSTUVWXYZABCD
     5  F  FGHIJKLMNOPQRSTUVWXYZABCDE
     6  G  GHIJKLMNOPQRSTUVWXYZABCDEF
     7  H  HIJKLMNOPQRSTUVWXYZABCDEFG
     8  I  IJKLMNOPQRSTUVWXYZABCDEFGH
     9  J  JKLMNOPQRSTUVWXYZABCDEFGHI
    10  K  KLMNOPQRSTUVWXYZABCDEFGHIJ
    11  L  LMNOPQRSTUVWXYZABCDEFGHIJK
    12  M  MNOPQRSTUVWXYZABCDEFGHIJKL
    13  N  NOPQRSTUVWXYZABCDEFGHIJKLM
    14  O  OPQRSTUVWXYZABCDEFGHIJKLMN
    15  P  PQRSTUVWXYZABCDEFGHIJKLMNO
    16  Q  QRSTUVWXYZABCDEFGHIJKLMNOP
    17  R  RSTUVWXYZABCDEFGHIJKLMNOPQ
    18  S  STUVWXYZABCDEFGHIJKLMNOPQR
    19  T  TUVWXYZABCDEFGHIJKLMNOPQRS
    20  U  UVWXYZABCDEFGHIJKLMNOPQRST
    21  V  VWXYZABCDEFGHIJKLMNOPQRSTU
    22  W  WXYZABCDEFGHIJKLMNOPQRSTUV
    23  X  XYZABCDEFGHIJKLMNOPQRSTUVW
    24  Y  YZABCDEFGHIJKLMNOPQRSTUVWX
    25  Z  ZABCDEFGHIJKLMNOPQRSTUVWXY
```

Fig. 4-22. Vigenère table.

Key word		Plaintext							Key word		Ciphertext						
E	C	R	U	L	B	S	D	Y	E	G	V	Y	P	F	H	W	C
N	A	Y	T	A	W	N	D		N	N	L	G	W	J	A	Q	
D	R	O	P	N	E	E	A		D	U	R	S	Q	H	H	D	

The ciphertext is thus

GNU VLR YGS PNQ FJH HAH WQD C

To decipher a polyalphabetic substitution the recipient must know the key word, and he must also know that the ciphertext was based on a Vigenère table.

Reversing the process requires writing the ciphertext in a vertical route transposition against the key word. By going to a key alphabet in the Vigenère table, finding the ciphertext letter, and then going up to the top of the table, the plaintext letter is found.

Suppose we have this ciphertext message to decipher:

TUAEIGTUEISBLNCCUAS

If the key word is RUN, the ciphertext is written alongside it following a vertical route transposition. By entering the Vigenère table from the key letter side, finding the ciphertext character, and following up to the top of the table, the plaintext letter is found. The direction is as follows:

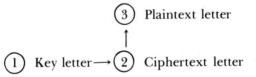

For the previous ciphertext the intermediate deciphering is as follows:

Key word		Ciphertext						Plaintext					
R	T	E	T	I	L	C	S	C	N	C	R	U	L	B
U	U	I	U	S	N	U		A	O	A	Y	T	A
N	A	G	E	B	C	A		N	T	R	O	P	N

The deciphered message appears in plaintext as follows:

CANNOT CARRY OUT PLAN B

As long as multiple alphabets are available, polyalphabetic substitutions can be used. Such substitution ciphers are possible using the decimated alphabets shown in Fig. 4-19 and Fig. 4-21.

With several decimated alphabets (each having a different key), another encryption procedure is possible using two or more of these alphabets. This is done with a key, such as 1 3 5. Each digit represents

```
10 REM PROGRAM FOR VIGENERE TABLE ENCRYPTION
20 DIM B(100),C(100),K(100)
30 READ A$
40 DATA CARRYOUTPLANBWEDNESDAY
50 PRINT "PLAINTEXT IS:"
60 PRINT A$
70 CHANGE A$ TO B
80 PRINT "YOUR KEYWORD IS";
90 INPUT K$
100 CHANGE K$ TO K
110 LET J=0
120 FOR I= 1 TO B(0)
130      GO SUB 250
140      IF B(I) > 90-K THEN 170
150          LET C(I) = B(I)+K
160          GO TO 180
170      LET C(I) = (B(I)+K-90) + 64
180 NEXT I
190 PRINT
200 LET C(0)=B(0)
210 CHANGE C TO E$
220 PRINT "VIGENERE TABLE CIPHERTEXT IS:"
230 PRINT E$
240 STOP
250      LET J=J+1
260      IF J>K(0) THEN 290
270      LET K=K(J)-65
280      RETURN
290          LET J=1
300          LET K=K(J)-65
310          RETURN
320 END

RUN

PLAINTEXT IS:
CARRYOUTPLANBWEDNESDAY
YOUR KEYWORD IS ?END

VIGENERE TABLE CIPHERTEXT IS:
GNUVLRYGSPNQFJHHAHWQDC
```

Fig. 4-23. Program for Vigenère table encryption.

a different single-number-key decimated alphabet. For each plaintext character a substitution is made from a specific cipher alphabet. The process, using the alphabets in Fig. 4-19 or Fig. 4-21, looks like this:

Plaintext:	C	L	E	A	R		M	E	S	S	A	G	E
Alphabet key:	1	3	5	1	3		5	1	3	5	1	3	5
Ciphertext:	C	J	Y	A	B		M	E	E	Q	A	U	Y

With this process the alphabet key numbers are repeated under the plaintext characters. The ciphertext characters are then drawn from the respective decimated alphabet.

Encryption with polyalphabetic substitution by computer requires appropriate programs for the particular procedure to be used, that is, either a Vigenère table or decimated alphabets. To illustrate with Vigenère encryption, the program in Fig. 4-23 was developed. This program is a revision of the Caesar cipher encryption program in Fig. 4-13. You will recall that a Vigenère table is comprised of 26 Caesar alphabets. A *subroutine* has been added to perform the encryption of a plaintext following the Vigenère process. The subroutine is shown in Lines 250 through 310. This program (Fig. 4-23) allows the user to enter a word key up to the length of the plaintext. This word key serves to pick those alphabets that will be used to encrypt the plaintext. Such word keys provide added security since, for example, a three-character word key picked from the 26 alphabet letters is one of 15,600 different three-letter keys that can be used.* Added security comes from the fact that with such a large number of possible keys, it is difficult for someone not knowing the real key to find it by trial and error.

To test this program, the plaintext CARRYOUT PLAN B WEDNESDAY and the word key END were entered in the Vigenère encryption program. The output shown in Fig. 4-23 agrees with that obtained previously, when the plaintext was encrypted by hand using the table in Fig. 4-22.

To develop a program to decipher messages encrypted by the program in Fig. 4-23 requires the addition of one statement. This additional statement,

$$135 \qquad \text{LET} \quad K=26-K$$

will reverse the Vigenère table encryption process. Question 24 calls for such a decryption program.

Just as a computer program was created for Vigenère table encryption, a program for polyalphabetic substitution using decimated alphabets can also be written. To develop such a program, see question 25.

Diagraphic Substitution

In *digraphic substitution* the plaintext is broken up into pairs of letters, and each pair is replaced by a substitution pair to form a ciphertext. One of the most popular systems of digraphic encipherment was developed in the nineteenth century by Sir Charles Wheatstone. The system is known as the *Playfair cipher.* It was named after Lord Lyon Playfair, who sponsored it for use by the British Foreign Office.

This cipher uses a 5×5 square containing the letters of the alphabet. Such a square may place the alphabet in a clockwise manner as follows:

* $_{26}P_3 = 26!/(26 - 3)! = 26 \times 25 \times 24 = 15,600$ different three-letter keys.

A	B	C	D	E
F	G	H	I	J
K	L	M	N	O
P	Q	R	S	T
U	V	W	X	Y

In this particular square, the letter Z is omitted. Another square may have the I and J combined in a single cell so that the Z can be included.

The rules for enciphering can vary. One set of rules follows:

1. If the two letters of the pair are in the same row, their cipher equivalents are the letters immediately to their right, for example:

    Plaintext: AC   *Ciphertext:* BD

When a plaintext letter is at the end of a row, we substitute the letter at the opposite end of the same row, for example:

    Plaintext: ST   Ciphertext: TP
    Plaintext: KO   Ciphertext: LK

2. If the two letters are in the same column, their cipher equivalents are the letters immediately below each one, for example:

    Plaintext: CH   *Ciphertext:* HM

When a plaintext letter is at the bottom of a column, we substitute the letter at the opposite end of the column, for example:

    Plaintext: IX   *Ciphertext:* ND
    Plaintext: YE   Ciphertext: EJ

3. If the two letters are in opposite corners of an imaginary rectangle, diagonally opposite each other, their cipher equivalents are the letters of the opposite diagonal. The substitution starts with the first plaintext letter, substituting the ciphertext letter in the same row; for example:

    Plaintext: EK   *Ciphertext:* AO
    Plaintext: SE   *Ciphertext:* TD

Applying the Playfair enciphering rules to the message USE PLAN TODAY, we have:

    Plaintext: US EP LA NT OD AY
    Ciphertext: XP AT KB OS NE EU

Deciphering a Playfair ciphertext requires that the receiver know the contents of the 5×5 square as well as the enciphering rules to reverse the process.

To vary the 5×5 square, start the characters by placing a code word or key in the square and then completing the square by using the remaining alphabet characters. The following square starts with the key word CODE and finishes with the remaining letters in a clockwise pattern.

C	O	D	E	A
B	F	G	H	I
J	K	L	M	N
P	Q	R	S	T
U	V	W	X	Y

Enciphering the previous plaintext using this square, we have

Plaintext:	US	EP	LA	NT	OD	AY
Ciphertext:	XP	CS	ND	TY	DE	IA

Given such rules as these, it would be possible to create a computer program to encipher messages using the Playfair cipher. Such a program is required in question 26.

Summary

In addition to transposition cipher systems, there is another type of cipher system using substitution of characters for those characters in a plaintext. Morse code is an example of a substitution cipher. Other substitutions can be made with numbers, such as A=1, B=2, and so on. A standard computer substitution uses ASCII (American Standard Code for Information Interchange) values of 65 for A, 66 for B, and so forth.

When single alphabets are used to supply substitution characters for a plaintext based on the normal alphabet, we have what is known as a monoalphabetic substitution. Such substitutions can be based on systems that use a reversed or reciprocal alphabet where the first character in the alphabet is Z, the next is Y, then X, W, and so on. More advanced monoalphabetic substitution cipher systems can be based on a Caesar cipher or a decimated alphabet.

With a Caesar cipher the alphabet used has a fixed shift or displacement based on a key value, usually from 1 to 26. A key of 1 would signify that the letters of the normal alphabet have moved up one place to form an alphabet starting at B, C, D, and so forth. The Caesar alphabet follows a consecutive sequence. However, an alphabet can be developed having a nonconsecutive sequence. Such an alphabet is said to be decimated. It uses a key value such as 1, 3, or 5 to produce a pattern that does not have a constant shift. A key of 3 would cause a normal alphabet to be rearranged so that, for example, A becomes C, B becomes F, and Y becomes W.

When a cipher substitution system uses more than one alphabet to produce a ciphertext, the system is referred to as a polyalphabetic cipher system. These systems produce a ciphertext by using more than one Caesar cipher alphabet, or several decimated alphabets, keyed to a specific word. A Vigenère table is a polyalphabetic substitution device that incorporates 26 Caesar cipher alphabets. A key word is used to enter the table and provide the appropriate substitution character.

Digraphic substitution produces a ciphertext by replacing pairs of plaintext letters with other letter pairs. The Playfair cipher is a popular digraphic cipher system.

This chapter illustrates that with modern computer systems and programming techniques, it is possible to develop software for rapid and accurate encryption or decryption of messages using character substitution principles.

Questions

1. How do *substitution* cipher systems differ from *transposition* cipher systems?
2. What is the plaintext for the following Morse code cipher text?

       —   · · · ·   · ·   — ·   — · —   · · ·

       ·   — · — ·   · · —   · — ·   · ·   —

       — · —   · —   —   · —   · — · ·

       · — · ·   —   · ·   — —   ·   · · ·

3. What is the plaintext for each of the following numeric ciphertexts?

   (a) 5   16   12   21   18   9   2   21   19   21   14   21   13

   (b) 19   5   3   21   18   9   20   25   4   5   16   5
        14   4   19   15   14   16   5   15   16   12   5   14
        15   20   3   15   13   16   21   20   5   18   19

4. What is the ASCII value equivalent for the word ENCRYPTION?
5. What is the plaintext for the following ASCII ciphertext?

        69   78   67   73   80   72   69   82
        83   69   78   83   73   84   73   86   69
        73   78   70   79   82   77   65   84   73   79   78

6. Think of a large message and encipher it by using the program in Fig. 4-8.
7. In looking at the output in Fig. 4-8, you will notice the value 32 appears quite often. What does this value represent?
8. What is the reciprocal ciphertext for the following plaintext?

   KEEP FIGHTING HELP IS ON THE WAY

9. What is the plaintext for the following reciprocal ciphertext (use Fig. 4-11)?

RYVORVEVRMWVNLXIZXBYVXZFHVRGIVOVZHVH
GSVVMVITRVHLUVEVIBSFNZMYVRMT

10. Using the program in Fig. 4-12, encipher the plaintext ADVANCE AT DAWN with a key of
    (a) 8
    (b) 27

11. If a key of K=30 is used in a Caesar cipher, will such a key work? What is the shift of characters with such a key?

12. Decipher the following ciphertexts:
    (a) EHJLQRSHUDWLRQEDUEDURVVDMXQHWZHQWBWZR
       (Hint: K=3)
    (b) YZGXZUVKXGZOUTUBKXRUXJPATKYODZN   (Hint: K=6)

13. Revise the Caesar cipher decryption program in Fig. 4-15 to carry out either encryption or decryption within a single program.

14. In Fig. 4-13 the Caesar ciphertext output shows # characters. Why have these characters been generated, and what are the plaintext equivalents for them?

15. In Fig. 4-15 the plaintext output shows the character ":".Why has this character been generated?

16. Why is a *decimated alphabet* preferable to a *Caesar alphabet* for encryption?

17. Develop a decimated cipher alphabet for K=29.

18. Using the decimation process, or the program in Fig. 4-20, and a key of K=5
    (a) Encipher this plaintext:

       NEED ADVICE ON ACTION TO TAKE

    (b) Decipher this ciphertext:

       DWHHWKBHERJLESQYUNYJST

19. Using the decimation process, or the program in Fig. 4-21, and a key of K=9, encipher this message:

    STOP NEGOTIATIONS BY WEDNESDAY

20. Using the Vigenère table in Fig. 4-22 with the key word SPY, encipher this message:

    PROTECT DATA BY ENCRYPTION

21. Decipher the Vigenère message using the key word BELL:

    QVZN METX MMMP SXJE IVZF HLZF UEWW ULPW
    BROF OXZL MPES FMYS BFTE BRED ULPC FSQ

22. Using either the Vigenère table in Fig. 4-22 or the program in Fig. 4-23, encipher this message, using the key END RUN AROUND THE BLOCK:

    CARRY OUT PLAN B WEDNESDAY

23. How many different word keys can be derived from the normal alphabet if the key has
    (a) Four characters?
    (b) Five characters?
24. Revise the program in Fig. 4-23 to perform Vigenère table decryption.
25. Develop a decimated polyalphabetic substitution program by revising Fig. 4-20 to accept a three-digit number key. (*Hint:* See Fig. 4-23.)
26. Using the rules given for the Playfair cipher, develop an enciphering program.
27. Using this Playfair square

A	B	C	D	E
F	G	H	I	J
K	L	M	N	O
P	Q	R	S	T
U	V	W	X	Y

encipher these messages:
    (a) BUY   NOW
    (b) SEND   HELP   SOON
    (c) DELAY   DEPARTURE
28. Using the Playfair square in question 27, decipher these messages:
    (a) PLAYFAIR   CIPHER: CPSHYBOKKO
    (b) PLAYFAIR   CIPHER: EAUFSPEPKODA
    (c) PLAYFAIR   CIPHER: EMEARDFSJCSTDKEDKNUAYJST
29. Using this Playfair square

C	O	D	E	A
B	F	G	H	I
J	K	L	M	N
P	Q	R	S	T
U	V	W	X	Y

decipher these messages:
    (a) PLAYFAIR   CIPHER: RJIAIOGT
    (b) PLAYFAIR   CIPHER: XPAODEHX
    (c) PLAYFAIR   CIPHER: XHBCSDECYI
    (d) PLAYFAIR   CIPHER: EDVAYJAAELAKAX

References

Bennett, William R., Jr. *Introduction to Computer Applications for Non-Science Students (BASIC)*. Englewood Cliffs, New Jersey: Prentice-Hall, Inc., 1976.

Chesson, Frederick W. "Computers and Cryptology." *Datamation,* vol. 19, no. 1 (January 1973): 62–64, 77–81.

Hoffman, Lance J. *Modern Methods for Computer Security and Privacy.* Englewood Cliffs, New Jersey: Prentice-Hall, 1977.

Kahn, David. "Modern Cryptology," *Scientific American,* vol. 215, no. 1 (July 1966): 38–46.

Sass, C. Joseph. *BASIC Programming and Applications.* Boston, Mass.: Allyn and Bacon, Inc., 1976.

Sinkov, Abraham. *Elementary Cryptanalysis: A Mathematical Approach.* New York: Random House, 1968.

Van Tassel, Dennis. *Computer Security Management.* Englewood Cliffs, New Jersey: Prentice-Hall, Inc., 1972.

5

Cryptography and Computer Operations

Introduction

In the two previous chapters the processes and methods of transposition and substitution cipher systems were described. Many of these processes were incorporated within computer programs. One advantage of the computer is that encryption and decryption can be both accurately and rapidly carried out.

In this chapter we will build upon the material described earlier. No new cipher systems will be shown. Instead, various computer operations to provide better security will be explored. The computer can provide random numbers to generate random keys and random alphabets. Using the computer, it will be possible to generate different encryption tables like the Vigenère table.

The computer enables us to combine arithmetic, algebraic, and matrix operations to improve code and cipher systems. After exploring these techniques, we will be able to scramble files and programs to make sure their contents are not easily understood by unauthorized persons.

Generating Random Word Keys

In Chapter 2 it was shown how code words could be computer-generated in a random manner (see Fig. 2-7). Many of the cipher systems described in Chapter 4 required a key. Using the ASCII character set, a program has been written to produce an alphabetic key of up to 26 characters. This random key word program is shown in Fig. 5-1.

To illustrate random word keys of varying lengths, the program in Fig. 5-1 has been modified by adding a FOR/NEXT loop:

```
30      FOR  K  =  1  TO  26

180     NEXT  K
```

This loop causes the program to generate 26 different word keys with

```
10 RANDOM KEYWORD PROGRAM
20 DIM B(30),C(30)
25 RANDOMIZE
30 READ A$
40 DATA ABCDEFGHIJKLMNOPQRSTUVWXYZ
50 CHANGE A$ TO B
60 PRINT "HOW MANY CHARACTERS IN THE KEY";
70 INPUT K
80 FOR N= 1 TO K
90     LET R=INT(26*RND(X)+1)
100     IF B(R)=-999 THEN 90
110         LET C(N) = B(R)
120         LET B(R)=-999
130 NEXT N
140 LET C(0)=B(0)
150 CHANGE C TO C$
160 PRINT
170 PRINT "KEYWORD IS: ";
180 PRINT C$
190 END

RUN

HOW MANY CHARACTERS IN THE KEY ?5

KEYWORD IS: PFVBZ
```

Fig. 5-1. Random key word program.

lengths of 1 to 26 characters. The complete output and program are illustrated in Fig. 5-2.

Generating Random Alphabets

Caesar cipher alphabets and decimated cipher alphabets, such as those shown in Chapter 4, are based on a specific procedure that *can* be broken by unauthorized persons. This is possible because such alphabets have a repetitive cycle.

An alphabet that can provide greater security when used in a cipher system is one that has no known cycle that can be easily discovered. With a normal alphabet of 26 letters, it is possible to rearrange the letters in a random, unsequenced manner n! possible ways. That is 26!, or $26 \times 25 \ldots \times 3 \times 2 \times 1$ different alphabets.

These alphabets would be best used in a polyalphabetic cipher process rather than as a single, monoalphabetic cipher system. In the next chapter you will see how the single alphabetic cipher is easily broken. The monoalphabetic is more difficult to unravel.

To produce (by computer) random alphabet ciphers, the program in Fig. 5-1 has been modified as follows:

```
30      FOR  P  =  1  TO  10
70      FOR  N  =  1  TO  26

180     NEXT  P
```

```
10 RANDOM KEYWORD OF VARYING LENGTH PROGRAM
20 DIM B(30),C(30)
25 RANDOMIZE
30 FOR K= 1 TO 26
40      READ A$
50      DATA ABCDEFGHIJKLMNOPQRSTUVWXYZ
60      CHANGE A$ TO B
70      FOR N= 1 TO K
80          LET R=INT(26*RND(X)+1)
90          IF B(R)=-999 THEN 80
100             LET C(N) = B(R)
110             LET B(R)=-999
120      NEXT N
130      LET C(0)=B(0)
140      CHANGE C TO C$
150      PRINT "KEYWORD IS: ";
160      PRINT C$
170      RESTORE
180 NEXT K
190 END

RUN

KEYWORD IS: Q
KEYWORD IS: SQ
KEYWORD IS: NKU
KEYWORD IS: HPTI
KEYWORD IS: EAQPS
KEYWORD IS: ARVYCF
KEYWORD IS: LTNMFCA
KEYWORD IS: WAFGLKQZ
KEYWORD IS: GRSYNOBTH
KEYWORD IS: EKUDTHFWJO
KEYWORD IS: YROKJTGVPWS
KEYWORD IS: KELCMAUPROJG
KEYWORD IS: OBKUDQRIWGSNY
KEYWORD IS: XBGYJSVKZIFCHP
KEYWORD IS: EMIXHSNUAYKGBCJ
KEYWORD IS: JSEOFWAHNMBCTPID
KEYWORD IS: VNBAQPXTMIULKFOSW
KEYWORD IS: NKRMVOYEGZJHCUTQIS
KEYWORD IS: NWLDPMRUAZVQYBHKXSE
KEYWORD IS: LDXEAPIQYSTFBRJWCZMN
KEYWORD IS: GXDRSKVNYUHTBCFIJEWAZ
KEYWORD IS: YZJKFNSMTOBVGLIHCWDAXR
KEYWORD IS: GIWFKPYEOAXJDULRNCBZMTS
KEYWORD IS: ULOMYGZJTAQCVESPKWFIBDNH
KEYWORD IS: TXWZVRQJDBKFHPLOUYSNCIEAG
KEYWORD IS: LGODXRYNPWBJUCEMIHSVTZAKQF
```

Fig. 5-2. Random key word (varying-length) program.

As a result of these added lines, ten random cipher alphabets are produced by the program in Fig. 5-3.

Computer-Generated Encryption Tables

So far we have seen that Vigenère tables and other polygraphic alphabets result in substitutions of one alphabetic character by another

```
10 RANDOM CIPHER ALPHABET PROGRAM
20 DIM B(30),C(30)
25 RANDOMIZE
30 FOR P= 1 TO 10
40      READ A$
50      DATA ABCDEFGHIJKLMNOPQRSTUVWXYZ
60      CHANGE A$ TO B
70      FOR N= 1 TO 26
80           LET R=INT(26*RND(X)+1)
90           IF B(R)=-999 THEN 80
100               LET C(N) = B(R)
110               LET B(R)=-999
120      NEXT N
130      LET C(0)=B(0)
140      CHANGE C TO C$
150      PRINT 'ALPHABET'P,
160      PRINT C$
170      RESTORE
180 NEXT P
190 END

RUN

ALPHABET 1      QWLURBFCVZNHPXKITODAMJEYGS
ALPHABET 2      NRFLQVEAOKMGSWHZJUDXBTYIPC
ALPHABET 3      CTVFSKDYLPQHZIJUXGAMRWOBEN
ALPHABET 4      SVKAPFBJTGQNOYZMWXDLEHUCRI
ALPHABET 5      KLUVYFGATINBCRMPZQSOJDXHWE
ALPHABET 6      QGYJNZDBAOCKMLSHXUVFEPWTIR
ALPHABET 7      XFIDZLSHEPVQOMJUGKRWYABNCT
ALPHABET 8      AFIXPJWYGVDMSBUKOQRNTHLZEC
ALPHABET 9      ZBMIQEGUTYXPRHLKVFWNOJSCDA
ALPHABET 10     IWFKOBQZDUPLJYTAHVEXSCNMRG
```

Fig. 5-3. Random cipher alphabet program.

alphabetic character. The plaintext is composed of normal characters A through Z, and the ciphertext is composed of substituted characters drawn from these same letters.

Computers enable us to have a larger than normal alphabet for messages. They also make it possible to use a set of substitution characters different from those in the normal alphabet. For example, the *normal alphabet* may consist of these 39 characters:

A	K	U	4
B	L	V	5
C	M	W	6
D	N	X	7
E	O	Y	8
F	P	Z	9
G	Q	0	?
H	R	1	$
I	S	2	
J	T	3	

These 39 *substitution characters* can be used:

A	K	U	5
B	L	V	#
C	M	W	$
D	N	X	%
E	O	Y	&
F	P	Z	*
G.	Q	1	+
H	R	2	@
I	S	3	–
J	T	4	

These substitution characters will be randomly scrambled to provide 40 different alphabets. Figure 5-4 is a program that generates a substitution table for the normal alphabet just given. The table has the normal alphabet on top. A word key is not practical for this table since characters may repeat themselves along the leftmost column. A number key based on the digits 1 to 40 is suggested. Line 1 represents digit 1, Line 2 represents digit 2, and so on.

```
10 REM SUBSTITUTION TABLE 40 ALPHABETS
20 DIM B(100),C(100),S(100)
25 RANDOMIZE
30 READ S$
40 DATA ABCDEFGHIJKLMNOPQRSTUVWXYZ12345#$%&*+@-
50 READ A$
60 DATA ABCDEFGHIJKLMNOPQRSTUVWXYZ0123456789?$,
70 PRINT TAB(4);A$
80 PRINT
90 CHANGE A$ TO B
100 FOR I= 1 TO 40
110     CHANGE S$ TO C
120     FOR T= 1 TO 39
130         LET R= INT(39*RND(X)+1)
140         IF C(R) =-999 THEN 130
150         LET S(T) =C(R)
160         LET C(R) =-999
170     NEXT T
180     LET S(0)=C(0)
190     CHANGE S TO C$
200     PRINT I; TAB(4);C$
210     RESTORE
220     READ S$
230 NEXT I
240 END
```

Fig. 5-4. Substitution table program.

Using the table in Fig. 5-4 with a key of 36–3–22–8 indicates that a plaintext message such as

```
RUN

ABCDEFGHIJKLMNOPQRSTUVWXYZ0123456789?$*

 1  TU1KXG32@-EJRDNOFWH+CAY4&ILMPB$%Z5Q#VS*
 2  #UAM%GLK-BXFRS*H2&CEJ+P$QW@NOTZ4IY53D1V
 3  GFPC4-DZBMVR5S+LNHEAU$YW3Q%XIJ2*#O@K1&T
 4  -TB4GFS#J&$CX%5D+P@NEUAQOM3*ZLIVKH21YWR
 5  N-&DR4Y@FBAQ3W5VPOHSET$JG%1*KUCI2Z+X#LM
 6  &TFLOYR-@+%SI4#QGJCH*1ADMBPVXKNZ$UW5E23
 7  *@UPYKB2-XNVF&CTMQ5%L$O#AE1IGS+ZD4JHR3W
 8  @RCP#KN1&IQW3T+EJF$MS*VDG-UA4HLOXB%Z25Y
 9  C$P+I&Q1GMZXYLRFD24TEH#@%J3KV*B-5UNOWAS
10  ICMQYJ3HVTB5-K2$4*Z#NDX1S%&WRGP+FO@EULA
11  2ES#V+JMZ$5N&@BQPFI-DXAG41T%KHOUYC*R3WL
12  2ST#PB1WH3UYAN%-+&RDME*Z4XOJ@VIKQ5GLCF$
13  &41G@J$%2TVQI3+U5XDFNEPM#*LWKSB-YRHCZAO
14  #YOX4L+MPV$3A1TJNIG&DBWEU@Q-F%5RHSZ2K*C
15  FO+V-CR5L$SEM&T#I4J*3@GHXKQBPZU%2D1ANWY
16  ZMF%AN#DKHG1WRPQ+2VCS-E$@5OUJ&*XTB3I4LY
17  NP2ZVS+O4FC%X$GWB-EAHQKJMID5UL#@&T31Y*R
18  TEG&4Y+*UARWM2NKPZ3QHI$JB%#CFLV@D5-S1OX
19  %1KW-#+GV52CDEAYH@SJ$BUX*4MN3LPZRFQ&OIT
20  +EOJ@3XD42PW-#I*ST1U&HQ$CVLBNZRAMK%GFY5
21  KU4$I3OZW5R+CPAXETS1FYDGQLH@#JBM%VN2-*&
22  ZBMS+FWDHJ#T3XG1PEV&AIK%L@CU*Q-45$02RNY
23  K*-2N4OAZXMWHP+Q#RY%$SFJI@1B3GVC5LUDTE&
24  5#4HQ%IYCJ&F+ORM1Z@*KWGDBSPVEUNA$3X2-LT
25  $SRQUKC%W2F4V3M51DX+HYA*JBTL#NGO&P@-IEZ
26  &NCBGYJ4PWORM%LA2S1DIUK*+TF@5#XE$QZHV-3
27  $P4ALX@MRHBZTECS&02QGDVJ5#UNFIWK-+Y1*%3
28  +DHMGB4L*5S@OYIXQP-#K%2V&JENTCU1WR3ZA$F
29  KJDITHMUF@*%A#-WVE2C&Y3ZSL+154OB$XGRNFQ
30  D42PC5IJXMY3$LOH#GTFUWQR@SB1&VK*EN-ZA%+
31  V4W3DBRQPX-FA&E1UNKM5Y@C+OIZ*%THGSJ#*2L
32  34-DVXZTFQK*$C#N2IM@RSBE&%WAU5GJ1LP+HYO
33  +O#T1VHMD4ZJQSA5W2PC&X3*BLI%N$-REFYGU@K
34  LR-@$KENA*S5T2ZBMVPU#&C4%XQGJDOWF+3YH1I
35  G*EQS1UAHLC3&Y*KPW%JVRD+O5MNZ4F-@XB2T$I
36  TAVJQS@YD%NW3F4LB+$G*H-ZCUK#&R5OI21PMEX
37  +EGC&2LOV%MF@Y3AINHJU5PTWKZXQB4#R-SD1$*
38  LYC#JHBTXGV51M%KWERZ&UA+2I-4$*3ONSF@DPQ
39  &R3J*KV#%UTFNBXLOQ-5AEWS1MCY$4PIG2Z+H@D
40  HJ3EM4ZBO$YIXQV*N@1-5LUK%DR&PW#2CGFS+AT
```

Fig. 5-4. Substitution table program (cont'd)

USE COMPUTER CRYPTOGRAPHY TO ACHIEVE SECURITY

is to be enciphered using random substitution alphabets 36–3–22–8. As shown in Chapter 4, you must first write the key, then next to it you write the plaintext vertically transposed, and finally you pick out the substitution characters.

Key		Plaintext									Ciphertext								
36	U	O	T	R	O	P	O	I	S	R	*	4	G	+	4	L	4	D	$	+
3	S	M	E	Y	G	H	A	E	E	I	E	5	4	3	D	Z	G	4	4	B
22	E	P	R	P	R	Y	C	V	C	T	+	1	E	1	E	L	M	I	M	&
8	C	U	C	T	A	T	H	E	U	Y	C	S	C	M	@	M	1	#	S	G

The end result of this transposition and substitution is this ciphertext message:

*E+C 451S G4EC +31M 4DE@ LZLM 4GM1 D4I# $4MS +B&G

Another tabular approach would be to take the 39 characters previously listed (A, B, C, . . ., ?, $, .) to develop a Vigenère-type table consisting of the characters randomly scrambled by the program in Fig. 5-5. The output shows the encryption table with 39 alphabets. The key is entered on the left side of the table, and the normal alphabet goes across the top.

Encryption of a plaintext requires a key to show which alphabets are used. For example, we will use the key word 2DAY$6 to encipher the following message:

A USEFUL SECURITY MEASURE IS THE ENCRYPTION
OF CUSTOMER FILES

To encipher this plaintext using the table in Fig. 5-5, the message is rewritten against the key. The ciphertext substitution characters are taken from each key alphabet and also listed.

Key		Plaintext								Ciphertext								
2	A	L	I	S	T	R	N	T	I	K	7	F	1	C	E	5	C	F
D	U	S	T	U	H	Y	O	O	L	E	$	N	E	5	O	4	4	C
A	S	E	Y	R	E	P	F	M	E	H	X	8	W	X	O	G	R	X
Y	E	C	M	E	E	T	C	E	S	U	R	V	U	U	?	R	U	X
$	F	U	E	I	N	I	U	R	X	H	8	J	X	M	X	8	E	?
6	U	R	A	S	C	O	S	F	X	8	1	?	P	5	A	P	V	9

```
10 REM RANDOM ALPHABET ENCRYPTION TABLE
15 RANDOMIZE
20 DIM B(100),C(100),S(100)
30 READ S$
40 DATA ABCDEFGHIJKLMNOPQRSTUVWXYZ0123456789?$.
50 PRINT TAB(3);S$
60 PRINT
70 FOR I= 1 TO 39
80     CHANGE S$ TO C
90     FOR T= 1 TO 39
100        LET R= INT(39*RND(X)+1)
110        IF C(R) =-999 THEN 100
120        LET S(T) =C(R)
130        LET C(R) =-999
140     NEXT T
150     LET S(0)=C(0)
160     CHANGE S TO C$
170     PRINT SUB$(S$,I);"  ";C$
180     RESTORE
190     READ S$
200 NEXT I
210 END
```

Fig. 5-5. Random alphabet encryption table program.

```
RUN

ABCDEFGHIJKLMNOPQRSTUVWXYZ0123456789?$.

A    TUOKXG21$.EJRDNOFWH?CAY38ILMPB67Z4Q5VS9
B    5UAM7GLK.BXFRS9H18CEJ?P6QW$NOTZ3IY42DOV
C    GFPC3.DZBMVR4S?LNHEAU6YW2Q7XIJ1950$KO8T
D    .TB3GFS5J86CX74D?P$NEUAQOM29ZLIVKH1OYWR
E    N.8DR3Y$FBAQ2W4VPOHSET6JG7O9KUCI1Z?X5LM
F    8TFLOYR.$?7SI35QGJCH9OADMBPVXKNZ6UW4E12
G    9$UPYKB1.XNVF8CTMQ47L6O5AEOIGS?ZD3JHR2W
H    $RCP5KNO8IQW2T?EJF6MS9VDG.UA3HLOXB7Z14Y
I    C6P?I8QOGMZXYLRFD13TEH5$7J2KV9B.4UNOWAS
J    ICMQYJ2HVTB4.K1639Z5NDXOS78WRGP?FO$EULA
K    1ES5V?JMZ64N8$BQPFI.DXAG3OT7KHOUYC9R2WL
L    1ST5PBOWH2UYAN7.?8RDME9Z3XOJ$VIKQ4GLCF6
M    830G$J671TVQI2?U4XDFNEPM59LWKSB.YRHCZAO
N    5YOX3L?MPV62AOTJNIG8DBWEU$Q.F74RHSZ1K9C
O    FO?V.CR4L6SEM8T5I3J92$GHXKQBPZU71DOANWY
P    ZMF7AN5DKHGOWRPQ?1VCS.E6$4OUJ89XTB2I3LY
Q    NP1ZVS?O3FC7X6GWB.EAHQKJMID4UL5$8T20Y9R
R    TEG83Y?9UARWM1NKPZ2QHI6JB75CFLV$D4.SOOX
S    7OKW.5?GV41CDEAYH$SJ6BUX93MN2LPZRFQ80IT
T    ?EOJ$2XD31PW.5I9STOU8HQ6CVLBNZRAMK7GFY4
U    KU36I2OZW4R?CPAXETSOFYDGQLH$5JBM7VN1.98
V    ZBMS?FWDHJ5T2XGOPEV8AIK7L$CU9Q.34601RNY
W    K9.1N3OAZXMWHP?Q5RY76SFJI$0B2GVC4LUDTE8
X    453HQ7IYCJ8F?ORMOZ$9KWGDBSPVEUNA62X1.LT
Y    6SRQUKC7W1F3V2M4ODX?HYA9JBTL5NGO8P$.IEZ
Z    8NCBGYJ3PWORM7LA1SODIUK9?TF$45XE6QZHV.2
0    6P3ALX$MRHBZTECS801QGDVJ45UNFIWK.?YO972
1    ?DHMGB3L94S$OYIXQP.5K71V8JENTCUOWR2ZA6F
2    KJDITHMUF$97A5.WVE1C8Y2ZSL?O43OB6XGRNPQ
3    D31PC4IJXMY26LOH5GTFUWQR$SBO8VK9EN.ZA7?
4    V3W2DBRQPX.FA8EOUNKM4Y$C?OIZ97THGSJ651L
5    23.DVXZTFQK96C5N1IM$RSBE87WAU4GJOLP?HYO
6    ?O5TOVHMD3ZJQSA4W1PC8X29BLI7N6.REFYGU$K
7    LR.$6KENA9S4T1ZBMVPU58C37XQGJDOWF?2YHOI
8    G9EQSOUAHLC28Y5KPW7JVRD?O4MNZ3F.$XB1T6I
9    TAVJQS$YD7NW2F3LB?6G9H.ZCUK58R4OI1OPMEX
?    ?EGC81LOV7MF$Y2AINHJU4PTWKZXQB35R.SD069
$    LYC5JHBTXGV4OM7KWERZ8UA?1I.36920NSF$DPQ
.    8R2J9KV57UTFNBXLOQ.4AEWSOMCY63PIG1Z?H$D
```

Fig. 5-5. Random alphabet encryption table program (cont'd)

The final result is this ciphertext:

```
KEHUH8  7$XR81  FN8VJ?  1EWUXP  C5XUM5  EOO?XA  54GR8P
C4RUEV  FCXX?9
```

Computational Cryptography

By applying mathematics and the computer to encryption techniques, it is possible to go beyond the standard cryptographic techniques examined so far. Computations that can be applied to the techniques previously described include the arithmetic operations of addition, subtraction, multiplication, and division. In addition, algebraic and matrix operations can be incorporated into the traditional encryption techniques. Each of these computational operations will be examined in this section.

Arithmetic Operations

A plaintext message can be easily enciphered using an arithmetic operation as a key. To illustrate, we will use the message

CHANGE KEYS TODAY

If each character is replaced by its ASCII value equivalent, the plaintext becomes a substitution cipher in the form of a series of two-digit numbers as follows:

Plaintext	ASCII value					
CHANGE	67	72	65	78	71	69
KEYS	75	69	89	83		
TODAY	84	79	68	65	89	

As these numbers may be recognized as ASCII values and thus give away the enciphered message, we can apply one or more arithmetic operation to disguise them. By subtracting 50 from each ASCII value we get:

Plaintext	(ASCII value) − 50					
CHANGE	17	22	15	28	21	29
KEYS	25	19	39	33		
TODAY	34	29	18	15	39	

If we multiply by .20, we get a series of values as follows:

Plaintext	.20 × (ASCII value)					
CHANGE	13.4	14.4	13.0	15.6	14.2	13.8
KEYS	15.0	13.8	17.8	16.6		
TODAY	16.8	15.8	13.6	13.0	17.8	

What is shown here suggests that a plaintext can be encrypted by using one of four keys based on the ASCII values. These four keys are:

1. (ASCII value) + constant → cipher character
2. (ASCII value) − constant → cipher character
3. (ASCII value) × constant → cipher character
4. (ASCII value) ÷ constant → cipher character

Figure 5-6 shows a program that permits the user to choose one of the four keys as an arithmetic operation. The constant value must be

```
10 DIM B(100)
20 REM ENCRYPTION WITH ARITHMETIC OPERATIONS
30 PRINT "WHAT IS YOUR PLAINTEXT:";
40 INPUT P$
50 CHANGE P$ TO B
60 PRINT "WHAT ARITHMETIC OPERATION IS TO BE"
70 PRINT "PERFORMED:ENTER 1 FOR +; 2 FOR -;"
80 PRINT "3 FOR X; 4 FOR /";
90 INPUT A
100 PRINT"WHAT IS THE KEYCONSTANT TO BE USED";
110 INPUT K
120 FOR I= 1 TO B(0)
130    ON A GO TO 140,160,180,200
140       PRINT B(I)+K;
150    GO TO 210
160       PRINT B(I)-K;
170    GO TO 210
180       PRINT B(I)*K;
190    GO TO 210
200       PRINT B(I)/K;
210 NEXT I
220 END

RUN

WHAT IS YOUR PLAINTEXT: ?CHANGEKEYSTODAY
WHAT ARITHMETIC OPERATION IS TO BE
PERFORMED:ENTER 1 FOR +; 2 FOR -;
3 FOR X; 4 FOR / ?1
WHAT IS THE KEYCONSTANT TO BE USED ?50
CIPHERTEXT:
 117  122  115  128  121  119  125  119  139  133  134  129  118  115
 139

RUN

WHAT IS YOUR PLAINTEXT: ?CHANGEKEYSTODAY
WHAT ARITHMETIC OPERATION IS TO BE
PERFORMED:ENTER 1 FOR +; 2 FOR -;
3 FOR X; 4 FOR / ?2
WHAT IS THE KEYCONSTANT TO BE USED ?50
CIPHERTEXT:
 17  22  15  28  21  19  25  19  39  33  34  29  18  15  39

RUN

WHAT IS YOUR PLAINTEXT: ?CHANGEKEYSTODAY
WHAT ARITHMETIC OPERATION IS TO BE
PERFORMED:ENTER 1 FOR +; 2 FOR -;
3 FOR X; 4 FOR / ?3
WHAT IS THE KEYCONSTANT TO BE USED ?50
CIPHERTEXT:
 3350  3600  3250  3900  3550  3450  3750  3450  4450  4150  4200
 3950  3400  3250  4450

RUN

WHAT IS YOUR PLAINTEXT: ?CHANGEKEYSTODAY
WHAT ARITHMETIC OPERATION IS TO BE
PERFORMED:ENTER 1 FOR +; 2 FOR -;
3 FOR X; 4 FOR / ?4
WHAT IS THE KEYCONSTANT TO BE USED ?50
CIPHERTEXT:
 1.34  1.44  1.3  1.56  1.42  1.38  1.5  1.38  1.78  1.66  1.68  1.58
 1.36  1.3  1.78
```

Fig. 5-6. Arithmetic operation encryption program.

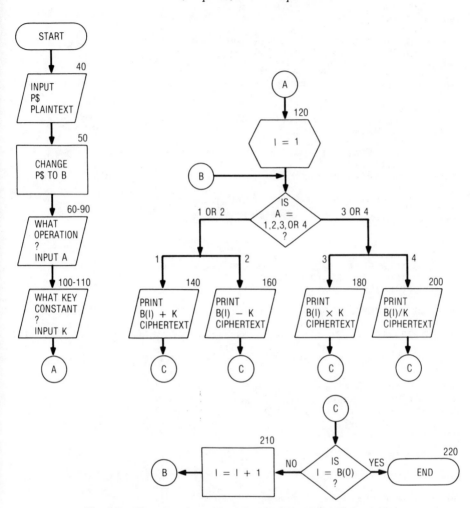

Fig. 5-7. Flowchart for arithmetic operation encryption program.

entered in response to an INPUT statement in Line 90. The program has been run with the message CHANGE KEYS TODAY, using a key constant of 50 through each of the four arithmetic operations. A flowchart for this program is shown in Fig. 5-7.

The ciphertext messages resulting from these arithmetic operations are not very secure in terms of cryptanalysis, or deciphering without knowledge of the key. The weakness is that although a substitution occurs, each number value is being modified by the *same* constant. For example, all E characters become 19 (69–50) when the key of 50 is subtracted.

Such weaknesses will be made more apparent in Chapter 6. However, for the moment, a better computational approach would involve a

```
10 REM ENCRYPTION WITH ALL 4 ARITHMETIC OPERATIONS
20 DIM B(100)
30 PRINT "WHAT IS YOUR PLAINTEXT:"
40 INPUT P$
50 PRINT "WHAT IS YOUR KEY CONSTANT";
60 INPUT K
70 PRINT
80 PRINT "PLAINTEXT IS:"
90 PRINT P$
100 CHANGE P$ TO B
110 PRINT"CIPHERTEXT IS:"
120 FOR I=1 TO B(0) STEP 4
130     PRINT B(I)+K;B(I+1)-K;B(I+2)*K;B(I+3)/K;
140 NEXT I
150 END

RUN

WHAT IS YOUR PLAINTEXT:
?CHANGEKEYSTODAYX
WHAT IS YOUR KEY CONSTANT ?50

PLAINTEXT IS:
CHANGEKEYSTODAYX
CIPHERTEXT IS:
 117   22   3250   1.56   121   19   3750   1.38   139   33   4200   1.58   118
 15   4450   1.76
```

Fig. 5-8. Four-arithmetic operation encryption program.

key that is not a *constant* but a *variable*. A possible approach would be to include all four arithmetic operations in the encryption process, producing a stream of digits for the ciphertext like those shown in the output of Fig. 5-8. The plaintext message is CHANGE KEYS TODAYX, with X serving as a *null* character. You might want to compare the output from this program with that of Fig. 5-6.

A program to decipher a message encrypted by the program in Fig. 5-8 is shown in Fig. 5-9. In the encryption program, Line 130, which causes the ciphertext to be printed out, looks like this:

```
130     PRINT  B(I)+K;  B(I+1)-K;  B(I+2)*K;  B(I+3)/K;
```

where B(I) is an ASCII number equivalent and K is a constant.

In the decryption program (Fig. 5-9), Lines 160–190 reverse the encryption process.

Rather than having both an encryption and a decryption program, a more practical approach would be to have a single program for both operations. Such a program would be available to senders and receivers, who would then enter the message to be processed, either enciphering it or deciphering it. Figure 5-10 is such a program, requiring the user to input a 1 for enciphering or a 2 for deciphering (Line 40). This figure shows output for both operations, with the original plaintext inputted with Line 70. To illustrate the deciphering process, the ciphertext has

```
10 REM DECRYPTION PROGRAM 4-ARITHMETIC OPERATIONS
20 DIM B(100)
30 PRINT"WHAT IS YOUR KEY CONSTANT";
40 INPUT K
50 PRINT "CIPHERTEXT IS:"
60 FOR I= 1 TO 100
70      READ B(I)
80      IF B(I) = 32 THEN 140
90      PRINT B(I);
100 NEXT I
110 DATA 117,22,3250,1.56,121,19,3750,1.38
120 DATA 139,33,4200,1.58,118,15,4450,1.76
130 DATA 32
140 LET B(0) = I
150 FOR I= 1 TO B(0) STEP 4
160      LET B(I) =B(I)-K
170      LET B(I+1)=B(I+1)+K
180      LET B(I+2)=B(I+2)/K
190      LET B(I+3)=INT(B(I+3)*K+.05)
200 NEXT I
210 PRINT
220 PRINT
230 PRINT "PLAINTEXT IS:"
240 CHANGE B TO A$
250 PRINT A$
260 END

RUN

WHAT IS YOUR KEY CONSTANT ?50
CIPHERTEXT IS:
 117   22   3250   1.56   121   19   3750   1.38   139   33   4200   1.58   118
 15   4450   1.76

PLAINTEXT IS:
CHANGEKEYSTODAYX
```

Fig. 5-9. Four-arithmetic operation decryption program.

been placed into the program in data Lines 290 and 300 and then run to produce the output shown.

Algebraic Operations

In the discussion that follows, the procedures and operations to produce ciphertexts from plaintext go beyond the simple arithmetic operations of addition, subtraction, multiplication, and division. Earlier arithmetic expressions such as

$$B(I) + C$$

where $B(I)$ is an ASCII number equivalent and C represents a constant contain only a single elementary operation—addition. The use of more than a single operation provides us with *algebraic* expressions that can produce improved and more secure substitution ciphers.

Fig. 5-10. Arithmetic operations encryption/decryption program (opposite page).

```
10 REM ENCRYPTION/DECRYPTION PROGRAM FOR ARITHMETIC OPERATIONS
20 DIM B(100)
30 PRINT "TYPE '1' TO ENCIPHER, OR '2' TO DECIPHER: 1 OR 2";
40 INPUT X
50 IF X=2 THEN 190
60      PRINT "WHAT IS YOUR PLAINTEXT";
70      INPUT P$
80      PRINT "WHAT IS YOUR KEY CONSTANT";
90 INPUT K
100 PRINT
110 PRINT "PLAINTEXT IS:"
120 PRINT P$
130 CHANGE P$ TO B
140 PRINT"CIPHERTEXT IS:"
150 FOR I=1 TO B(0) STEP 4
160     PRINT B(I)+K;B(I+1)-K;B(I+2)*K;B(I+3)/K;
170 NEXT I
180 STOP
190 PRINT"CIHPERTEXT SHOULD BE ENTERED IN DATA LINES"
200 PRINT "BETWEEN LINES 285 AND 305."
210 PRINT "WHAT IS YOUR KEY CONSTANT";
220 INPUT K
230 PRINT "CIPHERTEXT IS:"
240 FOR I= 1 TO 50
250     READ B(I)
260     IF B(I)=32 THEN 320
270     PRINT B(I);
280 NEXT I
290 DATA 117,22,3250,1.56,121,19,3750,1.38
300 DATA 139,33,4200,1.58,118,15,4450,1.76
310 DATA 32
320 LET B(0) = I
330 FOR I= 1 TO B(0) STEP 4
340     LET B(I) =B(I)-K
350     LET B(I+1)=B(I+1)+K
360     LET B(I+2)=B(I+2)/K
370     LET B(I+3)=INT(B(I+3)*K+.05)
380 NEXT I
390 PRINT
400 PRINT
410 PRINT "PLAINTEXT IS:"
420 CHANGE B TO A$
430 PRINT A$
440 END

RUN

TYPE '1' TO ENCIPHER, OR '2' TO DECIPHER: 1 OR 2 ?1
WHAT IS YOUR PLAINTEXT ?CHANGEKEYSTODAYX
WHAT IS YOUR KEY CONSTANT ?50

PLAINTEXT IS:
CHANGEKEYSTODAYX
CIPHERTEXT IS:
 117   22   3250   1.56   121   19   3750   1.38   139   33   4200   1.58   118
 15   4450   1.76

RUN:

TYPE '1' TO ENCIPHER, OR '2' TO DECIPHER: 1 OR 2 ?2
CIHPERTEXT SHOULD BE ENTERED IN DATA LINES
BETWEEN LINES 285 AND 305.
WHAT IS YOUR KEY CONSTANT ?50
CIPHERTEXT IS:
 117   22   3250   1.56   121   19   3750   1.38   139   33   4200   1.58   118
 15   4450   1.76

PLAINTEXT IS:
CHANGEKEYSTODAYX
```

Linear Equations

A familiar algebraic expression is the equation for a straight line:

$$y = a + bx$$

where a is the value of y when x is zero, or the y intercept; b is the slope; x is a value; and y is the result. Any given value for x, which then leads to y, provides a point x,y on a graph.

How can such an algebraic expression as $y = a + bx$ be used for encryption? Generally, we wish to disguise the ciphertext result so that it is difficult for unauthorized individuals to analyze it. Yet we want a simple process for encryption, as well as a simple process for decryption. An algebraic expression such as the previous one can help us arrive at a simple process. To illustrate this approach, the algebraic expression $y = a + bx$ requires that two constants be provided. These constants are, in fact, the key required for encryption in decryption. If it is decided that the key will be 2, ½, then

$$y = 2 + \tfrac{1}{2}x$$

and x will be an ASCII number equivalent after a message is changed from a string to ASCII value.

To explain this procedure, let us say that the message to be enciphered is

```
10 REM ALGEBRAIC EXPRESSION ENCIPHERING PROGRAM
20 DIM X(100)
30 READ A$
40 DATA CHANGEKEYSTODAY
50 PRINT"WHAT IS THE KEY:A,B";
60 INPUT A,B
70 PRINT
80 PRINT "PLAINTEXT IS:"
90 PRINT A$
100 CHANGE A$ TO X
110 PRINT
120 PRINT "CIPHERTEXT IS:"
130 FOR I = 1 TO X(0)
140     LET N= A + B*X(I)
150     PRINT N;
160 NEXT I
170 END

RUN

WHAT IS THE KEY:A,B ?-15,2

PLAINTEXT IS:
CHANGEKEYSTODAY

CIPHERTEXT IS:
 119  129  115  141  127  123  135  123  163  151  153  143  121  115
 163
```

Fig. 5-11. Linear function encryption program.

CHANGE KEYS TODAY

This plaintext, when changed into two-digit ASCII values, becomes

Plaintext	ASCII value					
CHANGE	67	72	65	78	71	69
KEYS	75	69	89	83		
TODAY	84	79	68	65	89	

These ASCII values will be transformed into a new set of cipher values by the following process:

$$\text{New value} = 2 + \tfrac{1}{2}\,(\text{ASCII value})$$

For example, the letter C equals 67 in ASCII, so that the process gives the new value

$$2 + \tfrac{1}{2}\,(67) = 2 + 33.5 = 35.5$$

We can then develop a new value for each plaintext character, and these new values can serve as our ciphertext. The complete ciphertext for the above message is

Plaintext	Ciphertext					
CHANGE	35.5	38	34.5	41	37.5	36.5
KEYS	39.5	36.5	46.5	43.5		
TODAY	44	41.5	36	34.5	46.5	

Unless an unauthorized person knows the algebraic expression used to develop this ciphertext, only a lucky guess could decipher it. In the next chapter you will be shown techniques that can be used to analyze and solve such messages without knowing the key.

Our ciphertext has both whole numbers as well as fractional values. A value such as 35.5 might be a clue that some algebraic encryption process was used.

To conceal that we may be using an algebraic expression in the encryption process, a key may be used that results only in whole numbers. With an expression such as $y = a + bx$, there is an infinite number of possibilities for the key of a, b to produce whole number cipher values. All that is required is that both a and b are integers or whole numbers. Either a or b, or both, could also be a negative integer. If a key of $-15, 2$ were used for the plaintext, the results would be as follows:

Plaintext	Ciphertext					
CHANGE	119	129	115	141	127	123
KEYS	135	123	163	151		
TODAY	153	143	121	115	163	

A program to incorporate the expression $y = a + bx$ as a cipher process is shown in Fig. 5-11. In this figure, Line 140,

LET N = A + B * X(I)

represents the algebraic expression $y = a + bx$. With the key A and B entered in Line 60 as INPUT A,B, the program will generate the desired ciphertext. The process is illustrated as follows, using the word CHANGE:

Plaintext word		C	H	A	N	G	E
ASCII value, X(I)		67	72	65	78	71	69
B*X(I), B = 2		134	144	130	156	142	138
N = A+B*X(I), A = −15		119	129	115	141	127	123

To decipher a message based on number values derived from an algebraic process requires a reversal of the process. For our example, the return from ciphertext to plaintext follows this process:

Ciphertext $\rightarrow$ Deciphering $\rightarrow$ Original $\rightarrow$ Change to
values   equation   ASCII   plaintext
                                  values

To get a deciphering equation we must algebraically solve the enciphering equation. This equation was the expression

$$y = a + bx$$

where x was supplied to produce y.

Now we start with y and try to find x. Shifting terms, we have

$$bx = y - a$$

and therefore

$$x = (y - a)/b$$

In Fig. 5-11 we used the statement

140   LET N = A + B*X(I)

for enciphering. In Fig. 5-12 (the deciphering program) the statement

100   LET X(I) = (N−A)/B

is used to reverse the process. This process is illustrated in Fig. 5-12 by using as data the ciphertext from the program in Fig. 5-11. The final result is a plaintext with blanks put in as follows:

Ciphertext: 119   129   115   141   127   (123)   135   (123)
             163   151   153   143   121   115   163

Plaintext: CHANGE KEYS TODAY

Because a repetition of a ciphertext may provide a cryptanalyst with a clue to breaking our ciphers, it is advantageous to further disguise

```
10 REM DECRYPTION PROGRAM FOR ASCII ALGEBRAIC PROCESS
20 DIM B(100),X(100)
30 PRINT "WHAT IS THE KEY: A,B";
40 INPUT A,B
50 PRINT "CIPHERTEXT IS:"
60 FOR I= 1 TO 100
70      READ N
80      IF N=-999.99 THEN 150
90      PRINT N;
100     LET X(I)=(N-A)/B
110 NEXT I
120 DATA 119,129,115,141,127,123,135,123
130 DATA 163,151,153,143,121,115,163
140 DATA -999.99
150 LET X(0)=I
160 PRINT
170 PRINT
180 PRINT "PLAINTEXT IS:"
190 CHANGE X TO A$
200 PRINT A$
210 END

RUN

WHAT IS THE KEY: A,B ?-15,2
CIPHERTEXT IS:
 119   129   115   141   127   123   135   123   163   151   153   143   121   115
 163

PLAINTEXT IS:
CHANGEKEYSTODAY
```

Fig. 5-12. Linear function decryption program.

the results so that all plaintext E characters will not be enciphered as the number 123. This was the case when a key of $a = -15$, $b = 2$ was used. It can also be seen by examining the output of Fig. 5-11.

One possible way to accomplish this disguise is to add a different value to each ciphertext value, but in a way that makes it simple to decipher the final ciphertext. The easiest way would be to add the index I to the encryption statement in Fig. 5-11. In that figure, these lines carry out the encryption process:

```
130     FOR I = 1 to X(0)
140     LET N = A+B*X(I)
150     PRINT N;
160     NEXT I
```

By changing Line 140 with I added, we have

```
130     FOR I = 1 TO X(0)
140     LET N = A+B*X(I)+I
150     PRINT N;
160     NEXT I
```

Going back to the plaintext used before, the ciphertext is

```
10 REM ALGEBRAIC EXPRESSION (+I) ENCIPHERING PROGRAM
20 DIM X(100)
30 READ A$
40 DATA CHANGEKEYSTODAY
50 PRINT"WHAT IS THE KEY:A,B";
60 INPUT A,B
70 PRINT
80 PRINT "PLAINTEXT IS:"
90 PRINT A$
100 CHANGE A$ TO X
110 PRINT
120 PRINT "CIPHERTEXT IS:"
130 FOR I = 1 TO X(0)
140     LET N= A + B*X(I) +I
150      PRINT N;
160 NEXT I
170 END

RUN
WHAT IS THE KEY:A,B ?-15,2

PLAINTEXT IS:
CHANGEKEYSTODAY

CIPHERTEXT IS:
 120   131   118   145   132   129   142   131   172   161   164   155   134   129
 178
```

Fig. 5-13. Modified linear function decryption program.

Plaintext	Ciphertext				
CHANGE	119	131	118	145	132	(129)
KEYS	142	(131)	172	161		
TODAY	164	155	134	129	178	

Note how the plaintext character E takes on a different ciphertext substitution value so that in CHANGE, E is 129, and in KEYS, E is 131.

An alternate approach to the addition of a variable value to the encryption function in Line 140 would be to subtract such a variable. Line 140 would look like this:

$$140 \quad LET \quad N \;=\; A+B*X(I)-I$$

and the result in the ciphertext would be

Plaintext	Ciphertext				
CHANGE	118	127	112	137	122	(117)
KEYS	128	(115)	154	141		
TODAY	142	131	108	101	148	

In this result, the plaintext character E also takes on a different ciphertext substitution—117 in CHANGE and 115 in KEYS.

By modifying the program in Fig. 5-11 to include the lines 130–160 shown here, the program in Fig. 5-13 will produce a ciphertext with a nonrepeating pattern of cipher numbers for the plaintext characters.

Nonlinear Equations

So far we have examined the possibility of using the linear function $y = a + bx$ as an encryption process. Anoher possible function that can be used is the *nonlinear* equation. This function has terms that are raised to some power other than one. For example,

$$y = a + bx^2$$

is a nonlinear function with x raised to the second power. If this function were used in a program, such as the one in Fig. 5-11, Line 140 would look like this:

LET N = A+B*(X(I)↑2)

where N is the ciphertext character; A and B are key values; and X(I) is an ASCII value for each plaintext character. To encrypt a word such as CHANGE using this nonlinear function, the following steps are used with a key of A = −15, B = 2:

Plaintext	C	H	A	N	G	E
ASCII value, X(I)	67	72	65	78	71	69
X(I)↑2	4489	5184	4225	6084	5041	4761
B*(X(I)↑2), B=2	8978	10368	8450	12168	10082	9522
N=A+B(X(I)↑2), A=−15	8963	10353	8435	12153	10067	9507

Deciphering a ciphertext based on a nonlinear function requires the use of a nonlinear deciphering equation. In the case where the enciphering function is

$$y = a + bx^2$$

we must solve for x, so that

$$y - a = bx^2$$

Then,

$$x^2 = \frac{y - a}{b}$$

and the deciphering equation is

$$x = \sqrt{\frac{y - a}{b}} \quad \text{or} \quad x = \left(\frac{y - a}{b}\right)^{1/2}$$

If the enciphering program in Fig. 5-11 were revised to use

140   LET N = A+B*(X(I)↑2)

then the program in Fig. 5-12 could be revised for deciphering with a new Line 100:

100   LET X(I) = ((N−A)/B)↑.5

This will provide a set of programs for nonlinear functions (see question 7 or 8).

When using nonlinear functions, it is more practical to start with an enciphering expression that has terms raised to positive integer values, such as x^2, x^3, and so forth. Deciphering will then entail getting the root of these expressions.

If a nonlinear enciphering function such as

$$y = a + b\sqrt{x} \qquad \text{or} \qquad a + bx^{1/2}$$

is to be used, we can readily convert a plaintext to a ciphertext. However, returning the ciphertext to a plaintext presents a problem, particularly when computer operations are to be used. To illustrate, we can use $y = a + b\sqrt{x} = a + bx^{1/2}$ in the form of

$$N = A + B*(X(I)\uparrow.5)$$

N will be the ciphertext value derived; the key will be A = 0, B = 1; and the plaintext word will be QUEST. Then we have the following:

Plaintext:	Q	U	E	S	T
ASCII value, X(I)	81	85	69	83	84
$N = \sqrt{X(I)}$	9.00000	9.21954	8.30662	9.11043	9.16515

The plaintext QUEST has been enciphered into a series of values (N) with a precision of five decimal places.

To decipher this ciphertext of N values requires reversing the enciphering process. For this case, we would square N; that is, with A = 0 and B = 1, then:

$$X(I) = N\uparrow 2$$

If these values of N are placed into a deciphering program to be converted back into ASCII integer values and then into alphabetic characters, a difficulty arises. First, let's square each ciphertext (N) value:

Ciphertext (N)	9.00000	9.21954	8.30662	9.11043	9.16515
$N\uparrow 2$	81.0000	84.9999	68.9999	82.9999	83.9999

You will note that except for the value 81.0000, all the other results are not completely reversed to the original ASCII integer values. The values of $N\uparrow 2$ are close to, but not *exactly* the same as, the original values. The computer does not automatically round off 84.9999 to 85 or 68.9999 to 69, and so on. What can be done to bring about a reversal of ciphertext to plaintext? How can we get these squared values rounded to the correct integer? To do this requires programming revisions so that a small amount, such as .05, will be added to the right side of the function, and the integer (INT) part of the result will return it to the correct ASCII integer value. Then the appropriate deciphering function will be

$$\text{LET} \quad X(I) = \text{INT} \quad (((N-A)/B)\uparrow 2 + .05)$$

```
10 REM NON-LINEAR EXPRESSION ENCIPHERING PROGRAM
20 DIM X(100)
30 READ A$
40 DATA QUEST
50 PRINT"WHAT IS THE KEY:A,B";
60 INPUT A,B
70 PRINT
80 PRINT "PLAINTEXT IS:"
90 PRINT A$
100 CHANGE A$ TO X
110 PRINT
120 PRINT "CIPHERTEXT IS:"
130 FOR I = 1 TO X(0)
140     LET N= A + B*(X(I)^.5)
150     PRINT N;
160 NEXT I
170 END

RUN

WHAT IS THE KEY:A,B ?0,1

PLAINTEXT IS:
QUEST

CIPHERTEXT IS:
 9.   9.21954  8.30662  9.11043  9.16515
```

Fig. 5-14. Nonlinear function encryption program.

The next two figures illustrate this discussion of nonlinear functions. Figure 5-14 is an enciphering program using the function $y = a + b\sqrt{x}$, with a key of $a = 0, b = 1$. Figure 5-15 is a deciphering program for the previous function where

$$x = \left(\frac{y - a}{b}\right)^2$$

and the key is $a = 0, b = 1$.

Matrix Operations

Where a computer is capable of working with alphabetic or string characters in a table or matrix, encryption or decryption processes may be developed using the concepts of *matrix algebra.*

In a matrix the plaintext is changed to ASCII number values. With these numerical values, various transformations can be performed on the matrix. For example, it can be multiplied by a constant to form a new matrix, thus producing a number ciphertext in a way similar to an algebraic transformation.

Another matrix operation that can be used for encryption is the matrix transposition operation. Here the plaintext is transformed into substitution values. Using a matrix transpose operation, a new ciphertext

```
10 REM DECRYPTION PROGRAM FOR ASCII ALGEBRAIC PROCESS
20 DIM B(100),X(100)
30 PRINT "WHAT IS THE KEY: A,B";
40 INPUT A,B
50 PRINT "CIPHERTEXT IS:"
60 FOR I= 1 TO 100
70     READ N
80     IF N=-999.99 THEN 140
90     PRINT N;
100    LET X(I)= INT (((N-A)/B)^2+.05)
110 NEXT I
120 DATA 9.,9.21954,8.30662,9.11043,9.16515
130 DATA -999.99
140 LET X(0)=I
150 PRINT
160 PRINT
170 PRINT "PLAINTEXT IS:"
180 CHANGE X TO A$
190 PRINT A$
200 END

RUN:

WHAT IS THE KEY: A,B ?0,1
CIPHERTEXT IS:
 9   9.21954  8.30662   9.11043   9.16515

PLAINTEXT IS:
QUEST
```

Fig. 5-15. Nonlinear function decryption program.

is developed. This type of ciphertext is a *compound* ciphertext. That is, it is based on both substitution and transposition processes.

In addition, other matrix operations may be programmed to provide plaintext encryption. A ciphertext can be developed by using matrix inversion on the ASCII value matrix.

These three matrix operations just described are illustrated here using the plaintext word DATA. Each illustration follows the conversion of the following matrix

$$\begin{pmatrix} D & A \\ T & A \end{pmatrix}$$

into ASCII values of

$$\begin{pmatrix} 68 & 65 \\ 84 & 65 \end{pmatrix}$$

Encryption by Matrix Multiplication

If the matrix of ASCII values is given the label V, then when multiplied by a constant value or key K, the result is a new ciphertext matrix, C. Then

$$C = (K) \times V$$

so that if the key is $K = 2$, we have

$$C = 2 \times \begin{pmatrix} 68 & 65 \\ 84 & 65 \end{pmatrix} = \begin{pmatrix} 136 & 130 \\ 168 & 130 \end{pmatrix}$$

The final ciphertext, if taken off from C horizontally, becomes a series of numbers

$$136 \qquad 130 \qquad 168 \qquad 130$$

standing for the plaintext word DATA.

Encryption by Matrix Transposition

The algebra of matrix transposition is

$$C = V^T$$

where V^T indicates that the rows and columns of matrix V are to be interchanged. This means that the ASCII value matrix

$$V = \begin{pmatrix} 68 & 65 \\ 84 & 65 \end{pmatrix}$$

becomes the ciphertext matrix

$$C = V^T = \begin{pmatrix} 68 & 84 \\ 65 & 65 \end{pmatrix}$$

and, if the values in C are taken off horizontally, the result is a compound ciphertext (both substitution and transposition)

$$68 \qquad 84 \qquad 65 \qquad 65$$

for the plaintext word DATA.

Encryption by Matrix Inversion

The inverse of a matrix is analogous to finding the reciprocal of a value. Thus, if $x = 4$, the reciprocal x^{-1} equals $1/x$ or $1/4$. To produce a ciphertext using a matrix inversion of ASCII values, we have symbolically

$$C = V^{-1}$$

which indicates that the matrix V should be inverted. This inverse is

$$C = \begin{pmatrix} -.0625 & .0625 \\ .0808 & -.0654 \end{pmatrix}$$

With the values taken off horizontally, this produces a ciphertext of

$$-.0625 \qquad .0625 \qquad .0808 \qquad -.0654$$

```
10 REM INFINTIE KEY ENCRYPTION PROGRAM
20 DIM B(100),K(100),C(100)
30 READ A$
40 PRINT "PLAINTEXT IS:"
50 PRINT A$
60 PRINT
70 DATA MESSAGE ENCRYPTION IS PART OF SECRET COMMUNICATION
80 CHANGE A$ TO B
90 PRINT "INFINTIE KEY IS:"
100 FOR N= 1 TO B(0)
110      LET K(N)=INT(100*RND(X))
120      PRINT K(N);
130 NEXT N
140 PRINT
150 PRINT
160 PRINT "CIPHERTEXT IS:"
170 FOR I= 1 TO B(0)
180      LET C(I)=B(I)+K(I)
190      PRINT C(I);
200 NEXT I
210 END

RUN

PLAINTEXT IS:
MESSAGE ENCRYPTION IS PART OF SECRET COMMUNICATION

INFINTIE KEY IS:
 49  52  67  27  60  15  52  73  69  53  97  98  15  10  23  43  50
 11   8  51  33  36  14  58  19  94  93   6   0  44  63  76  87  34  21
 17  12  17  95  15  34  63  74  71  61  27  13  28  49  44

CIPHERTEXT IS:
126 121 150 110 125  86 121 105 138 131 164 180 104  90
107 116 129  89  40 124 116  68  94 123 101 178 125  85  70
 76 146 145 154 116  90 101  44  84 174  92 111 148 152 144
128  92  97 101 128 122
```

Fig. 5-16. Infinite key encryption program.

for the plaintext word DATA. Matrix inversion can be carried out only on a square matrix. However, not all square matrices have inverses. Since matrix algebra is beyond the scope of this book, interested readers should consult specific texts on the subject.

Infinite Key Transformation

It is possible to increase the security of a ciphertext by enciphering with a key of endless or infinite length. Near the end of Chapter 4 a program (Fig. 4-22) was presented that permitted such an *infinite key* to be used. The key was a word with a length up to that of the plaintext. To make a system work with an infinite word key, both sender and receiver must know it. With a rather long message it becomes impractical to remember the key word. To solve this problem, both parties can agree on a single book, say the *Almanac*, as a supplier of keys. If we assume each message is a page in length, both sender and receiver can agree that each page of the *Almanac* would be used in consecutive order and serve as both enciphering and deciphering keys. With a different page used as a word key each time, we have what is known as a *one-time system*. The same key is never repeated again. Each key is used only once. This cipher system is considered to be unbreakable and has been used by secret agents, diplomatic missions, the military, and international organizations.

These systems using a nonrepeating key are referred to as *Vernam systems*. The basic idea is to *add* another *pulse* or value to the plaintext character to develop the ciphertext. To reverse the process requires the pulse to be subtracted.

Another approach to a Vernam-type system with a *one-time key* would be to use a computer operation to generate a different random key each time a message is to be enciphered. Both the sender and receiver would have the same encryption and decryption programs, as well as the same random number generation routines. The key would then be the *seed* that starts the random number sequence. Each party would have to know this key seed to encipher/decipher a message. Figure 5-16 provides a program to generate a random key the length of the plaintext. In this example, the pulses to be added are integer values from 0 to 99. Each plaintext character is converted to an ASCII value, and a random key value added to it (Line 180) to develop a new ciphertext value. The end result is a ciphertext that appears as a stream of two- and three-digit numbers. A flowchart for this program is shown in Fig. 5-17.

To reverse the process requires a program that begins with the ciphertext in digit form and, given the correctly seeded random number function, causes these numbers to be subtracted from the ciphertext. The values that result from this subtraction process will be ASCII character equivalents that, when changed, will produce a plaintext message. This entire decryption process has been programmed and is found in Fig. 5-18.

The original Vernam system is based on the work of Gilbert S. Vernam, who in 1917 was a young engineer with AT&T working with Teletype communications. It called for the addition of pulses to disguise messages. In terms of present-day computer operations, we can attach another pulse to create a ciphertext by using the arithmetic and algebraic operations previously described. Thus we could develop programs that, say, subtract rather than add a random key value (see question 13).

Encryption of Files

A *file* can be viewed as data not included in a specific program but accessible for use by a program or obtained by requesting a listing.

In most business organizations computer files exist for processing payrolls, as well as for various accounting operations. Other operations

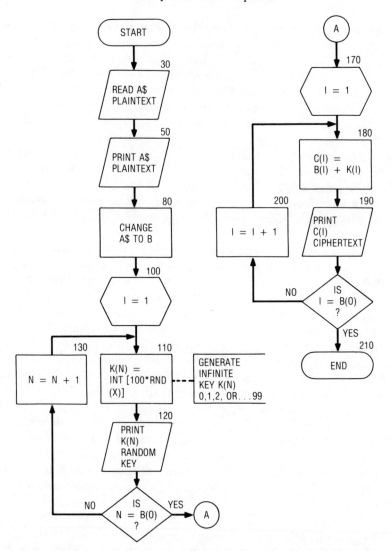

Fig. 5-17. Flowchart for infinite key encryption program.

using data files may involve inventory systems, management information systems, customer inquiry systems, and so forth.

It becomes apparent from this discussion that files in general contain important and valuable information. Specifically, files may contain confidential information on employee salaries, customer names and addresses, formulas or ingredients of a product, marketing and sales information, or future plans and forecasts. Because of the valuable nature of such information, it may be desirable to protect it from unauthorized individuals.

```
100 REM INFINTIE KEY DECRYPTION PROGRAM
110 DIM B(100),K(100),C(100)
120 PRINT "CIPHERTEXT IS:"
130 FOR I= 1 TO 100
140     READ C(I)
150     IF C(I) =-9999 THEN 200
160     PRINT C(I);
170     LET K(I)=INT(100*RND(X))
180     LET B(I)=C(I)-K(I)
190 NEXT I
200 LET B(0)=I-1
210 PRINT
220 PRINT
230 PRINT "PLAINTEXT IS:"
240 CHANGE B TO A$
250 PRINT A$
260 DATA 126,121,150,110,125,86,121,105,138,131,164,180,104,90
270 DATA 107,116,129,89,40,124,116,68,94,123,101,178,125,85,70
280 DATA 76,146,145,154,116,90,101,44,84,174,92,111,148,152,144
290 DATA 128,92,97,101,128,122
300 DATA -9999
310 END

RUN

CIPHERTEXT IS:
 126   121   150   110   125    86   121   105   138   131   164   180   104   90
 107   116   129    89    40   124   116    68    94   123   101   178   125    85   70
  76   146   145   154   116    90   101    44    84   174    92   111   148   152  144
 128    92    97   101   128   122

PLAINTEXT IS:
MESSAGE ENCRYPTION IS PART OF SECRET COMMUNICATION
```

Fig. 5-18. Infinite key decryption program.

To apply cryptographic techniques to data files is not very different from dealing with data within a program. Any of the transposition, substitution, or computer operations described in the preceding chapters may be applied to files. To illustrate, a file containing the names and addresses of ten very special accounts will be used. This information is as follows:

Account number	Name	Address	
101	Jones Tool Co.	Chicago, IL	60605
102	HAL Computers, Inc.	Armonk, NY	10504
103	Going Systems Group	Seattle, WA	98124
104	TOH Steel Co.	Pittsburgh, PA	15213
105	Cipher Systems, Inc.	Arlington, VA	22209
106	G & O Co., Inc.	Houston, TX	77002
107	LSI Co., Inc.	New Haven, CT	06520
108	I/O Devices Corp.	Holmdel, NJ	07733
109	CRT Inc.	Fresno, CA	93710
110	Crypto Systems, Ltd.	Rockville, MD	20852

```
PTF LIST

101 JONES TOOL CO. CHICAGO IL 60605
102 HAL COMPUTERS INC. ARMONK NY 10504
103 GOING SYSTEMS GROUP SEATTLE WA 98124
104 TOH STEEL CO. PITTSBURGH PA 15213
105 CIPHER SYSTEMS INC. ARLINGTON VA 22209
106 G&O CO. INC. HOUSTON TX 77002
107 LSI CO. INC. NEW HAVEN CT 06520
108 I/O DEVICES CORP. HOLMDEL NJ 07733
109 CRT INC. FRESON CA 93710
110 CRYPTO SYSTEMS LTD. ROCKVILLE MD 20852
```

```
10 REM ASCII VALUE FILE ENCRYPTION PROGRAM
20 DIM B(100)
30 OPEN:CTF:10000
40 FOR L= 1 TO 10
50 REM ENTER CLEAR FILE LINE BY LINE
60      INPUT:PTF:A$
70 REM CHANGE PTF TO ASCII CODE VALUES
80      CHANGE A$ TO B
90      FOR I= 1 TO B(0)
100          PRINT:CTF:B(I);
110      NEXT I
120 NEXT L
130 CLOSE:CTF:
140 END
```

```
CTF LIST
74 79 78 69 83 32 84 79 79 76 32 67 79 46 32 67 72
73 67 65 71 79 32 73 76 32 54 48 54 48 53 72 65 76
32 67 79 77 80 85 84 69 82 83 32 73 78 67 46 32 65
82 77 79 78 75 32 78 89 32 49 48 53 48 52 71 79 73
78 71 32 83 89 83 84 69 77 83 32 71 82 79 85 80 32
83 69 65 84 84 76 69 32 87 65 32 57 56 49 50 52 84
79 72 32 83 84 69 69 76 32 67 79 46 32 80 73 84 84
83 66 85 82 71 72 32 80 65 32 49 53 50 49 51 67 73
80 72 69 82 32 83 89 83 84 69 77 83 32 73 78 67 46
32 65 82 76 73 78 71 84 79 78 32 86 65 32 50 50 50
48 57 71 38 79 32 67 79 46 32 73 78 67 46 32 72 79
85 83 84 79 78 32 84 88 32 55 55 48 48 50 76 83 73
32 67 79 46 32 73 78 67 46 32 78 69 87 32 72 65 86
69 78 32 67 84 32 48 54 53 50 48 73 47 79 32 68 69
86 73 67 69 83 32 67 79 82 80 46 32 72 79 76 77 68
69 76 32 78 74 32 48 55 55 51 51 67 82 84 32 73 78
67 46 32 70 82 69 83 79 78 32 67 65 32 57 51 55 49
48 67 82 89 80 84 79 32 83 89 83 84 69 77 83 32 76
84 68 46 32 82 79 67 75 86 73 76 76 69 32 77 68 32
50 48 56 53 50
```

Fig. 5-19.   ASCII value file encryption program.

This information will be stored in a file named PTF, which stands for plaintext file. The encryption programs will access this file and develop the contents of a file called CTF, or ciphertext file. Several routines based on substitution encryption procedures described earlier in this chapter will be shown. These include simple ASCII value substitution, scrambling a file randomly, Vigenère table substitution with a key word, and key word table substitution with a random shift.

Files as ASCII Values

A simple and rather straightforward file encryption procedure involves the conversion by *substitution* of a file to ASCII value equivalents. Each line of the customer file, PTF, can be changed to ASCII values and the results placed into the ciphertext file, CTF. Figure 5-19 shows the original file PTF as a listing, an ASCII value encryption program, and then a listing of file CTF. This file is not printed out by the encryption program. The program transfers the processed results to file CTF, and to see its contents, the file must be listed. After examining file CTF (and assuming a decryption program exists), the original file, PTF, should be deleted from storage.

Note the file listing does not contain clearly defined boundaries for each line of the original file. That is, each ciphertext line is not exactly equal in physical length to the plaintext lines. In this way it becomes more difficult to readily know the contents of the CTF file. If each line of file CTF were as clearly defined as a line of PTF, an unauthorized individual might have little difficulty in unraveling the ciphertext.

In general, we have noted that direct ASCII code encryption is not a very secure approach. If greater security is desired, it is more practical to use other encryption processes.

Random File Scrambling

One approach to converting data files to a secure form not readily understandable is to *scramble* the contents of the file. The customer list file (PTF) is presently in readable form. If stored in its present shape, anyone obtaining an ASCII scrambling computer listing could discover its meaning. Earlier it was shown (Fig. 5-5) that a polyalphabetic substitution table for encryption could be developed with each alphabet generated by a random process.

This same kind of process can be applied to the contents of a plaintext data file. Each line of the file will be read sequentially and changed to ASCII values. For each value a random number will be picked and a substitution made. When all of the plaintext values have been scrambled amongst themselves, they are changed back to a string

```
PTF LIST

101 JONES TOOL CO. CHICAGO IL 60605
102 HAL COMPUTERS INC. ARMONK NY 10504
103 GOING SYSTEMS GROUP SEATTLE WA 98124
104 TOH STEEL CO. PITTSBURGH PA 15213
105 CIPHER SYSTEMS INC. ARLINGTON VA 22209
106 G&O CO. INC. HOUSTON TX 77002
107 LSI CO. INC. NEW HAVEN CT 06520
108 I/O DEVICES CORP. HOLMDEL NJ 07733
109 CRT INC. FRESON CA 93710
110 CRYPTO SYSTEMS LTD. ROCKVILLE MD 20852


10 REM RANDOM FILE SCRAMBLING PROGRAM
20 DIM C(100),S(100)
30 OPEN:CTF:2000
40 FOR L= 1 TO 10
50      INPUT:PTF:S$
60      CHANGE S$ TO C
70      FOR T = 1 TO C(0)
80          LET R= INT(C(0)*RND(X)+1)
90          IF C(R) =-999 THEN 80
100             LET S(T) =C(R)
110             LET C(R) =-999
120     NEXT T
130     LET S(0)=C(0)
140     CHANGE S TO C$
150     PRINT:CTF:C$
160 NEXT L
170 CLOSE:CTF:
180 END


CTF LIST

CHGOCS O5EO.N CITO6JAIO LOO 6 L
EONPNN5  .RRTLHA 100SM Y4ACKICOM U
2G UESLES1S PTR OGEYAATG94NWI8SOMT
3 RTC TPPIHS2 OSE UO1 1.BAELG5THT
AST2PALVCOIS.RIYCE  ONS2MG9 N  H2IETNR
NO CHN270XO &GTS.COO7. U OT I
I65 COVSEHNW.NO2.C O IL TNEAC
 D7S7E ONI.L3 OMELHDOR/JIEP  3CCVO
1RRF9C C3NNAOST .E7IOC
LDYLM V.2TTS R SP RC5KD8S2TIMOYEEOO LC
```

Fig. 5-20. Random file scrambling encryption program.

and the results printed to a new file (CTF). The process continues until each line of the plaintext is scrambled. This scrambling program is shown in Fig. 5-20. The figure shows a listing of the original file (PTF), the program, and a listing of the scrambled file (CTF).

This procedure does not have a specific word key. Rather, the process depends on the use of a random number function. Thus on some systems, using the function

$$RND(X)$$

implies that X is a specific starting point in the random number generation process, as though numbers were being picked from an exact location in a fixed table of random numbers. In this way RND(X) would provide the same set of numbers each time used, and a function RND(Y) would provide another set, and so on.

It is relevant that the set of random numbers for file encryption are reusable. If this were not possible, the decryption process would not be possible, and we would be left with a scrambled file that we could not understand.

With this random scrambling process, then, the key is the character placed in the RND function. It is this *seed* that must be kept confidential and not made available to unauthorized individuals.

Algebraic File Scrambling

In this chapter, a section was devoted to algebraic substitution techniques for encryption. The Vigenère substitution process described in Chapter 4 was also based on an algebraic technique. In general, the program in Fig. 4-23 used a Caeser cipher process, which required an algebraic function that looked like this:

$$C(I) = B(I) + K$$

where K was part of the key process. This particular program uses a key word to select the alphabets used in the encryption.

To encipher data files the ASCII characters were expanded to include all the characters from 32 to 90 shown in Fig. 4-7. Figure 4-23 was revised to take each line of the file PTF sequentially and scramble it using the Vigenère-Caesar process. The revised program appears in Fig. 5-21, which shows the plaintext customer file, the encryption program, and the listing of the ciphertext file (CTF).

To reverse the encryption procedure requires the addition of the line

$$130 \quad LET \quad K \ = \ 59-K$$

into the program in Fig. 5-21. By revising the encryption program, the ciphertext file (CTF) can be reversed with the program in Fig. 5-22. This figure shows the file CTF, the decryption program, and the plaintext file PTF.

Since Vigenère-Caesar encryption uses a process of *constant shift substitution* that leads to a built-in weakness of the end result, a modification to the process is suggested. To the shift computation, a random factor can be added (or subtracted). By such an addition, the shift is no longer constant. The algebraic encryption function can look like this:

$$C(I) = B(I) + K + RND(X)$$

To make such a change requires the addition of Lines 170 and 180,

```
PTF LIST

101 JONES TOOL CO. CHICAGO IL 60605
102 HAL COMPUTERS INC. ARMONK NY 10504
103 GOING SYSTEMS GROUP SEATTLE WA 98124
104 TOH STEEL CO. PITTSBURGH PA 15213
105 CIPHER SYSTEMS INC. ARLINGTON VA 22209
106 G&O CO. INC. HOUSTON TX 77002
107 LSI CO. INC. NEW HAVEN CT 06520
108 I/O DEVICES CORP. HOLMDEL NJ 07733
109 CRT INC. FRESON CA 93710
110 CRYPTO SYSTEMS LTD. ROCKVILLE MD 20852


10 REM ALGEBRAIC FILE SCRAMBLING ENCRYPTION PROGRAM
20 DIM B(100),C(100),K(100)
30 PRINT"WHAT IS YOUR KEYWORD";
40 INPUT K$
50 CHANGE K$ TO K
60 LET J=0
70 OPEN:CTF:200
80 FOR L= 1 TO 10
90      INPUT:PTF:A$
100       CHANGE A$ TO B
130       FOR I= 1 TO B(0)
140          GO SUB 260
150          IF B(I) > 90-K THEN 180
160             LET C(I) = B(I)+K
170             GO TO 190
180       LET C(I)=(B(I)+K-90)+31
190       NEXT I
200       LET C(0)=B(0)
210       CHANGE C TO E$
220       PRINT:CTF:E$
230 NEXT L
240 CLOSE:CTF
250 STOP
260      LET J=J+1
270      IF J>K(0) THEN 300
280      LET K=K(J)-32
290      RETURN
300         LET J=1
310         LET K=K(J)-32
320         RETURN
330 END

RUN

WHAT IS YOUR KEYWORD ?XAZ

CTF LIST

G5MB9ZQ5NIABLOZ@.H@'FLAHIA5-W/2
.@IABL3OR:DO9ZF4B+A@O3NK1ZK?Z.Q4-U
FL/MDARV9SB3RX-QL;OX9D>:SI+ZT'Z6YO/U
SL.ZP:DB2Z@5-X6HQ:R?;QD.ZM'Z.V1.T
BF6GB8ZP?RQ+LFAHK)-X'QI/MD:NKAU>A1/S/6
-%LABLOZF4B+AGL;RQ5MX:WXX6-Q1
I9HX)N+AHK)-X4DTAG><DKABQA/3V1-
/.LACB<H@+RX)NO6-X.NI3CB2ZKOZ-X60T
BO:ZF4B+AEO+RL4Z@'Z6T6.Q
BO?OQ5ZP?RQ+LPAKQ*-X8N@1UF2KBALAA1-Y4/
```

Fig. 5-21. Algebraic file scrambling encryption program.

PTF LIST

```
G5MB9ZQ5NIABLOZ@.H@'FLAHIA5-W/2
.@IABL3OR:DO9ZF4B+A@O3NK1ZK?Z.Q4-U
FL/MDARV9SB3RX-QL;OX9D>:SI+ZT'Z6YO/U
SL.ZP:DB2Z@5-X6HQ:R?;QD.ZM'Z.V1.T
BF6GB8ZP?RQ+LPAHK)-X'QI/MD:NKAU>A1/S/6
-%LABLOZF4B+AGL;RQ5MX:WXX6-Q1
I9HX)N+AHK)-X4DTAG><DKABQA/3V1-
/.LACB<H@+RX)NO6-X.NI3CB2ZKOZ-X6OT
BO:ZF4B+AEO+RL4Z@'Z6T6.Q
BO?OQ5ZP?RQ+LPAKQ*-X8N@1UF2KBALAA1-Y4/
```

```
10 REM ALGEBRAIC FILE SCRAMBLING DECRYPTION PROGRAM
20 DIM B(100),C(100),K(100)
30 PRINT "YOUR KEYWORD IS";
40 INPUT K$
50 CHANGE K$ TO K
60 LET J=0
70 OPEN:PT:2000
80 FOR L= 1 TO 10
90      INPUT:CTF:A$
100       CHANGE A$ TO B
110       FOR I= 1 TO B(0)
120          GO SUB 250
130          LET K=59-K
140          IF B(I) > 90-K THEN 170
150             LET C(I) = B(I)+K
160             GO TO 180
170          LET C(I)=(B(I)+K-90)+31
180       NEXT I
190       LET C(0)=B(0)
200       CHANGE C TO E$
210       PRINT:PT:E$
220 NEXT L
230 CLOSE:PT
240 STOP
250       LET J=J+1
260       IF J>K(0) THEN 290
270       LET K=K(J)-32
280       RETURN
290          LET J=1
300          LET K=K(J)-32
310          RETURN
320 END
```

RUN

YOUR KEYWORD IS ?XAZ

CTF LIST

```
JONES TOOL CO. CHICAGO IL 60605
HAL COMPUTERS INC. ARMONK NY 10504
GOING SYSTEMS GROUP SEATTLE WA 98124
TOH STEEL CO. PITTSBURGH PA 15213
CIPHER SYSTEMS INC. ARLINGTON VA 22209
G&O CO. INC. HOUSTON TX 77002
LSI CO. INC. NEW HAVEN CT 06520
I/O DEVICES CORP. HOLMDEL NJ 07733
CRT INC. FRESON CA 93710
CRYPTO SYSTEMS LTD. ROCKVILLE MD 20852
```

Fig. 5-22. Algebraic file scrambling decryption program.

```
170     LET  R  =  INT(6*RND(X))
180     LET  C(I)  =  C(I)+R
```

to the encryption program in Fig. 5-21. This modification will cause an integer of 0, 1, 2, 3, 4, or 5 to be added to the ASCII substitution values in the array C(I). Since the original set of values extends from 32 to 90 (see Fig. 4-7), with the RND function addition of integers 0 to 5, the ASCII character set is extended to 95. The additional values and character equivalents are

$$91 \ [\qquad 92 \ \backslash \qquad 93 \ ] \qquad 94 \ \uparrow \qquad 95 \ -$$

They will be encrypted by the program in Fig. 5-23. This figure shows the plaintext file (PTF), followed by the encryption program and the final ciphertext file (CTF).

Encryption of Programs

A *program* can be considered another type of file since it can be structured as a file. Thus any program can be scrambled in the same way that files were encrypted in the previous section.

We can take the program in Fig. 5-19 that performs ASCII character-to-value substitutions, and by treating the program as the plaintext file (PTA), perform an encryption on it. This process is shown in Fig. 5-24. The first item in the figure is the listing of the program as a file; the next item is the substitution program; and finally, we have the resulting ciphertext file listing (CTF).

By using the same procedure, any program treated as a file can be enciphered by any other encryption program. Another example of this is provided by Fig. 5-25. The first item in the figure is the simple ASCII character-value substitution program from Fig. 5-19. This program as a file will be processed by the random scrambling program (Fig. 5-20), the second item in the figure. The last item is the scrambled ciphertext file (CTF).

Note that this ciphertext file has the same line-by-line structure as the original program in Fig. 5-19. To further scramble the ciphertext, it could have been transposed to produce a compound ciphertext. Such a change could be produced by appending a comma to Line 150

```
150     PRINT:CTF:C$
```

to produce this revised line:

```
150     PRINT:CTF:C$,
```

When the random file scrambling program in Fig. 5-25 is run, the result will be a compound ciphertext based on a substitution and transposition process (see question 17).

PTF LIST

101 JONES TOOL CO. CHICAGO IL 60605
102 HAL COMPUTERS INC. ARMONK NY 10504
103 GOING SYSTEMS GROUP SEATTLE WA 98124
104 TOH STEEL CO. PITTSBURGH PA 15213
105 CIPHER SYSTEMS INC. ARLINGTON VA 22209
106 G&O CO. INC. HOUSTON TX 77002
107 LSI CO. INC. NEW HAVEN CT 06520
108 I/O DEVICES CORP. HOLMDEL NJ 07733
109 CRT INC. FRESON CA 93710
110 CRYPTO SYSTEMS LTD. ROCKVILLE MD 20852

```
10 REM RANDOM SHIFT FILE ENCRYTPION PROGRAM
20 DIM B(100),C(100),K(100)
30 PRINT"WHAT IS YOUR KEYWORD";
40 INPUT K$
50 CHANGE K$ TO K
60 LET J=0
70 OPEN:CTF:200
80 FOR L= 1 TO 10
90    INPUT:PTF:A$
100     CHANGE A$ TO  B
110     FOR I= 1 TO B(0)
120        GO SUB 260
130        IF B(I) > 90-K THEN 160
140            LET C(I) = B(I)+K
150            GO TO 170
160        LET C(I)=(B(I)+K-90)+31
170        LET R=INT(6*RND(X))
180        LET C(I)=C(I)+R
190     NEXT I
200     LET C(0)=B(0)
210     CHANGE C TO E$
220     PRINT:CTF:E$
230 NEXT L
240 CLOSE:CTF
250 STOP
260     LET J=J+1
270     IF J>K(0) THEN 300
280     LET K=K(J)-32
290     RETURN
300        LET J=1
310        LET K=K(J)-32
320        RETURN
330 END
```

RUNNH

WHAT IS YOUR KEYWORD ?XAZ

CTF LIST

```
I8QC<ZT9RLFGLO[B1H@*HNAKJF:-W15
2EKBCL4TR<GS=]G4C-CAP4OL1[M@Z2T5.Y
KQ1MFCSZ;VE7S]OTO?P]=E?<WJO^X)]9^21V
SLOZP:HB7[C:/Z9JU?SC@UI3ZO(]1Y41Y
EF:JB<ZQBTV+OPCJP)/]'QJOMF?QMEY@D4OT2;
2)OACQO[G9E,AJL=TV5N\<Z][9-V4
I9HX*S-FJL+.]6IVEJ?=IPCDSD25X12
1.PBFF=HEOR\-QQ81X3QI4CG2]M1Z1Z63U
FP?]I6B,BEROVN8ZE)[:W:1T
FR?TS6]QAST+PUANU--X:ND6UI2LFDNEE3-Y9/
```

Fig. 5-23. Random shift file encryption program.

```
PTA LIST

10 REM ASCII VALUE FILE ENCRYPTION PROGRAM
20 DIM B(100)
30 OPEN:CTF:10000
40 FOR L= 1 TO 10
50 REM ENTER CLEAR FILE LINE BY LINE
60      INPUT:PTF:A$
70 REM CHANGE PTF TO ASCII CODE VALUES
80      CHANGE A$ TO B
90      FOR I= 1 TO B(0)
100          PRINT:CTF:B(I);
110     NEXT I
120 NEXT L
130 CLOSE:CTF:
140 END


10 REM PROGRAM FOR ASCII ENCRYPTION OF ANOTHER PROGRAM
20 DIM B(100)
30 OPEN:CTF:2000
40 FOR L= 1 TO 14
50 REM ENTER CLEAR FILE LINE BY LINE
60      INPUT:PTA:A$
70 REM CHANGE PTF TO ASCII CODE VALUES
80      CHANGE A$ TO B
90      FOR I= 1 TO B(0)
100          PRINT:CTF:B(I);
110     NEXT I
120 NEXT L
130 CLOSE:CTF:
140 END
```

```
CTF LIST
82  69  77  32  65  83  67  73  73  32  86  65  76  85  69  32  70
73  76  69  32  69  78  67  82  89  80  84  73  79  78  32  80  82
79  71  82  65  77  68  73  77  32  66  40  49  48  48  41  79  80
69  78  58  67  84  70  58  49  48  48  48  48  70  79  82  32  76
61  32  49  32  84  79  32  49  48  82  69  77  32  69  78  84  69
82  32  67  76  69  65  82  32  70  73  76  69  32  76  73  78  69
32  66  89  32  76  73  78  69  73  78  80  85  84  58  80  84  70
58  65  36  82  69  77  32  67  72  65  78  71  69  32  80  84  70
32  84  79  32  65  83  67  73  73  32  67  79  68  69  32  86  65
76  85  69  83  67  72  65  78  71  69  32  65  36  32  84  79  32
66  70  79  82  32  73  61  32  49  32  84  79  32  66  40  48  41
80  82  73  78  84  58  67  84  70  58  66  40  73  41  59  78  69
88  84  32  73  78  69  88  84  32  76  67  76  79  83  69  58  67
84  70  58  69  78  68
```

Fig. 5-24. ASCII encryption program.

Summary

This chapter explores computer cryptography. Encryption and decryption using computer-generated random numbers, random keys, and random alphabets are illustrated, as well as encryption tables for polyalphabetic substitution produced by computer programs.

Computer programs can be used to apply the arithmetic operations of addition, subtraction, multiplication, and division to develop substitu-

PTB LIST

```
10 REM ASCII VALUE FILE ENCRYPTION PROGRAM
20 DIM B(100)
30 OPEN:CTF:10000
40 FOR L= 1 TO 10
50 REM ENTER CLEAR FILE LINE BY LINE
60     INPUT:PTF:A$
70 REM CHANGE PTF TO ASCII CODE VALUES
80     CHANGE A$ TO B
90     FOR I= 1 TO B(0)
100         PRINT:CTF:B(I);
110     NEXT I
120 NEXT L
130 CLOSE:CTF:
140 END
```

```
10 REM PROGRAM TO RANDOMLY SCRAMBLE ANOTHER PROGRAM
20 DIM C(100),S(100)
30 OPEN:CTF:2000
40 FOR L= 1 TO 14
50     INPUT:PTB:S$
60     CHANGE S$ TO C
70     FOR T = 1 TO C(0)
80         LET R= INT(C(0)*RND(X)+1)
90         IF C(R) =-999 THEN 80
100            LET S(T) =C(R)
110            LET C(R) =-999
120     NEXT T
130     LET S(0)=C(0)
140     CHANGE S TO C$
150     PRINT:CTF:C$
160 NEXT L
170 CLOSE:CTF:
180 END
```

CTF LIST

```
E PVCCITAMA I UESNIRMRROOIAL EPRYNF ELG
O(D OIM)B1
:OOFPNCOT:E100
OO O  F1T R1=L
EEBLYEEFTLC L IINEAM RR I LN EERN
:PFUI:NPTAT$
DOIGLEP REAESFH N O VMC ECATTA SIUC
B H$ EOATAN GC
FB  T 010=R O(I)
P:TIB:I)RN(;CTF
EITNX
L XNET
CELF:S:CTO
NED
```

Fig. 5-25. Random scrambling encryption program.

tion ciphers. Algebraic operations that can be easily programmed to produce linear and nonlinear substitution ciphers are also described. Ciphertext security can be improved by using a computer-derived infinite key transformation. This type of Vernam or one-time key system using a random number sequence is considered unbreakable.

Any encryption process applied to a plaintext can be used in appropriate computer software to encrypt either valuable computer files or computer programs.

Questions

1. Using the alphabets in Fig. 5-3, decipher this message:

    GYAYW   RATPB   PUOPB

    Alphabet 1 should serve as the normal alphabet. The key is 8–2–9–4–2.
2. Using the alphabets in Fig. 5-4, encipher the statement made by Wendell Philips (1811–84), American reformer and orator: "Eternal vigilance is the price of liberty."
3. Using the encryption table in Fig. 5-5
    (a) Encipher the message WILL LEAVE ON 5 MARCH AT 2 P.M. Use the key word TEN.
    (b) Decipher the message G$TCIF   R$.IJF   LI0NT0   MDWIYM using the key word IKE.
4. Using the program in Fig. 5-8, encipher the message in question 2 using a key of 10.
5. How would a key of 15, −2 alter the ciphertext in Fig. 5-11?
6. The following ciphertext was derived using the program in Fig. 5-13. What is the plaintext? The key is −150, 2.

    −15 4 −17 10 −3 −6 7 −4 37 26 29 20 −1 −6 43

7. Revise the program in Fig. 5-11 to use the nonlinear function $y = a + bx^2$. Run this revised program.
8. For the encryption program developed in question 7, develop a decryption program using the equation, $x = ((y - a)/b)^{1/2}$. Run this revised program.
9. What is the advantage to using a *one-time system* for communication security?
10. What is the basic idea of a Vernam system?
11. Which programs in this chapter use the idea of a Vernam system?
12. Here is a matrix of ASCII values:

$$V = \begin{pmatrix} 68 & 65 & 84 & 65 \\ 83 & 69 & 67 & 85 \\ 82 & 73 & 84 & 89 \end{pmatrix}$$

    (a) What is the plaintext contained in the matrix?
    (b) Develop a ciphertext using $C = (K) \times V$ where $K = 5$.
    (c) Develop a ciphertext using $C = V^T$.
13. Revise and run the algebraic enciphering program in Fig. 5-11 by using

    140   LET N = A+B*X−INT(300*RND(X))

    with a key of −20, 5.
14. Develop a decryption program to reverse the process of the program in

Fig. 5-19 that converts a file to ASCII value characters. *Hint:* See Figs. 5-18 and 4-6.

15. When using a program such as the one in Fig. 5-20 that scrambles a file, what is the nature of the key that is used? How does it differ from other types of keys used so far?

16. Can programs be secured by encryption?

17. To further scramble files or programs, a combination of substitution and transposition can be used. This approach produces a compound ciphertext. Revise the file scrambling program in Fig. 5-25 by using this line:

```
150     PRINT:CTF:C$,
```

Run the program and list the file CTF.

References

Branstad, D. K. "Data Protection through Cryptography." *Dimensions,* vol. 59, no. 9 (September 1975): 195–197.

Chesson, Frederick W. "Computers and Cryptology." *Datamation,* vol. 19, no. 1 (January 1973): 62–64, 77–81.

Clark, Fran J. *Mathematics for Data Processing.* Reston, Virginia: Reston Publishing Co., Inc., 1974.

Feistel, Horst. "Cryptography and Computer Privacy." *Scientific American,* vol. 228, no. 5 (May 1973): 15–24.

Girdansky, M. B. "Cryptology, the Computer, and Data Privacy." *Computers and Automation,* vol. 21, no. 4 (April 1972): 12–19.

Goldsmith, W. B., Jr. "Secret Message Coder/Decoder." *Personal Computing,* vol. 5, No. 3 (March 1981): 45–47.

Heidema, John H. "Computer Cryptography for Coded Communications." *Personal Computing,* vol. 4, No. 11 (November 1980): 66–68.

Hoffman, Lance J., ed. *Security and Privacy in Computer Systems.* Los Angeles, California: Melville Publishing Co., 1973.

Hoffman, Lance J. *Modern Methods for Computer Security and Privacy.* Englewood Cliffs, New Jersey: Prentice-Hall, Inc., 1977.

Kahn, David. "Modern Cryptology." *Scientific American,* vol. 215, no. 1 (July 1966): 38–46.

Martin, James. *Security, Accuracy, and Privacy in Computer Systems.* Englewood Cliffs, New Jersey: Prentice-Hall, Inc., 1973.

Pennington, Ralph H. *Introductory Computer Methods and Numerical Analysis.* 2d ed., New York: The Macmillan Company, 1970.

Shannon, C. E. "Communication Theory of Secrecy Systems." *Bell Systems Technical Journal* (October 1949).

Smith, Stephen. "Secrecy and your Personal Computer." *Personal Computing,* vol. 2, No. 8 (August 1978): 75–78.

Van Tassel, Dennis. "Advanced Cryptographic Techniques for Computers." *Communications of the ACM* (December 1969).

6

Cryptanalysis

Introduction

The previous chapters have been concerned with cryptography. Specifically, they have dealt with methods of converting a plaintext into a ciphertext to protect information. These methods dealing with code and cipher systems rendered a plaintext incomprehensible. To go from a ciphertext to a plaintext in an authorized way, both the sender and receiver must possess the means for decryption.

To go from a ciphertext to a plaintext in an unauthorized way is the realm of *cryptanalysis*. Cryptanalysis involves *breaking* the ciphertext when there is little or no knowledge about the system or key that was used to generate it.

This chapter is not intended as an in-depth coverage of crypt-analysis. Such a task would require a full-length text.* Rather, we will deal with several cryptanalytical approaches that are straightforward and involve computer operations.

Frequency Analysis

A most important tool in cryptanalysis is a simple statistical tech-nique based on the idea of relative frequency of occurrence of single letters in a ciphertext. In studying the English language, for example, it has been found that in a large plaintext the letters follow a specified relative frequency of occurrence. Figure 6-1 shows the 26 letters of the alphabet and their order of occurrence from E (the most frequent) to Z (the least frequent), based on a count of fifty thousand plaintext characters.

Doing a *frequency analysis* by hand can be a rather slow task. Large

* Interested readers are directed to the following books: Gaines, H. F. *Cryptanalysis*. New York: Dover Publications, Inc., 1956. Sinkov, A. *Elementary Cryptanalysis: A Mathematical Approach*. New York: Random House, 1968.

	Percent		Percent		Percent
E	13	L	3	W	1–2
T	9	H	2	V	1–2
N	7	C	2	B	1
R	7	F	2	X	0–1
O	7	P	2	Q	0–1
A	7	U	2	K	0–1
I	7	M	2	J	0–1
S	6	Y	1–2	Z	0–1
D	4	G	1–2		

Fig. 6-1. Letters and frequency of occurrence.

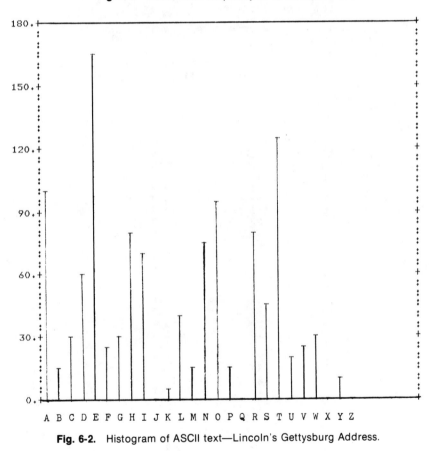

Fig. 6-2. Histogram of ASCII text—Lincoln's Gettysburg Address.

computer systems and time-sharing systems make the task one of entering the data and having a library routine do the necessary work. A page

```
10 REM LETTER FREQUENCY COUNT PROGRAM
20 DIM A$(26),T(26),B(100),C(100)
30 READ A$
40 DATA ABCDEFGHIJKLMNOPQRSTUVWXYZ
50 CHANGE A$ TO B
60 LET T(I)=0
70 LET X=0
80 INPUT:GBA:C$
82     FILEND:GBA:190
100      CHANGE C$ TO C
110      FOR J= 1 TO C(0)
120          FOR I= 1 TO 26
130              IF B(I)=C(J) THEN 150
140          NEXT I
150          LET T(I)= T(I)+1
160      NEXT J
170 GOTO 80
190 FOR I= 1 TO 26
200      LET X=X+T(I)
210 NEXT I
220 PRINT"CIPHER LETTERS","FREQUENCY","PERCENT"
230 CHANGE B TO A$
240 FOR I= 1 TO 26
250      PRINT USING 260,SUB$(A$,I),T(I),(T(I)/X)*100
260      FMT            ##        ###        ##.#
270 NEXT I
280 PRINT "            TOTAL"; X
340 END

RUN
```

CIPHER LETTERS	FREQUENCY	PERCENT
A	102	8.8
B	14	1.2
C	31	2.7
D	58	5.0
E	166	14.4
F	27	2.3
G	28	2.4
H	81	7.0
I	68	5.9
J	0	0.0
K	3	0.3
L	42	3.6
M	13	1.1
N	77	6.7
O	94	8.1
P	16	1.4
Q	1	0.1
R	80	6.9
S	44	3.8
T	126	10.9
U	22	1.9
V	24	2.1
W	28	2.4
X	0	0.0
Y	10	0.9
Z	0	0.0
TOTAL	1155	

Fig. 6-3. Letter frequency count program—Lincoln's Gettysburg Address.

of text, the Gettysburg Address, has been taken and processed in this way.* Only the letter characters have been analyzed. They have been transformed to ASCII values and sorted from high to low. From these sorted values the histogram in Fig. 6-2 was derived.

The Gettysburg Address was processed by a program written to analyze the relative frequency of letter characters in a message. The program in Fig. 6-3 changes each line of character string to ASCII value in the array B. Each value in the array is processed until all of them have been counted. The statement

150   LET   T(I)=T(I)   +   1

establishes 26 separate counters, one for each character value. The results are finally printed, showing each letter, the count, and the relative frequency (percent). Figure 6-4 is a flowchart for the frequency analysis program.

If a frequency analysis of a message shows that the letter characters

E   T   A   O   N   I   S   H

occur somewhat in accordance with the percents shown in Fig. 6-1, we could infer that some kind of transposition cipher has been used. Another possibility is that a simple substitution cipher has been used. It could be a monoalphabet Caesar cipher or a message reversal cipher, where the substitution alphabet has the same characters as the plaintext (normal) alphabet.

If the following single reversed alphabet was used for encryption of a large message,

Plaintext
alphabet: A B C D E F G H I J K L M N O P Q R S T U V W X Y Z

Ciphertext
alphabet: Z Y X W V U T S R Q P O N M L K J I H G F E D C B A

a frequency analysis of the ciphertext would show these letters occurring most often:

V   G   Z   L   M   R   I   H   S

These letters are the reciprocals of E T A O N I R S H. A *cryptanalyst*, upon seeing the letters V G Z L M R I H S form the greatest percent of letters, would know immediately that a reversed alphabet substitution was employed in the encryption process.

However, if these letters occurred as the most frequent in a cryptanalysis,

---

* Lincoln's Gettysburg Address, *Encyclopedia of American History* (Guilford, Conn.: Dushkin Pub. Group, Inc., 1973), p. 142.

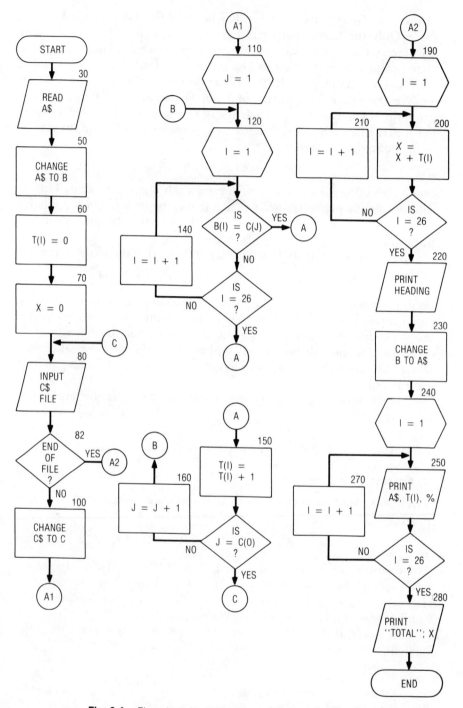

Fig. 6-4. Flowchart for letter frequency count program.

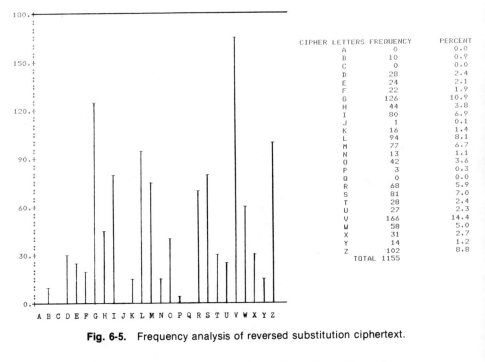

CIPHER LETTERS	FREQUENCY	PERCENT
A	0	0.0
B	10	0.9
C	0	0.0
D	28	2.4
E	24	2.1
F	22	1.9
G	126	10.9
H	44	3.8
I	80	6.9
J	1	0.1
K	16	1.4
L	94	8.1
M	77	6.7
N	13	1.1
O	42	3.6
P	3	0.3
Q	0	0.0
R	68	5.9
S	81	7.0
T	28	2.4
U	27	2.3
V	166	14.4
W	58	5.0
X	31	2.7
Y	14	1.2
Z	102	8.8
TOTAL	1155	

Fig. 6-5. Frequency analysis of reversed substitution ciphertext.

F U B P O J S T I

the cryptanalyst would know that a Caesar cipher alphabet with a key of K=1 was used for encryption.

Figure 6-5 shows the analysis of a Gettysburg Address ciphertext encrypted by using a reversed alphabet. When the ciphertext was processed by the frequency analysis program (Fig. 6-3), the results conformed to the letter frequency

V G Z L M R I H S

The Gettysburg Address as a ciphertext using a Caesar cipher alphabet and a key of K=1, when analyzed by the program in Fig. 6-3, produces a result confirming that in fact a Caesar cipher encryption was used. The output in Fig. 6-6 shows the most frequent letters to be

F U B P O J S T I

Even if a randomly produced substitute character alphabet is used for encryption, the frequency analysis would still point to the substitution relationship. For example, with this ciphertext substitution alphabet

Plaintext
alphabet: A B C D E F G H I J K L M N O P Q R S T U V W X Y Z

Ciphertext
alphabet: B T V 1 L X G U 4 2 + @ F J R E N O I * D S Z 5 H 3

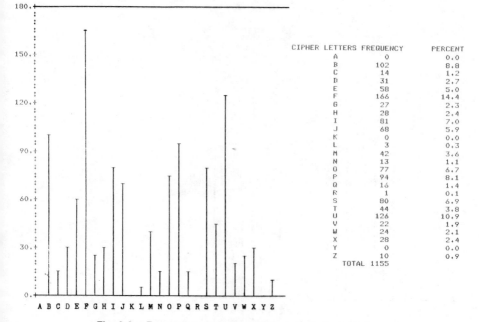

CIPHER LETTERS	FREQUENCY	PERCENT
A	0	0.0
B	102	8.8
C	14	1.2
D	31	2.7
E	58	5.0
F	166	14.4
G	27	2.3
H	28	2.4
I	81	7.0
J	68	5.9
K	0	0.0
L	3	0.3
M	42	3.6
N	13	1.1
O	77	6.7
P	94	8.1
Q	16	1.4
R	1	0.1
S	80	6.9
T	44	3.8
U	126	10.9
V	22	1.9
W	24	2.1
X	28	2.4
Y	0	0.0
Z	10	0.9
TOTAL	1155	

Fig. 6-6. Frequency analysis of Caesar ciphertext, K=1.

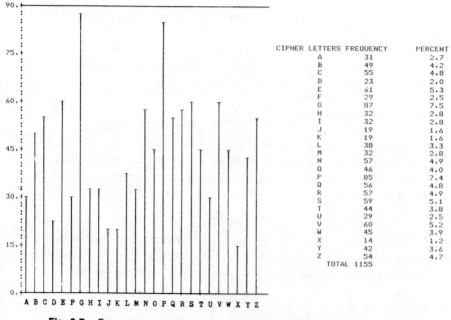

CIPHER LETTERS	FREQUENCY	PERCENT
A	31	2.7
B	49	4.2
C	55	4.8
D	23	2.0
E	61	5.3
F	29	2.5
G	87	7.5
H	32	2.8
I	32	2.8
J	19	1.6
K	19	1.6
L	38	3.3
M	32	2.8
N	57	4.9
O	46	4.0
P	85	7.4
Q	56	4.8
R	57	4.9
S	59	5.1
T	44	3.8
U	29	2.5
V	60	5.2
W	45	3.9
X	14	1.2
Y	42	3.6
Z	54	4.7
TOTAL	1155	

Fig. 6-7. Frequency analysis of a polyalphabetic substitution ciphertext.

a message, when analyzed, would produce these most frequently occurring characters,

L   *   B   R   J   4   O   I   U

conforming to the percents in Fig. 6-1. The cryptanalyst would then begin to construct a complete substitution alphabet and soon begin to decrypt the ciphertext.

When a ciphertext is produced by polyalphabetic substitution, a frequency analysis of the characters shows results that do not, and will not usually, conform to the percents in Fig. 6-1. This difference in percents gives the cryptanalyst the clue that possibly more than one alphabet was used. To see what percents may arise from polyalphabetic substitution, a Vigenère table encryption of the Gettysburg Address was carried out with the results shown in Fig. 6-7. A frequency analysis on the ciphertext indicates that no letter had a zero frequency of occurrence and that many letters occurred frequently. The overall pattern is very different from that found in Fig. 6-1.

Trial and Error

Computers provide us with the capability to repeat an operation a thousand times in a fraction of a second. Because of such power, much of the *trial and error* drudgery of cryptanalysis by hand can be eliminated by the computer.

Computer cryptanalysis can be illustrated by trying to *break* a Caesar ciphertext using trial and error methods. You will recall that to produce a Caesar ciphertext, a shift key of K character displacements is used (as described in Chapter 4). There are 25 possible keys, where K goes from 1 to 25. If we know that the ciphertext is derived from a Caesar process but do not know the key, we can break the code by trying each of the 25 possible keys. In effect, we could devise a program that would *run down* all possible keys until a workable plaintext appeared.

This approach is shown in Fig. 6-8. The ciphertext to be run down is

W   T   R   J

It is found in Line 50 of the Caesar cipher cryptanalysis program. The program generates 25 columns of output, corresponding to the number of possible keys. By examining each column it is found that the fourth column from the right end yields the plaintext word

R   O   M   E

the only legible word in the output. Thus a program, such as the one in Fig. 6-8, can "crack" a Caesar ciphertext message rather quickly and easily. The flowchart for this program is found in Fig. 6-9.

```
10 REM CAESAR CIPHER CRYPTANALYSIS PROGRAM
20 DIM B(26),C(100)
30 READ A$
40 CHANGE A$ TO B
50 DATA WTRJ
60 PRINT "CIPHERTEXT IS: ";A$
70 PRINT
80 PRINT "    PLAINTEXT IS FOUND DOWN ONE COLUMN:"
90 PRINT
100 FOR I= 1 TO B(0)
110      FOR J= 1 TO 90-B(I)
120          LET C(J) = B(I)+J
130      NEXT J
140      IF B(I)<>90 THEN 160
150          LET J=0
160      LET K=J
170      FOR J= 1 TO B(I)-65
180          LET C(K+J)= 64 + J
190      NEXT J
200      LET C(0) = 26
210      CHANGE C TO E$
220      PRINT SUB$(A$,I);": ";E$
230 NEXT I
240 END

RUNNH

CIPHERTEXT IS: WTRJ

    PLAINTEXT IS FOUND DOWN ONE COLUMN:

W: XYZABCDEFGHIJKLMNOPQRSTUV
T: UVWXYZABCDEFGHIJKLMNOPQRS
R: STUVWXYZABCDEFGHIJKLMNOPQ
J: KLMNOPQRSTUVWXYZABCDEFGHI
```

Fig. 6-8. Caesar cipher cryptanalysis program.

Summary

    In this chapter we have touched on cryptanalysis, the science of deciphering ciphertexts when the encryption process or key is not known. Without prior knowledge of the keys or methods by which the ciphertext was developed, it is necessary to analyze the ciphertext to discover how to "break" it. Such analysis can involve an examination of the letter frequency of a plaintext to determine if a transposition or substitution encryption process has been used. Trial and error of all possible keys can also be carried out. The computer can greatly speed up attempts at cryptanalysis and help to produce accurate results at a rate previously not attainable by hand.

Questions

1. Define the term *cryptanalysis*.
2. Take a fairly large plaintext of your own choosing and perform a frequency analysis on it.

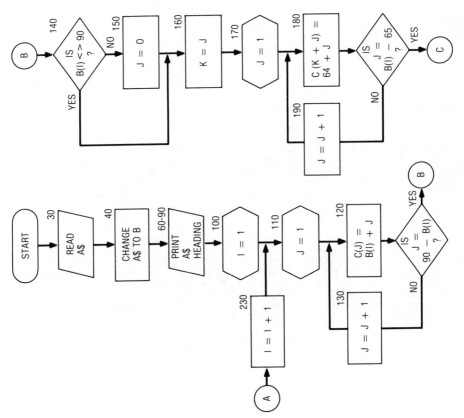

Fig. 6-9. Flowchart for Caesar cipher cryptanalysis program.

3. How does the frequency analysis shown in Fig. 6-2 compare with the expected letter frequencies shown in Fig. 6-1?

4. Analyze the letter frequencies in this ciphertext:

```
GPVST DPSFBOET    FWFOZFBST   BHPPVSGBUIFST    CSPVHIUGPSUIVQPOUIJT
DPOUJOFOU   BOFX  OBUJPODPODFJWFEJOMJCFSUZBOEEFEJDBUFEUPUIFQSPQPT
JUJPOUIBUBMMNFO   BSFDSFBUFEFRVBMOPX     X       FBSFFOHBHFEJOBHSFBUDJWJMX
BSUFT UJOHX IFUIFSUIBU   OBUJPOPSBOZPUIFSOBUJPOT PDPODFJWFEBOET
PEFEJDBUFDBOMPOHFOEVSFX     FBSF  NFUPOBHSFBUCUUMFHGJFMFPGUIBUX
BSX   FIBWFDPNFUPEFFEJDBUFBQPSUJPO  PGUIBUGJFMEBT    BGJOBMSFT
UJOHQMBDFPGGPSUIFJPT FX   IPIFSFIBWFUIFJSMJWFT   UIBU  UIBUOBUJPONJHIUNJWFJUJT
BMUPHFUIFSSGJUUJOHBOEQSQFSUIBUX    FT    IPVMEEPUIJT      CVUJOBNBSHFSF
FOT   FX    FDBOOPUFFEJDBUFX  FDBOOPUQDPOT FDSBUFX       FDBOOPUPVIBMMPX
        UIJT HSPVOEUIFCSBWFNFOFOMJWJJOHBOEEEFFBEX      IPT   USVHHMFIFEIFSFIBWFDPOT
FDSBUFE   JUGBSSBCPVFPVSQPPPSSQX    FSUPBEEPSPSEFUBDSIDUUJFX   PSMEX
JMMMJUUMFOPUFPUFFPPS MPOHSFNFNCFSX   IBUX  FT   BZIFSFCVUUJUDBOBOUGPBOFUFGOUIFUBHSFTHHSVUUFX
IBUUJFZEJEIFSFJFSFFSFUEJVJT       GPSVST  UIFMJJWJOHSBTUISBUIFSUFSFEIGBOUIUUGDVPOUUIF
VOGJOJST  IFEX   PSLX  IJDUUIFZFX  PSVFUIUFFEEJFSTGEBHUSTBSBTUU GBST
POPMCPNZBCEWBOFODFEF     JUUJT   SBUIFSFGPSSVSF UPCFTFFDEJ[NUDEBOUFEEEPUVFDUBWCGT
GSVBNBSBBMTUSTGEFOSQJCOSMEVL     UHUIFEUIFFJPESVSIPSFFFFFBCFFFFBEEX
FUBSFMFJIIGTEDFMICOJCOT     FEEFSVPVFPPUPUFBUFDBXUG      FGPS   X   IJDTDVUFEHBDSETGEDTS
UGUGMNOFGTES  FGPSUFDBPUUPVUFPX    FIFSSIFJMIGQTFU   PMFT   UIFFYFGC
FFFBEF  IBMUOCPUIBSBCWFEGFEJJFFOCJPOUIBUCUTTDD  GBCUFJOSTBUOSFT     IBCM
U        IBWFCPOX     CTJUSPGGGTFFFQNBOCPEEUOCVOFPVPDCUOFPUFMEUUGOCJFOFGQFNFPYBCJUAUGFPNF
GPSUFFGQFPNF       T       IBNNPPUPPPHFSSOT      IGTPSNOFUGGBSUI
```

5. Analyze the letter frequencies in this ciphertext:

```
ULFIH XLIVZMWH VEVMBVZIH ZTLLFIUZGSVIH YILFTSGULIGSFKLMGSRH
XLMGRMVMG ZMVD MZGRLMXLMXVREVWRMORYVIGBZMWWVWRXZGVWGLGSVKILKLH
RGRLMGSZGZOONVM ZIVXIVZGVWVJFZOMLD D VZIVVMTZTVWRMZTIVZGXREROD
ZIGVH GRMTD SVGSVIGSZG MZGRLML.IZMBLGSVIMZGRLMH LXLMXVREVWZMWH
LWVWRXZGVWXZMOLMTVMWFIVD VZIV NVGLMZTIVZGYZGGOVURVOWLUGSZGD
ZID VSZEVXLNVGLWVWRXZGVZVZKLIGRLM LUGSZGURVOWZH ZURMZOIVH
GRMTKOZXVULIGSLH VD SLSVIVTZEVGSVIRORVH GSZG GSZGMZGRLMNRTSGOREVRGRH
ZOGLTVGSVIURGGRMTZMWKILKVIGSZG VH SLFOWWLGSRH YFGRMZOZITVIH
VMH VD VXZMMLGWVWVWRXZGVD VXZMMLGXLMH VXIZGVD VXZMMLGSZOOLD
 GSRH TILFMWGSVYIZEVNVMORERMTZMWWVZWD SLH GIFTTOVWSVIVSZEVXLMH
VXIZGVW RGUZIZIYLEVLFIFIKLLIKLD VIGLZWWLIWVGIZXGGSVD
LIOWD ROOORGGOVMLGVMLI OLMTIVNVNYVID SZGD VH ZBSVIVYFGRGXZMMVEVIULITVGD
SZGGSVBWRWSVIVRGRH ULIFH GSVORERMTIZGSVIGLUGSVFMURMRXZGVWSVIVGLGSV
FMURMRH SVWD LIPD SRXSGSVD SLULFTSGSGSVIVSZEVXLMS
UZIH LMLYZWZVZMXVW RGRH IZGSVIULIFH GLYVSVIVWVWRXZGVWGLGSVTIVZGH
PIVNZRMRMTYVULIFH GSZGUILNGSVH VSLMLIVWWVZWD VGZPVRMXIVZH
VWWVELGRLMGLGSZGXZFH VULI D SRXSGSVBTZEVGSVOZH GUFOONVZH FIVFLMVZH
FIVLUWVWVELGRLMGSZGD VSVIVSRTSOBIVH LOEV GSZGSVH VWVZWH
SZOOMLGSZEVVRVWRVWRMVZRMGSZGGSRH MZGRLM.MFMWVITLWH SZOO
G SZEVZMVD YRIGSLUUIVVWLNZMWGSZGTLEVIMVMGLUGSVKVLKLVVYBGSVKVLKLV
ULIGSVKVLKLV H SZOOMLGKVIRH SUILNGSVVVZIGS
```

6. Show that this ciphertext is based on a polyalphabetic substitution process:

```
QWHTG NWEGOYQD    PDRPMPNCA    LOBQICSLBUGFD      MZBWUSGQWEVVFCZVGJWD
NWAVWYRYB   LVRY   YIGKCYPZVPGWGROQANWMRCBLCBOQPLVEQEROBBVVPCCWCQG
TBVQBEULBNNZXRY    LZREFPNEMQGEFNWVBY     H      PIEGSYTLORFWYNRZRCHNVGQYY
LZGGG EQAIK SMGJSCGSIG   YIGKCYBCIAACEUPZACHTBYA ZKBPQPVGMQCBOF
ZLRFWNNEMQEOYYZVTGBOHCMJ     PIEG  XMGQBLTCMNVPLGETRHWPYOWSVVLGH
LZJ   PPNXSNBXMGQRPQTKNVSLCZZGKCY   ZNGJOESTMYFOD     LNVPOWEPA
EQAIDWNNMSQFEUZA   PE    SWUGFPTLDRVVPVCTVXSD      EPNV   EPNVBLGTWAOWRUETVXSTGTA
LTGQUPGSMEHWEGTVTCBOCCWCGFEULBJ      PA    SWHNROBEPVU      MCGKBLYLZTGFD
PVF   PE    PKNPBZGOMQKQLGPE   PKNPBZGNWAU PKECHPJ      PKNPBZGSIYNCH
      EPVU  RZBWBOGSMOTOGRXMANWGVYONPRORLLJ      SWF   EZHIUWROPRTSSNGMPQBD
PKECHPQ     TBSCFLOZDRQICCZWERCH    PZGQOOQZZQGHCNNBGJSH    ZZYFK
TTYNWEGWMAQHPAZZ  WWAIFPZPUOGFH     SIGY  PA    LGUGFPOFBVVQLAYMIGFQBCORVK
SIGVVPLOQQJSCRTBVU          QWEWG EPRNWGVYOECHSRCBBDSOROQPCHPQSMEGHZGSM
FVSKBTF     SMQY  ZZXY  SQPJHSRJE   SWSQIRUEPRTSSNGMGJID    QIEU
ZVBDZJNODNPQPQ    TBVU  CIGJSCSZZHU EWOGVPEPLRFWNNEMQVCEUPOEGOEND
VZROOTATVTDSQBCMHU          EPNVTCBXBUGG     PPBPCCROLRCRH
PBNMSTANZRCG      PLQGJZGTWAVCEULBPCID     PNBT  H    SQPJHSRJONXSEUPTNU
ENHNZXRLA   FZRQTORGWGKCYGSIGY     PPRTSSVRPYAFPF    ZTIG  EPNVVPF
PLRCRD      SIYNBZGSIIGRTROQAXOTAEPNVHSVD YIGKCYHYLRTUZQD    SIYN
E     SIIGOYRH    MQEVVZSQZRGRZZLVQQVVLGRWIGFYZPVGQTEUPXRQDWRMGGJSARZXYG
QWEVVPCPWCNS      D    SIYNBZGAMEKG     SNEQAEUPMNTHS
```

7. Using a *trial and error* "run-down" process, cryptanalyze the following Caesar ciphertext:

ESTYVDJDEPXDPNFCTEJ

References

Calvocoressi, Peter. *Top Secret Ultra.* New York: Pantheon Books, 1981.

Chesson, Frederick W. "Computers and Cryptology." *Datamation,* vol. 19, no. 1 (January 1973): 62–64, 77–81.

Gaines, Helen Fouché. *Cryptanalysis.* New York: Dover Publications, Inc., 1956.

Gardner, Martin. "Mathematical Games." *Scientific American,* vol. 237, no. 2 (August 1977): 120–124.

Garliński, Józef. *Intercept, The Enigma War.* London: J. M. Dent & Sons, 1979.

Kahn, David. *The Codebreakers.* New York: The Macmillan Co., 1967.

Kennedy, Robert E. "Crypto." *Personal Computing,* vol. 5, no. 3 (March 1981): 48–54.

Peleg, Shmuel, and Rosenfeld, Azriel. "Breaking Substitution Ciphers Using a Relaxation Algorithm." *Communications of the ACM,* vol. 22, no. 11 (Nov. 1979): 598–605.

Shannon, C. E. "Communication Theory of Secrecy Systems." *Bell Systems Technical Journal* (October 1949): 656–713.

Sinkov, Abraham. *Elementary Cryptanalysis: A Mathematical Approach.* New York: Random House, 1968.

Smith, Laurence D. *Cryptography.* New York: Dover Publications, Inc., 1955.

Wilson, Charles J. "Solving Ciphers." *Personal Computing,* vol. 4, no. 6
    (June 1980): 78–79.
Winterbotham, F. W. *The Ultra Secret.* New York: Dell Publishing Company, Inc., 1974.

7

Security and the Data Encryption Standard

Introduction

The need to improve data and information security in computer systems is a direct result of the increased use of computers by government and private industry in processing, storing, and communicating valuable and sensitive data. In addition, we are seeing both public and legislative concern in the area of data and information privacy.

Data may consist of a group or collection of facts,statistics that constitute a record of an observation or event. *Information* can be viewed as data that has been processed so as to make it useful. The terms *data* and *information* are often assumed to be synonymous. *Security* is the protection of data and information so that they are

1. Not modified
2. Not destroyed
3. Not disclosed or compromised

either intentionally or accidentally.

The threats to data security are in two areas. First, we must consider the fact that more and more data is processed by computers and transmitted by electronic communications devices. Thus with data communications systems, we have threats of *eavesdropping* that cover a wide range of illegal activities including:

1. Interception of transmissions
2. Passive wiretapping; that is, "listening in on" or recording transmissions
3. Active wiretapping; that is, modification, deletion, falsification, substitution, or destruction of messages

These particular threats are cause for concern in the banking and financial community because of the increased use of electronic funds transfer systems (EFTS). This area of protection against threats to electronic communications is called *communications security.*

143

The second area of threats to data security involves the loss of materials by

1. Accident
2. Theft of movable storage media—a disk or tape reel, for example
3. Theft of materials from main storage

This area of protection against threats to information and data contained in storage media is called *file security.*

To counter the threats cited here, that is, to protect data passing through communications lines or data in storage media, the information in the data can be concealed. If the communication system or computer system *is* compromised and illegal access made, it would be both difficult and time-consuming for an individual to derive useful information for their efforts. Concealment of useful information in an unintelligible form is the realm of cryptography. In previous chapters the areas of cryptography, computer cryptographic techniques, and cryptanalysis have been explored. In this chapter we will look at the role of cryptography in communications security and file security.

Communication Security

Since it is easier to penetrate a communication system without being discovered, interest in providing data security is greater in this area than in the area of media security, where if physical items were missing, the loss would be noticed sooner or later.

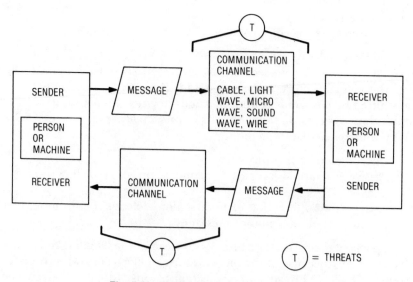

Fig. 7-1. The communication process.

The term *communication* can be defined as the transmitting or giving and receiving of information. Transmission may be by hand delivery; person-to-person over a communication device, or from computer-to-computer. The process of communication is shown in Fig. 7-1. The basic components of the process include

1. A sender/receiver at both ends
2. Message(s)
3. Communication channels

The threats to communication security surround the communication channels. Cryptographic methods can be used to protect communicated data and information from purposeful or accidental disclosure. To accomplish this protection, such techniques as the *Data Encryption Standard* (DES) have been developed.

The Development of a Data Encryption Standard

When it was recognized that a problem of data security was emerging, the National Bureau of Standards (NBS) requested in 1973 that encryption algorithms (procedures) for computer data protection be submitted. An algorithm developed by IBM personnel was submitted and published, and the proposed Data Encryption Standard (DES) became a federal standard. It is used by government agencies for data security.

A Brief Description of DES

The following is a brief description of the DES taken from the National Bureau of Standards publication *DIMENSIONS**:

> The Data Encryption Standard was issued in January 1977 as Federal Information Processing Standard Publication (FIPS PUB) 46. The DES, when implemented in electronic devices, provides cryptographic protection for computer data that are transmitted and stored in computer systems. Federal agencies and departments needing such protection can purchase commercially available DES implementations that have been validated by NBS as conforming to the standard.
>
> The DES is a complex non-linear ciphering algorithm that is capable of high-speed operation when implemented in hardware. Software implementations do not comply with the standard and are generally quite inefficient compared to hardware versions.

* J. Gait, "Encryption Standard: Validating Hardware Techniques," *DIMENSIONS*, vol. 62, no. 7/8 (July/August 1978): 22–23.

The DES algorithm converts 64 bits of plaintext to 64 bits of ciphertext under the action of a 56-bit keying parameter. The key is generated in such a way that each of the 56 bits used directly by the algorithm is random and the 8 error detecting bits are set to make the parity of each 8-bit byte of the key odd. Each member of a group of authorized users of encrypted data must have the key that was used to encipher the data in order to use it.

A block of data to be enciphered is subjected to an initial permutation, then to a complex key-dependent computation, and finally to a permutation which is the inverse of the initial permutation. The computation sequence is a series connection of sixteen rounds, one of which is depicted:

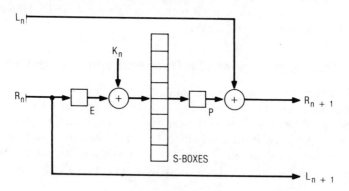

Each round uses 48 bits of the key in a sequence determined by a key schedule which provides for a thorough intermixing of the key bits for each round. With the exception of this difference in the round keys, the sixteen rounds are identical to one another. Each round receives an input of 64 bits; the 31-bit right half is expanded by the linear operator E to 48 bits and the result is mod two added to the round key; the 48 bit sum is divided into eight 6-bit blocks, each of which determines a 4-bit S-box entry; the resulting 32 bits are added mod two to the left half and the two halves are interchanged, thus producing 64 bits of output for the rounds.

The purpose of the permutations is to thoroughly mix the data bits so they cannot be traced back through the S-boxes, which are non-linear substitution tables. This technique strengthens the algorithm and makes it resistant to cryptanalytic attack.

As you can see from the description, the algorithm used in the DES is a rather involved process. For this reason we will not discuss it right now. Instead, we will first review some concepts from earlier chapters. In addition, we will examine the binary and modular arithmetic used in the DES, as well as the type of cipher system it is based on.

Some Review Concepts

It will be useful for future discussions to review at this point some cryptographic concepts covered in Chapters 3 and 4, specifically, the *compound cipher system* that uses both transposition and substitution operations to carry out a data encryption.

An example of a compound cipher system follows:

1. Take a data *input* as a plaintext and transpose the characters by reversing the message.

Plaintext: AB

Ciphertext: BA

2. Select a *key* to use with a Vigenère substitution table as shown in Fig. 4-22. The message to be processed in the table is the ciphertext BA

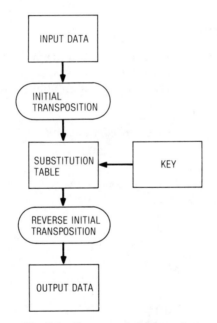

Fig. 7-2. Compound cipher system.

from (1). The key for the table is UN. Entering the table we have

	Message characters	
Key	**B**	**A**
U	V	—
N	—	N

The substitution for the transposition ciphertext BA is then VN.

3. Take the result VN from (2) and transpose it using the reverse of the process in (1). That is, use a message reversal transposition so that we have

$$VN \quad \rightarrow \quad NV$$

Then NV is the ciphertext *output*. We started with the plaintext AB and, using a compound cipher system, produced a ciphertext NV. Figure 7-2 shows this system.

Data Representation

Fully to understand the discussions to follow, it is necessary to explain how data is represented in binary form, how binary arithmetic is done, and how modular arithmetic can be used in cipher systems.

The Binary System

In the computer, numeric characters are represented by the binary digits 0 and 1. Figure 7-3 provides the binary equivalents for the decimal values 0 to 10. The term *binary digit* is often abbreviated as *bit*.

Decimal	Binary numeral
0	0 0 0 0
1	0 0 0 1
2	0 0 1 0
3	0 0 1 1
4	0 1 0 0
5	0 1 0 1
6	0 1 1 0
7	0 1 1 1
8	1 0 0 0
9	1 0 0 1
10	1 0 1 0

Fig. 7-3. Decimal and binary equivalents.

Binary Addition

The rules for binary addition are as follows:

$1 + 1 = 0$ and carry 1 to add to the next column
$1 + 0 = 1$
$0 + 1 = 1$
$0 + 0 = 0$

As an example of binary addition, we shall add 7 plus 3 using these rules and the binary values in Fig. 7-3.

Decimal	Binary	Carry-over
		1 1 1
7	0 1 1 1	0 1 1 1
+ 3	+ 0 0 1 1	+ 0 0 1 1
10	1 0 1 0	1 0 1 0

Note that there are three 1's carried over to the next left column. Thus in column two we have $1 + 1 + 1 = 1$; in column three we have $1 + 1 + 0 = 0$; and in column four we have $1 + 0 + 0 = 1$.

Modular Arithmetic

If we are working with a set of b integers 0 and 1, and if any positive integer a outside the set $\{0,1\}$ is reducible by some process to an integer b in the set, then the type of arithmetic that does this reduction is called *modular arithmetic*.

When using the binary system, we seek to reduce a positive integer 0 or 1 to another integer value in the set $\{0,1\}$. The term *modulus* refers to the number of integers in the process. Thus we will be dealing with modulus 2 or mod 2 operations. Specifically, we will be dealing with *addition modulo 2* for the bits 0 or 1. Such addition is similar to binary addition, but there is no carry-over to the next column. The symbol used for this type of addition is $\oplus$.

The rules for modulo 2 addition are as follows:

$$1 + 1 = 0$$
$$1 + 0 = 1$$
$$0 + 1 = 1$$
$$0 + 0 = 0$$

They can be summarized in this table with the results inside the rules and the values to be added outside:

$\oplus$	0	1
0	0	1
1	1	0

An example of addition modulo 2 using a binary message and key to produce a ciphertext is

Message:	1 0 0 1 1 0 1
$\oplus$ Key:	1 1 0 1 0 1 1
Ciphertext:	0 1 0 0 1 1 0

Addition modulo 2 has the property that subtraction is the same as addition. If the key used to encipher a message is "subtracted" from the ciphertext using the preceding rules, the original message is recovered. Taking our binary ciphertext and "subtracting" modulo 2 (the key), we have:

Ciphertext:	0	1 0 0	1 1 0
"–" Key:	1	1 0 1	0 1 1
Message:	1	0 0 1	1 0 1

The usefulness of modular arithmetic can be seen if we let

M = A binary message of n bits
K = A binary key of n bits
C = A ciphertext

To encrypt a message, we can use

$$M \oplus K = C$$

and to decrypt a ciphertext, we can use

$$C \oplus K = M$$

Concepts Relating to the DES

Permutation is another term for transposition. The number, letter, or character in a starting position is transposed or shuffled to another position using a specified scrambling key. One example is the following:

Character starting position	Transposition position	Moves to new position
1	4	1
2	3	2
3	5	3
4	6	4
5	1	5
6	2	6

The transposition has the fourth character in the first position, the third character in the second position, and so on with the second character in the last or sixth position.

With a word such as SYSTEM, the permutation-transposition works like this:

Starting position	Permutation position	Word	Result	New position
1	4	S	T	1
2	3	Y	S	2
3	5	S	E	3
4	6	T	M	4
5	1	E	S	5
6	2	M	Y	6

If a six-digit number (987654) is to be permuted/transposed, the sequence looks like this:

Starting position	Permutation position	Number	Results	New position
1	4	9	6	1
2	3	8	7	2
3	5	7	5	3
4	6	6	4	4
5	1	5	9	5
6	2	4	8	6

Given a binary character with a length of six bits, 011010 for example, following this process to permute/transpose yields these results:

Starting position	Permutation position	Go to position	Result	New position
1	4	0	0	1
2	3	1	1	2
3	5	1	1	3
4	6	0	0	4
5	1	1	0	5
6	2	0	1	6

This concept of transposition of characters by a fixed sequence appeared earlier in Chapter 3 with the discussion of columnar transpositions. In the current literature on computer cryptography the process of shuffling the positions of binary digits has been illustrated by a *permutation box* or *P-box*, such as the one in Fig. 7-4.

A *product-cipher* or *product transformation* involves a combination of both transposition and substitution to produce a ciphertext. Whereas transposition shuffles digits following a fixed sequence (as in a P-box), substitution should provide a nonlinear replacement. A substitution table is needed for a product-cipher system. Such tables are not new to us. They were described in Chapters 4 and 5 as Vigenère tables and substitution tables.

You will recall that a substitution table works with a key to replace an *input* character to derive an *output* character. The output characters need not bear any relationship to the input characters. The key controls the selection of characters, possibly based on the positions of the inputs. Inputs may be divided between two or more substitution tables.

Let's devise two such tables, each with three digits from the group 3, 4, 5, 6, 7, and 8 scrambled in them.

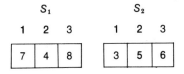

	S_1				S_2	
1	2	3		1	2	3
7	4	8		3	5	6

P-BOX

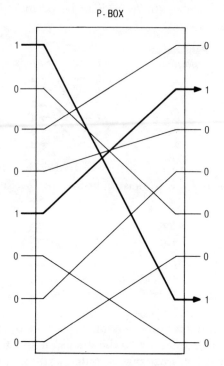

Fig. 7-4. Permutation box.

This process uses a key of 3–2–1. Input to S_1 and S_2 is as follows: The first three characters from a P-box are replaced by characters in S_1 following the key sequence; the next three characters from the P-box are replaced by the characters in S_2; and so on, back and forth, S_1, S_2, S_1, . . .

Using the word SYSTEM and the preceding permutation results, we have the following:

Word	Result	Key	S_1/S_2 replacement character
S	T	3	8
Y	S	2	4
S	E	1	7
T	M	3	6
E	S	2	5
M	Y	1	3

In this discussion, we started with the plaintext word SYSTEM, transposed it to become TSEMSY, and then replaced each character to develop the ciphertext 847653. This type of ciphertext based on both transposition and substitution operations is also called a *compound* ciphertext. It was described earlier in Chapter 5 during our discussion of matrix operations.

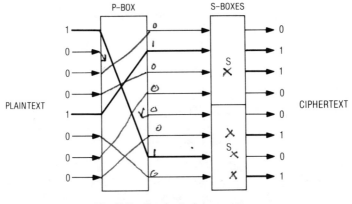

Fig. 7-5. Product-cipher system.

A product-cipher system is diagrammed in Fig. 7-5. Shown is binary plaintext going through a P-box and then through a group of substitution boxes or S-boxes. The P-box will shuffle the position of the 0,1 digits using a fixed sequence. The S-boxes will provide the substitution characters based on a key in a *nonlinear* way. That is, it is possible for more 1's to result in the ciphertext than began with the plaintext.

A Product-Cipher System Example

More complicated product-cipher systems can be developed by adding P- and S-boxes to the encryption process. Such systems increase data security. Trying to unravel the ciphertext by cryptanalysis or trial and error methods is a time-consuming and costly task.

Figure 7-6 represents a more involved product-cipher system having the basic characteristics of the Data Encryption Standard (DES). The system in Fig. 7-6 shows a plaintext converted to binary digits. These digits are scrambled by a P-box; the results have a key added to them using modulo 2 addition, as signified by the symbol ⊕. The resulting set of binary digits is divided into left and right halves to become the input into a left and right S-box. Here substitutions occur. The output from these S-boxes is then scrambled by a permutation box labelled P^{-1}. This box is an *inverse permutation box;* that is, it scrambles in a reverse sequence of the starting P-box. Finally, the bits of P^{-1} are converted into standard characters to produce a ciphertext. The discussion that follows uses three different examples, each one building on the prior one, to show step-by-step how the system in Fig. 7-6 works.*

Both the permutation box and the inverse permutation box are set for 14 bits of binary input. The binary input consists of two characters

---

* The system is presented solely for illustrative purposes. In its current form it does not present a usable cryptographic algorithm.

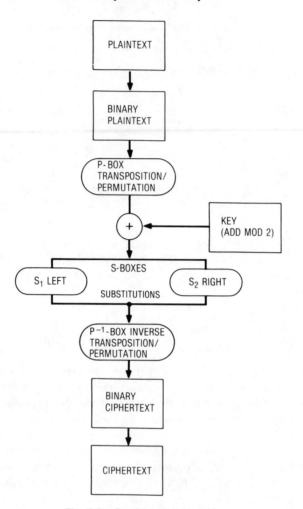

Fig. 7-6. Product-cipher system.

each seven bits in length. This gives us a basic *input block* of 14 bits. Figure 7-7 shows the permutation boxes P and P^{-1}. A 7-bit ASCII character code shown in Fig. 7-8 is used to convert plaintext characters to binary digits.

The key consists of a 14-bit block added (mod 2) each time to the 14 bits of binary output of the P-box. This output will enter two substitution boxes, shown in Fig. 7-9. Entry into the box is determined by the numerical value of the last three bits of each block of seven bits after the addition of the key. This is illustrated in Fig. 7-9.

Each substitution box has eight positions (0–7). The contents of each cell are the values 0, 1, 2, 3, 4, 5, 6, and 7, scrambled randomly.

	P				P^{-1}	
	Item in this column moves to		this position		Item in this column moves to	this position
1	10		1	1	7	1
2	8		2	2	3	2
3	2		3	3	5	3
4	5		4	4	10	4
5	3		5	5	4	5
6	14		6	6	8	6
7	1		7	7	9	7
8	6		8	8	2	8
9	7		9	9	12	9
10	4		10	10	1	10
11	13		11	11	14	11
12	9		12	12	13	12
13	12		13	13	11	13
14	11		14	14	6	14

Fig. 7-7. Permutation boxes.

Examples

These examples follow the product-cipher system process outlined in Fig. 7-6, along with the P- and S-boxes shown in Figs. 7-7 and 7-9, respectively.

EXAMPLE A

One block, 14 bits, and a word key

Plaintext: AB

Binary plaintext:

	A				B	
1	0 0 0	0 0 1	1	0 0 0	0 1 0

Permutation:

1	2 3 4	5 6 7	8	9 10 11	12 13 14	{Column position
1	0 0 0	0 0 1	1	0 0 0	0 1 0	{Binary position
10	8 2 5	3 14 1	6	7 4 13	9 12 11	{P-box
0	1 0 0	0 0 1	0	1 0 1	0 0 0	{Transposition

Key: The word key is EZ; when converted to binary digits it is added (mod 2) to the permutation/transposition.

7-bit ASCII	ASCII Char.	7-bit ASCII	ASCII Char.	7-bit ASCII	ASCII Char.
0 100 000	SP	1 000 000	@	1 100 000	\
0 100 001	!	1 000 001	A	1 100 001	a
0 100 010	"	1 000 010	B	1 100 010	b
0 100 011	#	1 000 011	C	1 100 011	c
0 100 100	$	1 000 100	D	1 100 100	d
0 100 101	%	1 000 101	E	1 100 101	e
0 100 110	&	1 000 110	F	1 100 110	f
0 100 111	'	1 000 111	G	1 100 111	g
0 101 000	(	1 001 000	H	1 101 000	h
0 101 001	)	1 001 001	I	1 101 001	i
0 101 010	*	1 001 010	J	1 101 010	j
0 101 011	+	1 001 011	K	1 101 011	k
0 101 100	,	1 001 100	L	1 101 100	l
0 101 101	-	1 001 101	M	1 101 101	m
0 101 110	.	1 001 110	N	1 101 110	n
0 101 111	/	1 001 111	O	1 101 111	o
0 110 000	0	1 010 000	P	1 110 000	p
0 110 001	1	1 010 001	Q	1 110 001	q
0 110 010	2	1 010 010	R	1 110 010	r
0 110 011	3	1 010 011	S	1 110 011	s
0 110 100	4	1 010 100	T	1 110 100	t
0 110 101	5	1 010 101	U	1 110 101	u
0 110 110	6	1 010 110	V	1 110 110	v
0 110 111	7	1 010 111	W	1 110 111	w
0 111 000	8	1 011 000	X	1 111 000	x
0 111 001	9	1 011 001	Y	1 111 001	y
0 111 010	:	1 011 010	Z	1 111 010	z
0 111 011	;	1 011 011	[	1 111 011	{
0 111 100	<	1 011 100	\	1 111 100	|
0 111 101	=	1 011 101	]	1 111 101	}
0 111 110	>	1 011 110	∧	1 111 110	¬
0 111 111	?	1 011 111	–	1 111 111	DEL

Fig. 7-8. ASCII character code.

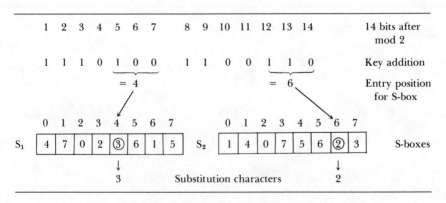

Fig. 7-9. S-boxes and entry.

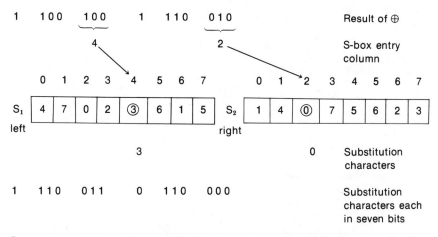

```
    0   1 0 0   0 0 1    0   1 0 1   0 0 0   Transposition
⊕   1   0 0 0   1 0 1    1   0 1 1   0 1 0   Key, EZ
    1   1 0 0   1 0 0    1   1 1 0   0 1 0   Result
```

S-boxes: Entry to the S-box uses the last three digits from the preceding result.

Inside the figure:

```
1   1 0 0   1 0 0   1   1 1 0   0 1 0                Result of ⊕

            4                   2                    S-box entry
                                                     column

    0  1  2  3  4  5  6  7      0  1  2  3  4  5  6  7

S₁  4  7  0  2  ③  6  1  5  S₂  1  4  ⓪  7  5  6  2  3
left                          right

            3                       0                Substitution
                                                     characters

1   1 1 0   0 1 1   0   1 1 0   0 0 0                Substitution
                                                     characters each
                                                     in seven bits
```

Inverse permutation: The two 7-bit characters are shuffled using the P^{-1}-box. A left and right 7-bit result is obtained from the transposition.

```
1   2 3 4   5 6 7   8 9  10 11 12 13 14    Column
                                           position

0   1 1 0   0 1 1   0 1   1 0 0 0 0         S-box
                                           results

7   3 5 10  4 8 9   2 12  1 14 13 11  6     P⁻¹-box

1   1 0 1   0 0 1   1 0   0 0 0 0 1         Transposition
```

Binary ciphertext: The output of the inverse permutation represents a binary ciphertext of two 7-bit characters.

Binary plaintext: 1   0 0 0   0 0 1   1   0 0 0   0 1 0

Binary ciphertext: 1   1 0 1   0 0 1   1   0 0 0   0 0 1

Note how the binary plaintext contains four 1's, and the binary ciphertext contains six 1's. The difference in the number of 1's is a result of the *nonlinear* nature of the S-boxes. By nonlinear we mean that the number of 1's in plaintext or ciphertext need not be equal.

Ciphertext: From Fig. 7-8 the binary ciphertext provides the characters i and A:

$$1 \quad 101 \quad 001 \qquad 1 \quad 000 \quad 001$$

$$\underbrace{\hspace{3cm}}_{\text{i}} \qquad \underbrace{\hspace{3cm}}_{\text{A}}$$

These characters give the ciphertext from the plaintext as shown below:

Plaintext: AB
Ciphertext: iA

EXAMPLE B

Two blocks of 14 bits each and a word key

Plaintext: A   B   U   T
Binary plaintext:

A		B		U		T	
1 000 001		1 000 010		1 010 101		1 010 100	

$$\underbrace{\hspace{5cm}}_{\text{A block of 14 bits}} \qquad \underbrace{\hspace{5cm}}_{\text{A block of 14 bits}}$$

Permutation: Since each 14-bit block is treated as a unit of input to the P-box, the first binary block representing the characters AB will be the same as in Example A. You need only shuffle the digits in the second block, representing UT.

1	2 3 4	5 6 7	8	9 10 11	12 13 14	
1	0 1 0	1 0 1	1	0 1 0	1 0 0	Binary plaintext: UT
10	8 2 5	3 1 4 1	6	7 4 1 3	9 12 11	P-box transposition
1	1 0 1	1 0 1	0	1 0 0	0 1 0	

Key: The key ZE is added in binary form, bit-by-bit (mod 2), to the P-box transposition. Only the second 14-bit block is processed with this key since the first block is the same as before. Note that in the actual NBS–DES algorithm (process), the *key* changes for each block.

	1	1 0 1	1 0 1	0	1 0 0	0 1 0	Transposition
⊕	1	0 1 1	0 1 0	1	0 0 0	1 0 1	Key, ZE
	0	1 1 0	1 1 1	1	1 0 0	1 1 1	Result

S-boxes:

0	1 1 0	1 1 1	1	1 0 0	1 1 1	
		7			7	S-box column, substitution character
S_1		5		S_2 3		
0	1 1 0	1 0 1	0	1 1 0	0 1 1	Substitution characters each in seven bits

Inverse permutation: Using the P^{-1}-box, we get the following:

0	1 1 0	1 0 1	0	1 1 0	0 1 1	S-box result

1	1 1 1	0 0 1	1	0 0 1	1 0 0	P-box transposition

Binary ciphertext: The entire two-block binary ciphertext is

1	101	001	1	000	001	1	111	001	1	001	100

Ciphertext: Using Fig. 7-8, the binary ciphertext becomes the following character ciphertext:

1 101 001	1 000 001	1 111 001	1 001 100
i	A	y	L

Plaintext: A   B   U   T

Ciphertext: i   A   y   L

EXAMPLE C

Two blocks of 14 bits each and a binary key

Rather than use a key word, a randomly generated key consisting of a binary digit stream can be used.

Plaintext: A   B   U   T

Binary plaintext:

1	000	001	1	000	010	:	AB
1	010	101	1	010	100	:	UT

Permutation:

0	100	001	0	101	000	:	AB
1	101	101	0	100	010	:	UT

Key:

0	110	100	1	101	100	:	Block 1 key
1	001	110	1	101	101	:	Block 2 key

For each block the bit-by-bit (mod 2) additions are

	0	1 0 0	0 0 0	0	1 0 1	0 0 0	: AB
⊕	0	1 1 0	1 0 0	1	1 0 1	1 0 0	: Block 1 key
	0	0 1 0	1 0 1	1	0 0 0	1 0 0	Result

	1	1 0 1	1 0 1	0	1 0 0	0 1 0	: UT
⊕	1	0 0 1	1 1 0	1	1 0 1	1 0 1	: Block 2 key
	0	1 0 0	0 1 1	1	0 0 1	1 1 1	Result

S-boxes:

	Block 1			Block 2			
	Left	Right		Left	Right		Results
	1 0 1	1 0 0		0 1 1	1 1 1		Last three digits
	5	4		3	7		S-box column
							substitution
S_1	6	S_2	5	S_1	2	S_2	3	character
0 110 110	0 110 101		0 110 010	0 110 011			S-box characters in seven bits

Inverse permutation: Using P^{-1} in Fig. 7-7, the inverse permutation and binary ciphertext then becomes two blocks of 14 digits each:

    0 111 001   1 010 001   0 101 001   1 001 101

Ciphertext: Based on the results of the P^{-1} transposition and Fig. 7-8, the four groups of seven bits produces the following ciphertext:

Plaintext: A   B   U   T

Ciphertext: 9   i   )   M

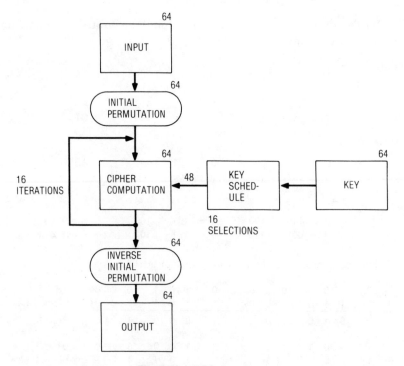

Fig. 7-10. DEA algorithm.

The DES Algorithm

The Data Encryption Standard (DES) consists of a Data Encryption Algorithm (DEA). An *algorithm* is a step-by-step procedure for solving a problem. The problem we are working with involves the enciphering and deciphering of blocks of data consisting of 64 bits. Input is in 64 bits, and output is in 64 bits. A key used in the process is also 64 bits in length. The DEA processes 64 bits of input in a *recirculating block cipher* as shown in Fig. 7-10. The DEA also consists of the pieces shown in Fig. 7-10 plus a

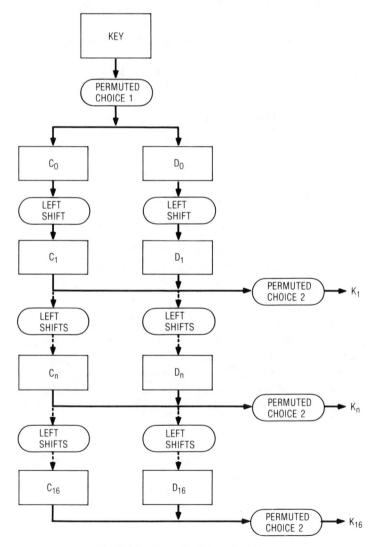

Fig. 7-11. Key schedule calculation.

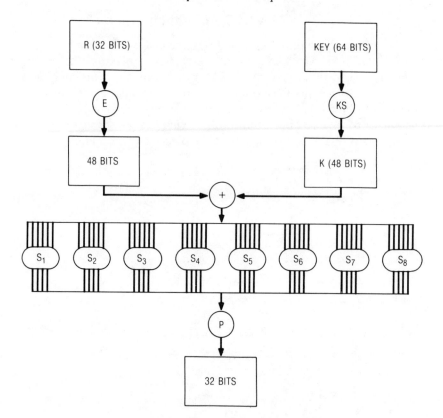

Fig. 7-12.   Cipher calculation, f(R,K).

key schedule that involves two *permuted choice* tables and a *left shift* table. Figure 7-11 gives an overview of the *key schedule* calculation. The *cipher computation* includes an *expansion table, key* addition, *S-box* substitution tables, and a *permutation* table. Figure 7-12 shows the cipher calculation. Beginning and ending the DEA is an *initial permutation* and an *inverse initial permutation,* respectively.

The overall computation is shown in Fig. 7-13. An explanation of some notations in this figure follows:

L_n = A left 32-bit block of input with n going from 0 to 16

R_n = A right 32-bit block of input with n going from 0 to 16.

K_n = A 48-bit key chosen from a 64-bit starting key (Fig. 7-11 shows the way this key is calculated.)

$\textcircled{f}$ = The cipher computation that is repeated 16 times, each time producing a 64-bit output (Fig. 7-12 shows how this computation is done.)

$\oplus$ = Bit-by-bit addition modulo 2

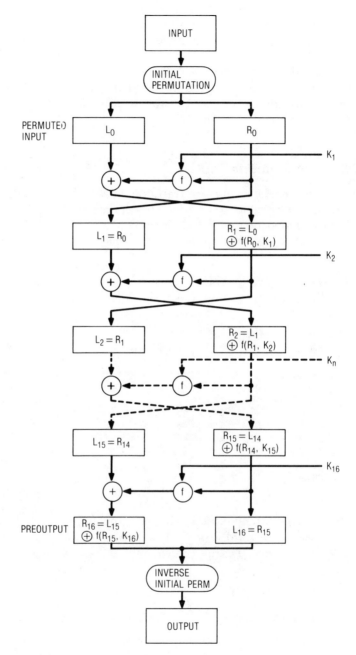

Fig. 7-13. Enciphering computation.

The DEA utilizes various tables to carry out the permutation, cipher computation, and key schedule selections shown in the previous figures. These tables will now be fully described. This discussion will draw on the source document for the DEA, that is, *Data Encryption Standard*, Federal Information Processing Standards Publication 46, National Bureau of Standards, January 15, 1977.

Some material will be quoted directly from the source document. In order of appearance, we use the following tables to complete the enciphering computation in Fig. 7-13.

IP: Initial Permutation Table

The 64 bits of data input are transposed according to the bit positions shown in the IP table to produce a 64-bit data block, divided into a left side with 32 bits and a right side with 32 bits. Each row of the table represents another eight bit positions. The table is used once for each input block.

The 64 bits of the input block to be enciphered are first subjected to the following permutation, called the *initial permutation,* IP:

Bit position	IP							
1– 8	58	50	42	34	26	18	10	2
9–16	60	52	44	36	28	20	12	4
17–24	62	54	46	38	30	22	14	6
25–32	64	56	48	40	32	24	16	8
33–40	57	49	41	33	25	17	9	1
41–48	59	51	43	35	27	19	11	3
49–56	61	53	45	37	29	21	13	5
57–64	63	55	47	39	31	23	15	7

That is, the permuted input has bit 58 of the input as its first bit, bit 50 as its second bit, and so on, with bit 7 as its last bit. The permuted input block is then the input to a complex key-dependent computation.

E: E Bit-Selection Table

This table expands 32 bits of input to 48 bits by shuffling the bits according to the positions indicated in the table. Note the repetition of bit positions, which provide the expansion. For example, the bits 1, 4, 5, 9, 16, and so on repeat one time each. This table is used 16 times and is symbolized by E in various figures.

Let E denote a function which takes a block of 32 bits as input and yields a block of 48 bits as output. Let E be such that the 48 bits of its output, written as 8 blocks of 6 bits each, are obtained by selecting the bits in its inputs in order, according to the following table:

Bit position	E Bit-Selection Table					
1- 6	32	1	2	3	4	5
7-12	4	5	6	7	8	9
13-18	8	9	10	11	12	13
19-24	12	13	14	15	16	17
25-30	16	17	18	19	20	21
31-36	20	21	22	23	24	25
37-42	24	25	26	27	28	29
43-48	28	29	30	31	32	1

Thus, the first three bits of $E(R)$ are the bits in positions 32, 1, and 2 of R while the last two bits of $E(R)$ are the bits in positions 32 and 1.

PC-1: *Permuted Choice Table-1*

This is a permutation table that shuffles the original 64-bit key to produce a 56-bit key consisting of two 28-bit parts: C_0 on the left and D_0 on the right. This table is used one time for each input block.

Permuted choice 1 is determined by the following table:

Bit position	PC – 1							
1- 7	57	49	41	33	25	17	9	
8-14	1	58	50	42	34	26	18	C_0
15-21	10	2	59	51	43	35	27	
22-28	19	11	3	60	52	44	36	
1- 7	63	55	47	39	31	23	15	
8-14	7	62	54	46	38	30	22	D_0
15-21	14	6	61	53	45	37	29	
22-28	21	13	5	28	20	12	4	

The table has been divided into two parts, with the first part determining how the bits of C_0 are chosen, and the second part determining how the bits of D_0 are chosen. The bits of *KEY* are numbered 1 through 64. The bits of C_0 are, respectively, bits 57, 49, 41,

. . . , 44 and 36 of *KEY*, with the bits of D_0 being bits 63, 55, 47, . . . , 12, and 4 of *KEY*.

LS: Left Shift Table

For each of the 16 iterations of the algorithm, a different key is used. Depending on the *iteration number,* the LS table will shift the 56-bit key either one or two positions to the left.

With C_0 and D_0 defined, we now define how the blocks C_n and D_n are obtained from the blocks C_{n-1} and D_{n-1}, respectively, for $n = 1$, 2, . . . , 16. That is accomplished by adhering to the following schedule of left shifts of the individual blocks:

Iteration number	Number of left shifts
1	1
2	1
3	2
4	2
5	2
6	2
7	2
8	2
9	1
10	2
11	2
12	2
13	2
14	2
15	2
16	1

For example, C_3 and D_3 are obtained from C_2 and D_2, respectively, by two left shifts, and C_{16} and D_{16} are obtained from C_{15} and D_{15}, respectively, by one left shift. In all cases, by a single left shift is meant a rotation of the bits one place to the left, so that after one left shift the bits in the 28 positions are the bits that were previously in positions 2, 3, . . . , 28, 1.

PC-2: Permuted Choice Table–2

This is a permutation table that shuffles the 56-bit key result of the LS table to produce a 48-bit key. This key is then added (mod 2) to the 48 bits derived from the E table. This table is used 16 times, once for each iteration.

Permuted choice 2 is determined by the following table:

Bit position	PC – 2					
1– 6	14	17	11	24	1	5
7–12	3	28	15	6	21	10
13–18	23	19	12	4	26	8
19–24	16	7	27	20	13	2
25–30	41	52	31	37	47	55
31–36	30	40	51	45	33	48
37–42	44	49	39	56	34	53
43–48	46	42	50	36	29	32

Therefore, the first bit of K_n is the 14th bit of C_nD_n, the second bit the 17th, and so on with the 47th bit the 29th, and the 48th bit the 32nd.

S: Substitution Boxes

There are eight substitution boxes: $S_1, S_2, \ldots, S_8$. Each box or table performs a separate substitution on a consecutive subblock of six bits of the 48-bit result from the operation $\textcircled{E} \oplus K_n$. The result is a 32-bit block. These eight tables are used 16 times, once for each iteration.

Each of the unique selection functions $S_1, S_2, \ldots, S_8$, takes a six-bit block as input and yields a four-bit block as output and is illustrated by using a table containing the recommended S_1:

$$S_1$$

Row no.	Column number															
	0	1	2	3	4	5	6	7	8	9	10	11	12	13	14	15
0	14	4	13	1	2	15	11	8	3	10	6	12	5	9	0	7
1	0	15	7	4	14	2	13	1	10	6	12	11	9	5	3	8
2	4	1	14	8	13	6	2	11	15	12⁻	9	7	3	10	5	0
3	15	12	8	2	4	9	1	7	5	11	3	14	10	0	6	13

If S_1 is the function defined in this table and B is a block of 6 bits, then $S_1 (B)$ is determined as follows: The first and last bits of B represent in base 2 a number in the range 0 to 3. Let that number be i. The middle 4 bits of B represent in base 2 a number in the range 0 to 15. Let that number be j. Look up in the table the number in the i'th row and j'th column. It is a number in the range 0 to 15 and is uniquely represented by a 4 bit block. That block is the output $S_1(B)$ of S_1 for the input B. For example, for input 011011 the row is 01, that is row 1, and the column is determined by 1101, that is column 13. In row 1 column 13 appears 5 so that the output is 0101.

Here are the other S-boxes:

S_2

15	1	8	14	6	11	3	4	9	7	2	13	12	0	5	10
3	13	4	7	15	2	8	14	12	0	1	10	6	9	11	5
0	14	7	11	10	4	13	1	5	8	12	6	9	3	2	15
13	8	10	1	3	15	4	2	11	6	7	12	0	5	14	9

S_3

10	0	9	14	6	3	15	5	1	13	12	7	11	4	2	8
13	7	0	9	3	4	6	10	2	8	5	14	12	11	15	1
13	6	4	9	8	15	3	0	11	1	2	12	5	10	14	7
1	10	13	0	6	9	8	7	4	15	14	3	11	5	2	12

S_4

7	13	14	3	0	6	9	10	1	2	8	5	11	12	4	15
13	8	11	5	6	15	0	3	4	7	2	12	1	10	14	9
10	6	9	0	12	11	7	13	15	1	3	14	5	2	8	4
3	15	0	6	10	1	13	8	9	4	5	11	12	7	2	14

S_5

2	12	4	1	7	10	11	6	8	5	3	15	13	0	14	9
14	11	2	12	4	7	13	1	5	0	15	10	3	9	8	6
4	2	1	11	10	13	7	8	15	9	12	5	6	3	0	14
11	8	12	7	1	14	2	13	6	15	0	9	10	4	5	3

S_6

12	1	10	15	9	2	6	8	0	13	3	4	14	7	5	11
10	15	4	2	7	12	9	5	6	1	13	14	0	11	3	8
9	14	15	5	2	8	12	3	7	0	4	10	1	13	11	6
4	3	2	12	9	5	15	10	11	14	1	7	6	0	8	13

$$S_7$$

4	11	2	14	15	0	8	13	3	12	9	7	5	10	6	1
13	0	11	7	4	9	1	10	14	3	5	12	2	15	8	6
1	4	11	13	12	3	7	14	10	15	6	8	0	5	9	2
6	11	13	8	1	4	10	7	9	5	0	15	14	2	3	12

$$S_8$$

13	2	8	4	6	15	11	1	10	9	3	14	5	0	12	7
1	15	13	8	10	3	7	4	12	5	6	11	0	14	9	2
7	11	4	1	9	12	14	2	0	6	10	13	15	3	5	8
2	1	14	7	4	10	8	13	15	12	9	0	3	5	6	11

P: Permutation Table

The 32-bit output of the S-boxes is shuffled according to the bit positions shown in the P table. The output is a 32-bit block symbolized by Ⓟ in various figures. This table is used 16 times for every input block.

The permutation function P yields a 32-bit output from a 32-bit input by permuting the bits of the input block. Such a function is defined by the following table:

Bit position	P			
1– 4	16	7	20	21
5– 8	29	12	28	17
9–12	1	15	23	26
13–16	5	18	31	10
17–20	2	8	24	14
21–24	32	27	3	9
24–28	19	13	30	6
29–32	22	11	4	25

The output $P(L)$ for the function P defined by this table is obtained from the input L by taking the 16th bit of L as the first bit of $P(L)$, the 7th bit as the second bit of $P(L)$, and so on until the 25th bit of L is taken as the 32nd bit of $P(L)$.

IP^{-1}: Inverse Initial Permutation Table

The 64 bits of output from the sixteenth iteration of the enciphering computation are transposed according to the bit positions shown in the IP^{-1} table. This table is used once for each input block.

The output of that computation, called the preoutput, is then subjected to the following permutation which is the inverse of the initial permutation:

Bit
position: IP^{-1}

1– 8	40	8	48	16	56	24	64	32
9–16	39	7	47	15	55	23	63	31
17–24	38	6	46	14	54	22	62	30
25–32	37	5	45	13	53	21	61	29
33–40	36	4	44	12	52	20	60	28
41–48	35	3	43	11	51	19	59	27
49–56	34	2	42	10	50	18	58	26
57–64	33	1	41	9	49	17	57	25

That is, the output of the algorithm has bit 40 of the preoutput block as its first bit, bit 8 as its second bit, and so on, until bit 25 of the preoutput block is the last bit of the output.

The DEA, Bit-by-Bit

In order to understand and appreciate the complexity of the Data Encryption Algorithm (DEA) outlined in the previous figures and description, a detailed step-by-step, bit-by-bit example will be presented.

Since the algorithm is repetitive (Figs. 7-10 and 7-13), going through 16 rounds using the same computational process (Figs. 7-11 and 7-12), only a single iteration is detailed. This iteration process is shown in Fig. 7-14 and should be followed carefully along with the example given.

1. Begin with an *input* block of 64 bits, as shown in Fig. 7-15.
2. Perform an *initial permutation* on the 64 bits by shuffling them using the following IP table, with the bit in position 58 of the input block going to position 1, the bit in position 50 going to position 2, and so on until the bit 1 in position 7 of the input block is transposed to position 64. The result, as shown in Fig. 7-16, is separated into a 32-bit left part L_0 and a 32-bit right part R_0.

IP

58	50	42	34	26	18	10	2
60	52	44	36	28	20	12	4
62	54	46	38	30	22	14	6
64	56	48	40	32	24	16	8
57	49	41	33	25	17	9	1
59	51	43	35	27	19	11	3
61	53	45	37	29	21	13	5
63	55	47	39	31	23	15	7

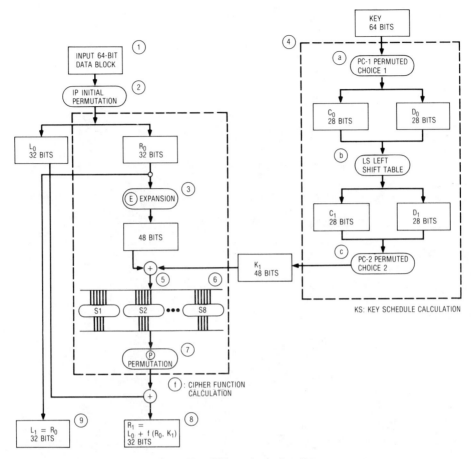

Fig. 7-14. DEA, a single iteration.

3. An *expansion* E of the rightmost 32 bits (R_0) occurs by using the following *E bit-selection table* to yield 48 bits of output. Bit 32 in R_0 (a 1) becomes bit 1 as a result of the expansion. The remaining bits of R_0 form a 48-bit block, as shown in Fig. 7-17, by falling into the column position as shown in the E bit-selection table. Note that many of the bit positions in the table repeat themselves. This makes the expansion possible.

E Bit-selection Table

32	1	2	3	4	5
4	5	6	7	8	9
8	9	10	11	12	13
12	13	14	15	16	17
16	17	18	19	20	21
20	21	22	23	24	25
24	25	26	27	28	29
28	29	30	31	32	1

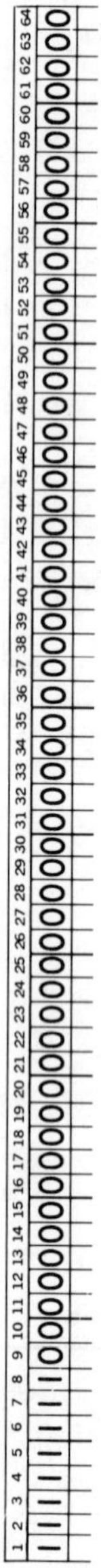

Fig. 7-15. Input block.

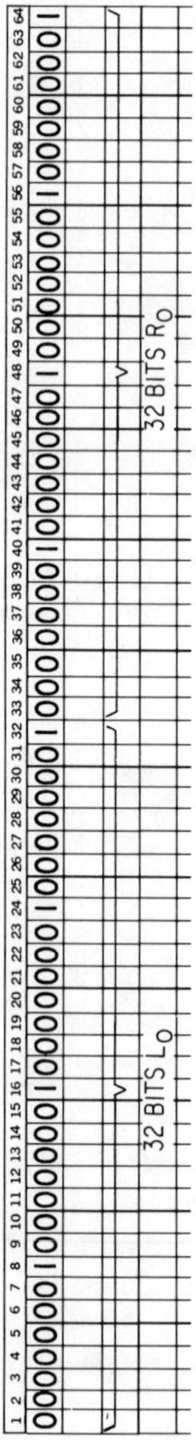

Fig. 7-16. Initial permutation.

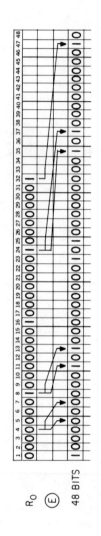

Fig. 7-17. Expansion.

4. A *key* (K_n) for round 1 is developed. This will be key K_1, derived from a 64-bit starting key. K_1 uses a key schedule (KS) described here in several steps. The 64-bit key is shown in Fig. 7-18.

(a) The 64-bit key enters the following *permuted choice table* (PC-1) and is reduced to 56 bits. Bits of the key are shifted to the positions indicated in PC-1. Key bit 57 (a 0) becomes bit 1 and so on. The 56-bit result is divided into two equal parts as shown in Fig. 7-19. The left part is labeled C_0 and the right part is D_0. Each part contains 28 bits.

PC − 1

57	49	41	33	25	17	9	
1	58	50	42	34	26	18	C_0
10	2	59	51	43	35	27	
19	11	3	60	52	44	36	
63	55	47	39	31	23	15	
7	62	54	46	38	30	22	D_0
14	6	61	53	45	37	29	
21	13	5	28	20	12	4	

(b) Each of the 28-bit blocks is shifted to the left, based on the following *left shift table* (LS).

Left Shift Table

Iteration number	Number of left shifts
1	1
2	1
3	2
4	2
5	2
6	2
7	2
8	2
9	1
10	2
11	2
12	2
13	2
14	2
15	2
16	1

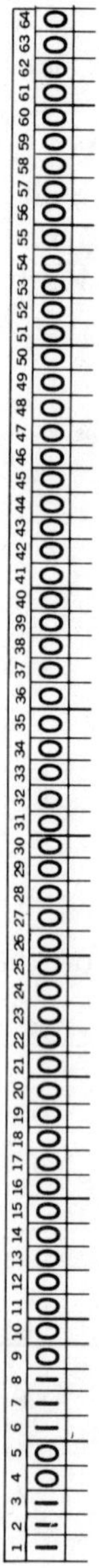

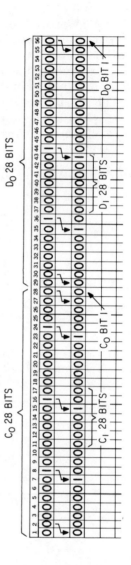

Fig. 7-18. 64-bit key.

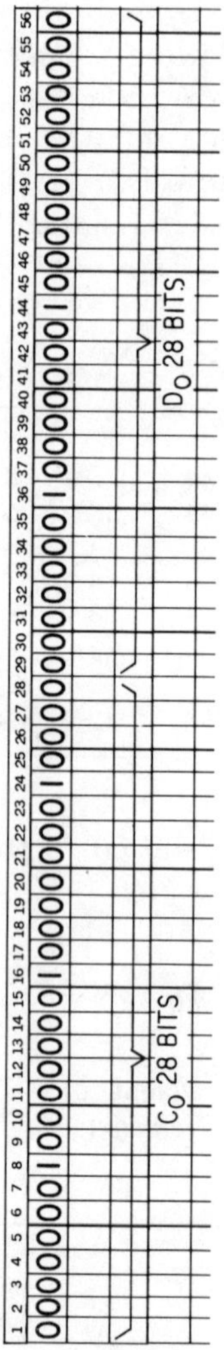

Fig. 7-19. 56-bit permutation.

Fig. 7-20. Result of left shift.

For iteration number 1, the number of left shifts is one bit position for C_0 and D_0. Bit 2 becomes bit 1; bit 3 becomes bit 2; and so on, with bit 1 becoming the last bit, 28. The result is C_1 and D_1, as shown in Fig. 7-20.

c. The 56-bit block of C_1 and D_1 enters the following *permuted choice table* (PC-2) where the bits are shuffled and reduced to a block of 48 bits. The 48-bit block shown in Fig. 7-21 is the key K_1.

PC-2

14	17	11	24	1	5
3	28	15	6	21	10
23	19	12	4	26	8
16	7	27	20	13	2
41	52	31	37	47	55
30	40	51	45	33	48
44	49	39	56	34	53
46	42	50	36	29	32

5. The 48-bit key (K_1) and the 48-bit expansion are added $\oplus$ (mod 2), as shown in Fig. 7-22.
6. The results of $E \oplus K_1$ are 48 bits of input for S-boxes 1 through 8. Each S-box takes six bits of input as row and column numbers to produce a substitution value from the table. The bits 1 and 6 locate the row, and the bits 2 through 5 locate the column, as shown below.

	Bits				Bits			
Row	1	6	Column	2	3	4	5
0	0	0	0	0	0	0	0
1	0	1	1	0	0	0	1
2	1	0	2	0	0	1	0
3	1	1	3	0	0	1	1
			4	0	1	0	0
			5	0	1	0	1
			6	0	1	1	0
			7	0	1	1	1
			8	1	0	0	0
			9	1	0	0	1
			10	1	0	1	0
			11	1	0	1	1
			12	1	1	0	0
			13	1	1	0	1
			14	1	1	1	0
			15	1	1	1	1

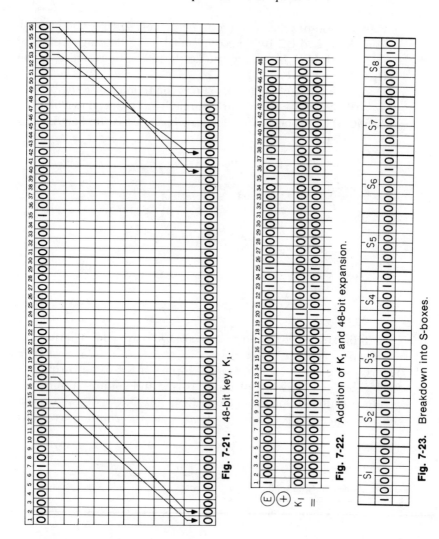

Fig. 7-21.   48-bit key, K₁.

Fig. 7-22.   Addition of K₁ and 48-bit expansion.

Fig. 7-23.   Breakdown into S-boxes.

The six bits for each S-box are as shown in Fig. 7-23. For S_1, the row bits 1 and 6 yield a 10 = row 2. The column bits 2 through 5 yield a 0000 = column 0. In table S_1, this gives a substitution number of 4.

S_1

Row	Column number															
no.	0	1	2	3	4	5	6	7	8	9	10	11	12	13	14	15
0	14	4	13	1	2	15	11	8	3	10	6	12	5	9	0	7
1	0	15	7	4	14	2	13	1	10	6	12	11	9	5	3	8
2	4	1	14	8	13	6	2	11	15	12	9	7	3	10	5	0
3	15	12	8	2	4	9	1	7	5	11	3	14	10	0	6	13

All S-box inputs and output are summarized here:

S-box	6-bit input	Row and column no.	Table number	4-bit output
1	100000	2, 0	4	0100
2	001010	0, 5	11	1011
3	000000	0, 0	10	1010
4	010010	0, 9	2	0010
5	100000	2, 0	4	0100
6	000010	0, 1	1	0001
7	100000	2, 0	1	0001
8	000010	0, 1	2	0010

7. The 32 bits of S-box output enter the following *permutation table* (P), producing 32 bits of output, as shown in Fig. 7-24.

P

16	7	20	21
29	12	28	17
1	15	23	26
5	18	31	10
2	8	24	14
32	27	3	9
19	13	30	6
22	11	4	25

8. The 32-bit result in (7) represents the first of the 16 cipher function, $f(R,K)$, calculations. The leftmost 32 bits (L_0), so far unmoved from (2), and $f(R,K)$ are added (mod 2) to form a new 32-bit block R_1, as shown in Fig. 7-25. The notation to express this is

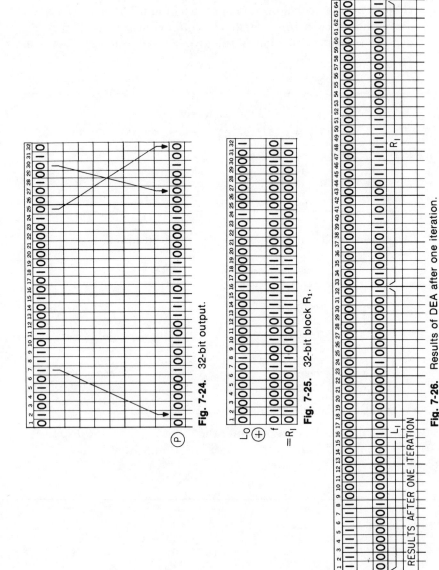

Fig. 7-24. 32-bit output.

Fig. 7-25. 32-bit block R_1.

Fig. 7-26. Results of DEA after one iteration.

$$R_1 = L_0 \oplus f(R_0 , K_1)$$

where L_0 = initial 32 leftmost bits in (2), and $f(R_0, K_1)$ indicates that a result was derived using R_0 and K_1, steps (3) through (7).

9. In step (2) the rightmost 32 bits are labeled R_0. This block starts the next iteration as L_1, the leftmost block. Figures 7-13 and 7-14 show two 32-bit blocks as

$$L_1 = R_0 \qquad R_1 = L_0 \oplus f(R_0, K_1)$$

Steps (3) through (9) are repeated, producing

$$L_2 = R_1 \qquad R_2 = L_1 \oplus f(R_1, K_2)$$

10. The process shown in Fig. 7-13 continues through to R_{16} and L_{16}, the *preoutput* block. Note that R_{16} is on the *left;* L_{16} is on the *right.* The *inverse initial perm* performs the reversing operation so that R_{16} will go to the right, and L_{16} will go to the left. This step produces a 64-bit *output* ciphertext.
11. The entire process, steps (1) through (10), is repeated for each 64-bit block of input.

DEA after One Iteration

We can now examine the results of the DEA after one iteration to see how the input block has been changed. Shown in Fig. 7-26 are the 64 bits of the input block and the 64 bits comprising L_1 and R_1.

Note how the input block has changed. Only one of the original 1 digits remains in the first eight bit positions. Most dramatic of the changes is the number of 1 bits. From the original eight there are now 17. This increase results from the expansion operation E and the nonlinear S-box substitutions. If the algorithm consisted of only one iteration, the results would be rather difficult to analyze by cryptanalysis without the key. With 16 iterations, the results cannot be readily "cracked."

Inverse Initial Permutation

To illustrate the last step of the enciphering computation, the *inverse initial perm* of Fig. 7-13, the outputs L_1 and R_1 derived from the bit-by-bit process will be used. In this illustration we start with the preoutput of R_{16} and L_{16}, using L_1 for R_{16} and R_1 for L_{16}.

Begin with the 64-bit preoutput block, and using the inverse of the initial permutation in the form of the IP^{-1} table, shuffle the bits. The result of this transposition is an output block of 64 bits. Figure 7-27 shows the inverse initial permutation step.

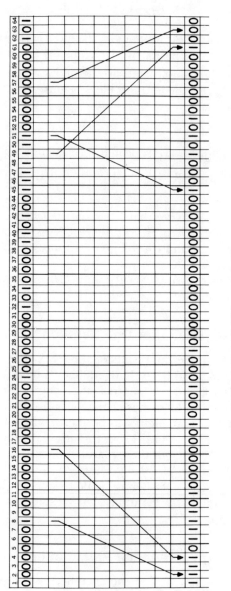

Fig. 7-27.   Inverse initial permutation.

IP^{-1}

40	8	48	16	56	24	64	32
39	7	47	15	55	23	63	31
38	6	46	14	54	22	62	30
37	5	45	13	53	21	61	29
36	4	44	12	52	20	60	28
35	3	43	11	51	19	59	27
34	2	42	10	50	18	58	26
33	1	41	9	49	17	57	25

Deciphering

To decipher output from the DEA, an enciphered message block must be entered into the algorithm. During the deciphering process, the same key (K_n), used during enciphering, must be used at each iteration. The processes for enciphering and deciphering are outlined in Fig. 7-28.

A bit-by-bit illustration will now follow. You will recall that after the initial permutation, the permuted input was L_0 and R_0. After one iteration of the enciphering computation the results were

$$L_1 = R_0 \qquad R_1 = L_0 \oplus f(R_0, K_1)$$

For illustration purposes only, we skipped down to the preoutput where we let $R_{16} = L_1$ and $L_{16} = R_1$. The ciphertext output then followed from the inverse initial permutation of the preoutput.

In Fig. 7-29 the bit-by-bit deciphering process is shown. It starts with the ciphertext output as input into the DEA. The final output is the plaintext input with which we began the bit-by-bit encryption.

DEA Summary

To summarize the DEA, the following material has been excerpted from FIPS Pub 46.*

Enciphering

Let the 64 bits of the input block to an iteration consist of a 32-bit block L followed by a 32-bit block R. Using the notation defined in the introduction, the input block is then LR.

Let K be a block of 48 bits chosen from the 64-bit key. Then the output $L'R'$ of an iteration with input LR is defined by:

(1) $$L' = R \qquad R' = L \oplus f(R,K)$$

where $\oplus$ denotes bit-by-bit addition modulo 2.

* *Data Encryption Standard*, U.S. Department of Commerce, National Bureau of Standards, Federal Information Processing Standards Publication 46 (January 15, 1977): 9–10.

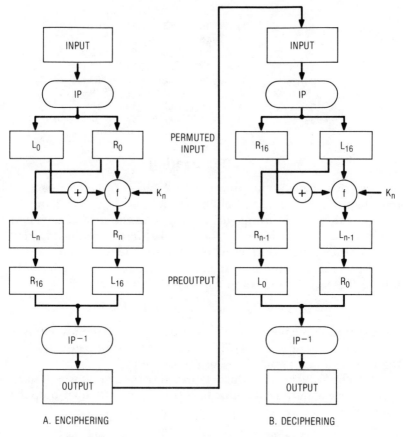

Fig. 7-28. Enciphering and deciphering processes.

As remarked before, the input of the first iteration of the calculation is the permuted input block. If $L'R'$ is the output of the 16th iteration then $R'L'$ is the preoutput block. At each iteration a different block K of key bits is chosen from the 64-bit key designated by KEY.

With more notation we can describe the iterations of the computation in more detail. Let KS be a function which takes an integer n in the range from 1 to 16 and a 64-bit block KEY as input and yields as output a 48-bit block K_n—a permuted selection of bits from KEY. That is,

$$(2) \qquad\qquad K_n = KS(n, KEY)$$

with K_n determined by the bits in 48 distinct bit positions of KEY. KS is called the key schedule because the block K used in the n'th iteration of (1) is the block K_n determined by (2).

As before, let the permuted input block be LR. Finally, let L_0 and R_0 be respectively L and R and let L_n and R_n be respectively L' and R' of (1)

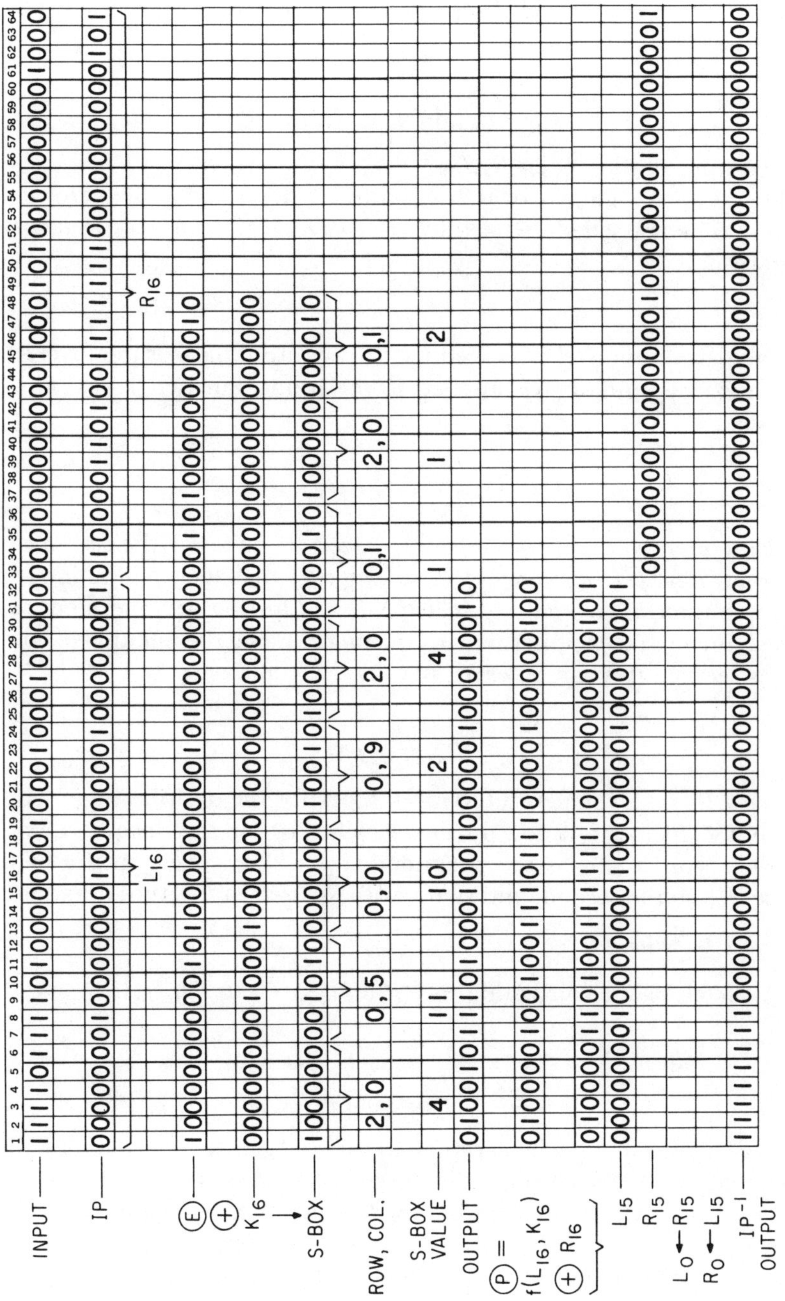

INPUT

IP

E ⊕ K₁₆

S-BOX

ROW, COL.

S-BOX VALUE

OUTPUT

P = f(L₁₆, K₁₆) ⊕ R₁₆

L₁₅

R₁₅

L₀ → R₁₅

R₀ → L₁₅

IP⁻¹

OUTPUT

Fig. 7-29. Bit-by-bit deciphering.

when L and R are respectively L_{n-1} and R_{n-1} and K is K_n; that is, when n is in the range from 1 to 16,

$$
(3) \qquad \begin{aligned} L_n &= R_{n-1} \\ R_n &= L_{n-1} \oplus f(R_{n-1}, K_n) \end{aligned}
$$

The preoutput block is then $R_{16}L_{16}$.

The key schedule KS of the algorithm is described above [and in Fig. 7-11]. The key schedule produces the 16 K_n which are required for the algorithm.

Deciphering

The permutation IP^{-1} applied to the preoutput block is the inverse of the initial permutation IP applied to the input. Further, from (1) it follows that:

$$
(4) \qquad \begin{aligned} R &= L' \\ L &= R' \oplus f(L', K) \end{aligned}
$$

Consequently, to *decipher* it is only necessary to apply the *very same algorithm to an enciphered message block,* taking care that at each iteration of the computation *the same block of key bits K is used* during decipherment as was used during the encipherment of the block. Using the notation of the previous section, this can be expressed by the equations:

$$
(5) \qquad \begin{aligned} R_{n-1} &= L_n \\ L_{n-1} &= R_n \oplus f(L_n, K_n) \end{aligned}
$$

where now $R_{16}L_{16}$ is the permuted input block for the deciphering calculation and L_0R_0 is the preoutput block. That is, for the decipherment calculation with $R_{16}L_{16}$ as the permuted input, K_{16} is used in the first iteration, K_{15} in the second, and so on, with K_1 used in the 16th iteration.

The Cipher Function f

A sketch of the calculation of $f(R,K)$ is given in Fig. 7-12.

DES Controversy

You will recall that when cryptanalysis was discussed in Chapter 6, it was pointed out that if an encryption process is known, then by trying all possible keys the ciphertext can be deciphered. With DES we all know how the algorithm works. However, the designers of the algorithm maintain that the present key of 64 bits is long enough to make it unprofitable to use trial-and-error techniques to break the ciphertext. The *work factor* to break the DEA is so large it could cost, according to some estimates, $200 million to try all 72 quadrillion possible keys.

Critics of the algorithm argue that at most it would take $20 million to build a special-purpose computer to exhaust the DEA key and break

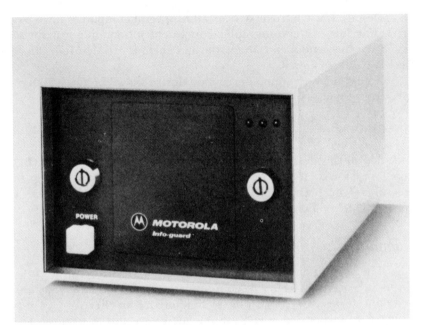

Fig. 7-30. Encryption devices, desk top and rack mount. (Courtesy of Motorola Inc.)

the algorithm. In addition, they have raised a political issue, claiming that the National Security Agency (NSA) is privy to DES development designs and "may" therefore know how to break any intercepted messages easily. The IBM developers of the algorithm insist there has been no such collusion between them and the NSA.

Despite this controversy over DES, several companies have begun marketing low-cost cryptographic equipment for communications security. Current vendors of these devices include IBM, Motorola, and Rockwell International.

A desk top encryption/decryption device shown in Fig. 7-30 has the following physical specifications:

height:	6.2 in.	depth:	15 in.
width:	7.2 in.	weight:	21 lb

Included in this device is a 24-key key-pad on the inside surface of the door. A rack-mount device with the key-pad can be seen in the figure. It measures 7 in. high, 19 in. wide, and 16 in. deep. These devices cost approximately $4,000 each.

Summary

The protection of data and information from threats and abuse covers two areas of security—communication systems/data transmission and data storage. Cryptographic techniques are an effective way of providing data security. A cryptographic algorithm in the form of a Data Encryption Standard (DES) has been adopted as a federal standard for data security. The algorithm is a complex product transformation. Commercially available devices for data encryption can now make a communication system more secure.

Questions

1. Define *data security*.
2. (a) What is meant by *communications security?*
   (b) What is meant by *file security?*
3. What is the purpose of DES?
4. What is a *compound cipher system?*
5. Solve the problem 7 + 5 = ? using a 4-bit set by
   (a) Binary addition
   (b) Addition modulo 2
6. Perform the operation indicated using a key of K = 1 000 100:
   (a) C = M $\oplus$ K, where M = 1 010 111
   (b) M = C $\oplus$ K, where C = 0 010 011
7. Transpose the word SECURITY using the permutation box:

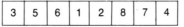

| 3 | 5 | 6 | 1 | 2 | 8 | 7 | 4 |

8. What is a *product cipher system?*
9. What is the function of
   (a) A P-box?
   (b) An S-box?
10. What is meant by *nonlinear* when referring to an S-box?
11. Using Example C as a guide, encipher the plaintext word ABLE.
12. In what ways does the DEA make use of P-boxes and S-boxes?
13. Using L_1 and R_1 in the DEA text example, carry out the deciphering process.

References

Branstad, Dennis K., ed. *Computer Security and the Data Encryption Standard.* Washington, D.C.: National Bureau of Standards, Department of Commerce, February 1978.

Branstad, Dennis K.; Gait, Jason; and Katzke, Stuart. *Report of the Workshop on Cryptography in Support of Computer Security.* Washington, D.C.: National Bureau of Standards, September 1977.

Bryce, Heather. "The NBS Data Encryption Standard: Products and Principles." *Mini-Micro Systems,* vol. 14, no. 3 (March 1981): 111–116.

Denning, Peter J., ed. "Special Issue: Cryptology." *ACM Computing Surveys,* vol. 11, no. 4 (December 1979).

Gait, Jason. "Encryption Standard: Validating Hardware Techniques." *Dimensions,* vol. 62, no. 7/8 (July/August 1978): 22–24.

Katzan, Harry, Jr. *Standard Data Encryption Algorithm.* New York: Petrocelli Books, Inc., 1977.

Kinnucan, Paul. "Data Encryption Gurus: Tuchman and Meyer." *Mini-Micro Systems,* vol. 11, no. 9 (October 1978): 54–60.

Lennon, R. E. "Cryptography Architecture for Security." *IBM Systems Journal,* vol. 17, no. 2 (1978): 138–150.

Meyer, Carl H., and Tuchman, Walter L. "Putting Data Encryption to Work." *Mini-Micro Systems,* vol. 11, no. 9 (October 1978): 46–52.

National Bureau of Standards. *Data Encryption Standard.* Washington, D.C.: NTIS, January 1977.

Solomon, Richard J. "The Encryption Controversy." *Mini-Micro* Systems, vol. 11, no. 2 (February 1978): 22–26.

Sykes, David J. "Protecting Data by Encryption." *Datamation,* vol. 22, no. 8 (August 1976): 81–85.

8

Public-Key Cryptography

Introduction

Research is currently directed toward development of another encryption algorithm that may soon rival the DES. This algorithm has been called the *public-key algorithm* or PKA.

Public-Key Algorithm

The DES algorithm and other encryption techniques use a single key for enciphering and deciphering a message. Both the sender and receiver must know the key and keep it confidential. In the case of DES the algorithm is known to all, but keys are kept secret.

A disadvantage of the DES in electronic mail and electronic funds transfer (EFT) applications may occur if a user must distribute secret keys to many correspondents. Such a distribution increases the risk that messages will be exposed or obtained by unauthorized persons.

The proposed public-key algorithm (PKA) is designed to minimize these risks by using two separate keys. One key is used for message encryption and is made *public* or published; the other key is used for message decryption and is kept secret.

The success of this algorithm results from the fact that the inverse of the enciphering functions, which are needed for deciphering, cannot be derived even if the enciphering function is known. This contrasts with other ciphers we have discussed in which the deciphering function can be determined by knowing the enciphering function. Not so with the PKA!

The PKA employs special mathematical functions known as *trapdoor one-way functions*. These one-way functions are easy to develop. The inverse of the function cannot be derived from a description of the function. To derive the inverse, you must know *how* the function was constructed. This special knowledge results in the *trapdoor*. A user will construct a one-way function and an inverse function. The one-way function, in effect the encryption key, is made available for public use. The inverse, or decryption key, is not made public. No one who sees the public encryption function can deduce its inverse.

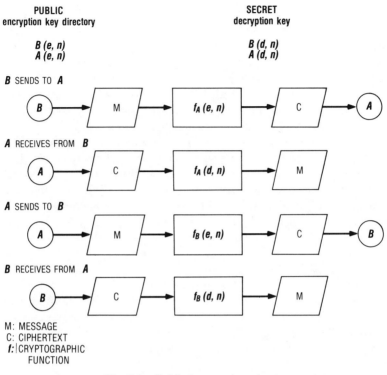

PUBLIC
encryption key directory

SECRET
decryption key

B (e, n)
A (e, n)

B (d, n)
A (d, n)

B SENDS TO *A*

A RECEIVES FROM *B*

A SENDS TO *B*

B RECEIVES FROM *A*

M: MESSAGE
C: CIPHERTEXT
f: CRYPTOGRAPHIC
     FUNCTION

Fig. 8-1. Public-key cryptosystem.

Public-Key Cryptosystem

In *public-key cryptosystem,* person *A* would publish his enciphering key (two numbers, *e* and *n*). Person *B* could send an enciphered plaintext message to *A* by using the trapdoor function *f*. This would produce the original plaintext message. Figure 8-1 shows such a system where

    M = Plaintext message
    C = Ciphertext
    f = Trapdoor function for encryption/decryption
    e,n = Encryption key (two positive integers)
    d,n = Decryption key (two positive integers)
    B = Sender/receiver
    A = Receiver/sender

Another useful feature of this public-key cryptosystem (PKS) in the area of electronic mail or funds transfer (EFT) is the *message signature.* Such a signature ensures the recipient that the sender was really the person he or she was supposed to be and not someone making an unauthorized request.

The message signature can be used to *sign* an EFT order. A sender in bank B enciphers a plaintext message with *his secret deciphering* key. This represents sender B's "signature." Sender B now enciphers this message signature again, but using receiver A's *public enciphering key*. This *double enciphered* ciphertext message is sent to A. Upon receiving the ciphertext, A uses his secret deciphering key to reverse the second coding of B's message. By applying B's *public enciphering key* to the first encipherment, the original plaintext message appears.

How does A really know if B sent the message? He knows because only B has knowledge of *his* secret deciphering key. Receiver A could understand the message because *his* secret deciphering key is known only to him. Someone else could send a message to A while masquerading as B, but A would be able to authenticate the sender by checking the message signature. Figure 8-2 shows how the message signature works, using the notation of the previous figure with S representing "signature."

The PKA has yet to be incorporated into a cryptographic device as has the DES algorithm. Work continues on developing the public-key algorithm into a practical data security system.

We will examine a public-key cryptosystem called the RSA, named after the designers Rivest, Shamir, and Adelman.* This system uses *prime numbers* and *modular arithmetic* to develop the public and private keys for encryption and decryption. The RSA system also permits the sending of a message signature.

Mathematical Prerequisites

To understand the workings of the RSA public-key cryptosystem we will review several mathematical concepts. These concepts involve prime numbers, factors, and modular arithmetic.

Prime Numbers

A number is prime if it is divisible only by itself and 1. If an integer is divisible by some other number, it is not prime. The division, when carried out, produces a whole number. For example, 10 is *not* prime because it can be divided by the integers 2 or 5. Is 11 prime? Yes it is because it can only be divided by 1 and itself. The following are examples of prime numbers:

2,   3,   5,   7,   11,   13,   17,   19,   23,   29,   31,   . . .

Greatest Common Divisor

The greatest common divisor (GCD) of a pair of integers is the largest integer that divides *both* numbers of the given pair. Thus 3 is the

---

* Ronald Rivest, Adi Shamir, and Len Adelman, "A Method for Obtaining Digital Signatures and Public-Key Cryptosystems," MIT Technical Memo LCS/TM82 (April 1977).

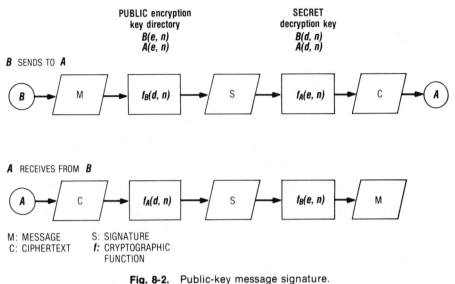

M: MESSAGE   S: SIGNATURE
C: CIPHERTEXT   *f:* CRYPTOGRAPHIC
                FUNCTION

Fig. 8-2. Public-key message signature.

GCD of the pair 6,15. We express this fact by writing the following:

$$GCD(6,15) = 3$$

To find the GCD we can first list the divisors of each number, including the number itself. Then we pick out the largest divisor appearing on both lists:

$$
\begin{aligned}
\text{Divisors of 6:} &\quad 1,\quad 2,\quad 3,\quad 6 \\
\text{Divisors of 15:} &\quad 1,\quad 3,\quad 5,\quad 15
\end{aligned}
$$

$$\therefore \quad GCD(6,15) = 3$$

The GCD can also be found using Euclid's algorithm. This algorithm leads to the GCD without having to list all possible divisors and is useful in cases where the numbers involved are very large. It is applied as follows: Given two numbers, 42 and 135, divide the *smaller* (42) into the *larger* (135). The remainder is 9. We can write

$$GCD(42,135) = GCD(9,42)$$

The process is repeated, stopping at the step before a division comes out even, leaving no remainder:

$$GCD(42,135) = GCD(9,42) = GCD(6,9) = GCD(3,6) = 3$$

We do not proceed beyond GCD(3,6) because

$$6 \div 3 \rightarrow 2 \text{ with } no \text{ remainder}$$

The final step is GCD(3,6), which gives 3 as the answer.

Modular Arithmetic

Modular arithmetic is part of a larger field of study commonly referred to as *number theory*. Our needs require the understanding of the relationship of three numbers expressed as

$$a \equiv b \text{ modulus } m$$

where a and b are two integers and m is a positive integer. This statement means that

$$a \text{ is the remainder of } m \div b$$

For example:

$$14(\text{mod } 12) = 2$$

or

$$
\begin{array}{r}
1 \\
12\overline{)14} \\
-\ 12 \\
\hline
R =\ \ 2 = \text{remainder}
\end{array}
$$

Other examples are as follows:

(A)
$$70(\text{mod } 15) = 10$$

$$
\begin{array}{r}
4 \\
15\overline{)70} \\
-\ 60 \\
\hline
R = 10
\end{array}
$$

(B)
$$9(\text{mod } 26) = 9$$

$$
\begin{array}{r}
0 \\
26\overline{)9} \\
-\ 0 \\
\hline
R = 9
\end{array}
$$

(C)
$$72(\text{mod } 26) = 20$$

$$
\begin{array}{r}
2 \\
26\overline{)72} \\
-\ 52 \\
\hline
R = 20
\end{array}
$$

The RSA Public-Key Cryptosystem

1. *Developing keys:* Two keys need to be developed. A public-key (e,n) and a secret key (d,n).

(a) To start, each receiver generates three numbers:

$$p = \text{A large prime number}$$
$$q = \text{A large prime number}$$
$$e = \text{A large number}$$

These numbers should be picked randomly.

(b) Calculate $n = p \times q$. The public-key is then (e,n).

(c) Next calculate the secret key value

$$d = e^{-1} \text{ modulo } \emptyset(n)$$

where $\emptyset(n) = (p - 1)(q - 1)$. The term $\emptyset(n)$ is known as Euler's quotient function. To compute d, use

$$d = \frac{\text{GCD}(\emptyset(n)) \times \emptyset(n) + 1}{e}$$

(d) Check if e and d are correct by seeing if

$$e \times d \;(\text{mod } \emptyset(n)) = 1$$

Note: It might be better to first find

$$\text{GCD}(\emptyset(n)) \times \emptyset(n) + 1$$

and the pair of values of $e \times d$ that show

$$e \times d = \text{GCD}(\emptyset(n)) \times \emptyset(n) + 1$$

The secret key is then (e,n).

2. *Developing a ciphertext:* The plaintext message (M) is converted to blocks of numbers using a substitution of number values for alphabetic characters. For example:

$$01 = A \qquad 02 = B \qquad 03 = C \;\ldots\; 26 = Z$$

Each block of numbers (M_1, M_2, and so forth)

$$M_1 = 01, \quad M_2 = 02, \quad \ldots$$

is converted to a ciphertext character

$$C_1, \quad C_2, \quad C_3, \text{ and so forth}$$

using the public-key (e,n) this way:

$$C_i = M_i^e \text{ modulo } n$$

Each block of numbers is raised to the e power and then reduced by modulo n to obtain a ciphertext character (C_1, C_2, . . ., and so forth). The ciphertext consisting of

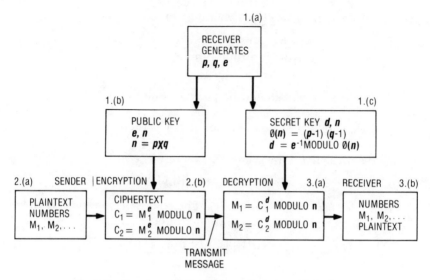

Fig. 8-3. Summary of the RSA public-key cryptosystem.

$$C_1 = M_1^e \text{ modulo } n$$
$$C_2 = M_2^e \text{ modulo } n$$

is transmitted to the receiver.

3. *Obtaining a plaintext:* For the ciphertext receiver, the secret key of the recipient (d,n) is used.

  (a) Reverse each ciphertext value (C_i) by using

$$M_1 = C_1^d \text{ modulo } n$$

where

$$M_1 = C_1^d \text{ modulo } n$$
$$M_2 = C_2^d \text{ modulo } n$$

and so on.

  (b) $M_1, M_2, \ldots$ are blocks of numbers that are converted back to plaintext characters using the appropriate substitution alphabet.

Figure 8-3 summarizes the RSA public-key cryptosystem.

An RSA Example

1. Develop keys (e,n) and (d,n)
  (a) Use the prime numbers $p = 3$ and $q = 17$. Let $e = 5$.
  (b) Calculate $n: p \times q = 3 \times 17 = 51$. The *public-key* is therefore $(e,n) = (5,51)$.

(c) Find $\emptyset(n)$ since $d = e^{-1}$ modulo $\emptyset(n)$:

$$\emptyset(n) = (p - 1)(q - 1)$$
$$= (2)(16) = 32$$

Calculate d, where

$$d = \frac{\text{GCD}(\emptyset(n)) \times \emptyset(n) + 1}{e}$$

and $\text{GCD}(2,16) = 2$:

$$d = [(2 \times 32) + 1]/5 = 65/5 = 13$$

(d) Does $e \times d(\text{mod } \emptyset(n)) = 1$?

$$5 \times 13(\text{mod } 32) = 1$$
$$65 \ (\text{mod } 32) = 1$$

The answer is yes. Therefore, the *secret key* is $(d,n) = (13,51)$.

2. Sender B wants to transmit to A the following message: ABC
   (a) The plaintext ABC is converted to number equivalents:

Message: ABC
M_i: 01,02,03

(b) B uses A's public-key $(e,n) = (13,51)$ to encipher $M_1 = 01$, $M_2 = 02$, $M_3 = 03$, using the following encryption algorithm:

$C_i = M_i^e \ (\text{mod } n)$
$C_1 = M_1^{13} \ (\text{mod } 51)$
$C_1 = 01^{13} \ (\text{mod } 51) = 1(\text{mod } 51) = 1$
$C_2 = 02^{13} \ (\text{mod } 51) = 8,192 \ (\text{mod } 51) = 32$
$C_3 = 03^{13} \ (\text{mod } 51) = 1,594,323 \ (\text{mod } 51) = 12$

The ciphertext 01, 32, 12 is transmitted to A.

3. A uses his secret key $(d,n) = (5,51)$ to decipher the ciphertext.
   (a) The decryption algorithm used is as follows:

$M_i = C_i^d \ (\text{mod } n)$
$M_1 = 1^5 \ (\text{mod } 51) = 1$
$M_2 = 32^5(\text{mod } 51) = 33,554,432 \ (\text{mod } 51) = 2$
$M_3 = 12^5(\text{mod } 51) = 248,832 \ (\text{mod } 51) = 3$

(b) The recovered message is as follows:

M_i:	01	02	03
Message:	A	B	C

In this example, the values of e, p, and q were chosen to make it easy to perform the computations involved. However, they are too small to provide real security. For real security against cryptanalytic attack the values of p, q, and e must be very large so that n ($= p \times q$) will be about 200 digits long.

PK Signature

The *sender* signs the ciphertext as follows:

1. He uses his own secret *deciphering* key (d,n) to compute the signature

$$S_i = M_i^d \text{ modulo } n$$

2. As an optional second step to ensure additional privacy, he enciphers the signature using the *receiver's* public-key. That is,

$$S = S_i^e \text{ modulo } n$$

Note: The signature can be a single signature or a signature for each message block (M) transmitted.

The *receiver* recovers M_i as follows:

1. He uses his own *secret* deciphering key (d,n) and

$$S_i = S^d \text{ modulo } n$$

2. Looking up the sender's public-key (e,n), he finds

$$M_i = S_i^e \text{ modulo } n$$

which will return the sender's signature and authenticate the origin of the ciphertext.

Figure 8-4 summarizes this public-key signature methodology.

An RSA Signature Example

B sends A a ciphertext. How can A authenticate that it was really B who sent the message? If B signed the message, say with his initial B, then A would have proof that the message was authentic. The RSA message signature procedure previously discussed will be used.

1. The sender will sign the ciphertext using the initial $B = 02$. The sender knows three keys—his public encryption key, the secret decryption key, and the public encryption key of the receiver.

	A	B
Public key (e,n):	(13,51)	(7,123)
Secret key (d,n):		(23,123)

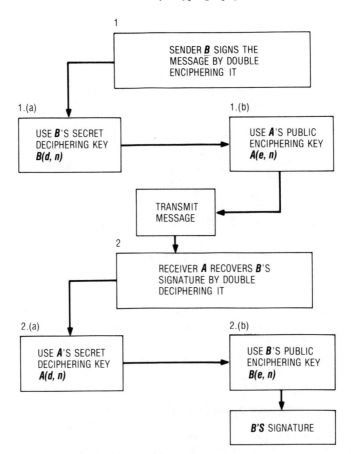

Fig. 8-4. Summary of the RSA public-key signature.

(a) *B* computes his signature,

$$S_i = M_i^d \text{ modulo } n$$

using his own secret deciphering key, $(d,n) = (17,55)$:

$$
\begin{aligned}
S_i &= 02^{23} \text{ (mod 123)} \\
S_i &= 8,388,608 \text{ (mod 123)} \\
S_i &= 8
\end{aligned}
$$

(b) Using the receiver's public encryption key, $(e,n) = (13,51)$, $S_i = 8$ is enciphered as follows:

$$
\begin{aligned}
S &= S_i^e \text{ modulo } n \\
S &= 8^{13} \text{ (mod 51)} \\
S &= 549,755,813,888 \text{ (mod 51)} \\
S &= 26
\end{aligned}
$$

The ciphertext message is *signed* by a 26.

2. The receiver A must recover $02 = B$ to authenticate the ciphertext he received. He also knows three keys—two public encryption keys and his own secret deciphering key:

	A	B
Public key (e,n):	(13,51)	(7,123)
Secret key (d,n):	(5,51)	

(a) A uses his secret deciphering key, $(d,n) = (5,51)$, to obtain

$$
\begin{aligned}
S_i &= S^d \text{ modulo } n \\
&= 26^5 \text{ (mod 51)} \\
&= 11{,}881{,}376 \text{ (mod 51)} \\
S_i &= 8
\end{aligned}
$$

(b) A applies B's public-key, $(e,n) = (7,123)$, to find M_i:

$$
\begin{aligned}
M_i &= S_i^e \text{ modulo } n \\
M_i &= 8^7 \text{ (mod 123)} \\
M_i &= 2{,}097{,}153 \text{ (mod 123)} \\
M_i &= 2
\end{aligned}
$$

The result, $M_i = 2$, is the value of $B = 02$, confirming that the sender of the ciphertext was B. A is sure of this because only B would have the secret decryption key that could produce a result to be deciphered using his own public-key.

Cryptanalysis of the RSA System

A modern cryptosystem must be able to resist an "attack" by a trained cryptanalyst working with a computer to find the secret key or trying to break the ciphertext in some other way. In the RSA cryptosystem if the cryptanalyst (knowing the public-key e and n) could *factor* $n (= p \times q)$ to find p and q, it would then be possible to compute $\emptyset(n)$ and then find the secret key component d.

As an illustration, you will recall that in the previous RSA example, the public-key was $e = 5$, $n = 51$. The factors of a two-decimal-digit number $n = 51$ can only be 3 and 17. Thus a small n can be easily factored and the secret key (d,n) found. This raises the following question: how easy would it be to factor n to determine the secret decryption key? As it turns out, if n is over 100 digits long, it could take 74 years with current computer techniques to determine the factors of n! The following table shows the time required to factor n for varying lengths in decimal digits.*

* *Ibid*, p. 11.

Digits	Time
50	3.9 hours
75	104 days
100	74 years
200	3.8×10^9 years
300	4.9×10^{15} years
500	4.2×10^{25} years

From this table it appears that to factor an n of 200 decimal digits is beyond current possibilities. Thus it is recommended that n be at least 200 digits in length. If the application required less security, a shorter n length could be used. Moderate security can be achieved if n is 80 digits long.

Thus the mathematics of the RSA cryptosystem (described earlier) appears to provide an encryption function that at present is resistant to attack.

Summary

Public-key cryptography is a new method of data encryption that uses an encryption algorithm called a trapdoor one-way function. Such a function requires two sets of keys—one public-key for the sender and one secret key for the receiver. Older methods of encryption require a single secret key known to both the sender and receiver.

One advantage of a public-key cryptosystem is that secret communications in a computer network can be carried out without having to control and manage the distribution of secret keys (as is necessary with other computer cryptosystems, such as the DES algorithm). Another advantage of a public-key cryptosystem, as shown with the RSA method, is the message signature, which is very useful in communication systems requiring authentication of the sender.

Proponents of public-key cryptography believe that the use of trapdoor one-way functions as encryption algorithms can provide systems that will resist cryptanalytical attack and give greater security than other presently proposed systems.

Questions

1. Compare and contrast the *Data Encryption Standard* and the *Public-Key Cryptosystem*.
2. List the five prime numbers beyond 31.
3. Which of the following numbers are prime?
   (a) 57   (b) 71   (c) 101   (d) 313   (e) 903

4. Find the GCD for each pair of numbers:
   (a) (4,18)   (b) (6,15)   (c) (8,20)   (d) (18,84)
   (e) (391,544)
5. In each case, find b (mod m):
   (a) 12 (mod 11)   (c) 8192 (mod 56)
   (b) 87 (mod 10)   (d) 2^5 (mod 26)
6. Write a program to determine if an integer is prime. Use the numbers in question 3 to test the program.
7. Write a program to find a when

$$a = b \text{ modulo } m$$

Use exercise 5 as your test data.
8. For the decimated cipher alphabets in Fig. 4-18 (Chapter 4) devise a modular expression to obtain the cipher value C when k is
   (a) 3   (b) 5   (c) 9
9. For each of the following find d and show that $e \times d \ (\text{mod} \phi(n)) = 1$:
   (a) $p = 5, q = 11, e = 3$ (c) $p = 5, q = 23, e = 59$
   (b) $p = 3, q = 41, e = 23$ (d) $p = 47, q = 59, e = 17$
10. Using a public-key of $(e,n) = (5,51)$, encipher the message ABE DEAD using 01 = A, 02 = B, . . . , and so forth.
11. Using a secret-key of $(d,n) = (13,51)$, decipher the message 4, 1, 5, 1.
12. Using a public-key of $(e,n) = (3,55)$, encipher the message BID HIGH using 01 = A, 02 = B, . . . , and so forth.
13. Using a secret-key of $(d,n) = (5,51)$, decipher the message 4,   20,   1,   4   20,   5,   4
14. Sign a message ED using 5,4 = ED, $B(d,n)$ = 7,39, and $A(e,n)$ = 5,21.
15. Verify that the signature values 17,1 are the initials of the sender (N.A.) using $A(d,n)$ = 5,21 and $B(e,n)$ = 5,51.

References

Feistel, Horst. "Cryptography and Computer Privacy." *Scientific American*, vol. 228, no. 5 (May 1973): 15–24.

Gaines, R. Stockton. "Secure Personal Computing in an Insecure Network." *Communications of the ACM*, vol. 22, no. 8 (August 1979): 476–482.

Hellman, Martin E. "The Mathematics of Public-Key Cryptography." *Scientific American*, vol. 241, no. 16 (August 1979): 146–157.

Jones, Burton W. *Modular Arithmetic*. New York: Blaisdell Publishing Co., 1964.

Kolata, Gina B. "Cryptography on the Brink of a Revolution?" *Science*, vol. 197 (August 19, 1977): 747–748.

Lempel, Abraham. "Cryptology in Transition." *ACM Computing Surveys*, vol. 11, no. 4 (December 1979): 285–304.

Maxfield, John E., and Maxfield, Margaret W. *Discovering Number Theory.* Philadelphia, Pa.: W.B. Saunders Co., 1972.

Rivest, R.; Shamir, A.; and Adelman, L. "A Method for Obtaining Digital Signatures and Public-Key Cryptosystems," Laboratory for Computer Science, MIT Technical Memo LCS/TM 82 (April 1977).

Rivest, R.; Shamir, A.; and Adelman, L. "A method for Obtaining Digital Signatures and Public-Key Cryptosystems." *Communications of the ACM,* vol. 21, no. 2 (Feb. 1978): 120–126.

Simmons, Gustavus J. "Symmetric and Asymmetric Encryption." *ACM Computing Surveys,* vol. 11, no. 4 (December 1979): 305–330.

Smith, Karl J. *The Nature of Modern Mathematics.* 2d ed. Monterey, California: Brooks/Cole Publishing Company, 1976.

9

Cryptographic Security Systems

Introduction

With the development of the Data Encryption Standard and the availability of low-cost cryptographic equipment, it is possible to develop and implement a *cryptographic security system*. There are two environments where such a system can be used. These environments are both independent and complementary to one another. They cover the areas of *communication security* and *file security*.

Communication security concerns the protection of data in motion. Such protection is important in a teleprocessing environment. *File security* concerns the protection of data in storage, particularly in media stored off premises or in unprotected areas. Figure 9-1 illustrates the threats to communication and file security.

There are two types of applications possible in the security environments mentioned—*private* or *system*. In a *private application* an individual acts to provide cryptographic protection independent of the system. This

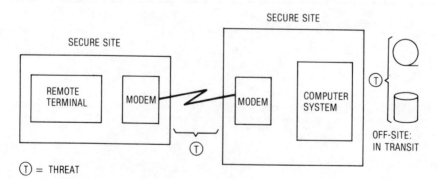

Fig. 9-1. Threats to communication and file security.

202

may involve the use of a private encryption/decryption algorithm to protect a data file, for example. In a *system application* all cryptographic operations are uniform, controlled, and managed with user involvement at a minimum.

We will examine the implementation of cryptography, first in communication security and then in file security.

Communication Security Implementation

There are three levels or approaches to the implementation of cryptography in data communication systems—link cryptography, session cryptography, and personal-key cryptography. *Link cryptography* involves the protection of data by encryption/decryption while the data is being transmitted between two directly communicating nodes or devices. This type of protection is typically used in electronic communications and is often referred to as *link-by-link* encryption. In link cryptography a pair of encryption devices brackets the line between two communication devices. Between each communicating device and its modem,* an encryption device is placed, as shown in Fig. 9-2.

In this approach the cryptographic device can be independent of the communications devices. The key does not have to be set by the system. The cryptographic devices are not necessarily under system control; both the key and encryption device can be under manual control. Link cryptography is the recommended approach when only a few links in a large network require protection.

The node-by-node scheme is an encryption approach similar to link-by-link. In such an arrangement there may be many links in a system, and each link or node has the encryption device attached to it. A different key is used to protect each link in the network so that a message crossing several nodes goes through many translations. A message entering the system can only be recovered at its destination. Figure 9-3 illustrates a node-by-node implementation.

Session cryptography involves data encryption/decryption where the data transmitted at a source remains unintelligible until reversed at its final destination. This type of cryptography is often referred to as *end-to-end*. In a communications system each end device incorporates a data encryption device. The system controls the key as well as the cryptographic device; that is, the system turns them on and off. The system will develop the key and transmit it to both sender and receiver. The session key will exist only for the session's duration. An end-to-end encryption

---

* *Modem* is an acronym for *mo*dulator-*dem*odulator. It is a device to link data processing equipment (CPU or terminals) to a telegraph or telephone line.

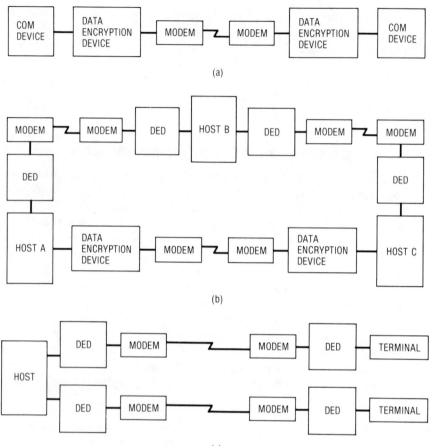

Fig. 9-2. Link cryptography: (a) Link-by-link, (b) point-to-point configuration, and (c) multipoint configuration.

system is shown in Fig. 9-4. Its advantages over the other approaches are as follows:

1. Only the sending and receiving nodes need cryptographic capability.
2. Greater security is achieved because messages remain encrypted until they reach their final destination.
3. It can support many links in a network.
4. It can support file security applications.

Personal-key cryptography involves encryption/decryption of data by an individual and an encryption device. The user maintains an exclusive key that need not be transmitted within the system. The key is completely personal. Two applications are possible. In one application the

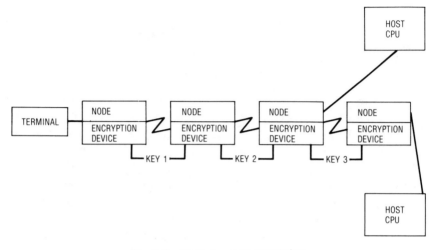

Fig. 9-3. Node-by-node encryption.

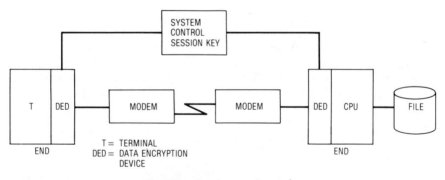

Fig. 9-4. Session cryptography.

user, through a terminal, manipulates data using his key. The system need not be aware that any cryptographic operations are being performed. If encrypted data remains within the system, any individual(s) sharing access to the data must also know the key.

In the second personal-key application the user's key is maintained by the system. The user must identify himself and enter his personal-key. Once a match is made of the key, communications during the session will be encrypted under that key. This approach is similar to session encryption with encryption/decryption taking place between the terminal and the host computers (see Fig. 9-4). Extending this approach to a session between two terminals with the host in between, the end users must either use the same key, or the system must validate two different personal keys.

File Security Implementation

Both communication security and file security seek to protect data. The need for encryption of data files arises when such data is

1. On-line
2. Going into the library
3. To be transported
4. In main storage

The difference between file security and communication security is the duration of the protection. Communication security is short. Protection is supplied only for the duration of the transmission. File security, on the other hand, provides data protection for longer periods of time. This is particularly true when data is placed in a library or shipped off premises to other locations. It is essential that each key used to encrypt a specific file be maintained throughout the life of that file. The topic of key management will be covered in the next section.

Developing a Cryptographic System

The DES and hardware devices that enable a common cryptographic algorithm to be used for data security are only one aspect in a system. Since the algorithm and devices incorporating it are not secret, it becomes necessary to develop a cryptographic system that includes *key security*. To do this, two functions must be defined—key generation and key management.

Key generation involves the selection or development of keys for the algorithm being used. Particular thought should be given to selecting keys to resist cryptanalytical attack based on analysis of both cleartext and ciphertext, as well as attempts to "try all possible keys." In the case of DES the algorithm is too strong and the key too large for a cryptanalytical attack to be successful.

Generally, keys should be generated randomly, as has been discussed and illustrated in previous chapters. A cryptographic system using a process or program to generate random keys should be secure against tampering or modeling that could compromise the system. When using pseudorandom number generators, care must be taken; such generators may produce a predictable pattern and, therefore, decrease the power of the key.

Key management involves the protection of the cryptographic keys. If a cryptographic system is to be of value, its keys must be protected. Such protection is an important management function and must not be left to chance.

Security of keys can be achieved by following these guidelines:

1. Keys in clear form must not exist within the system. This would not apply when the key is placed into an encryption device.
2. A separate key should be assigned to each data resource to be protected.
3. Keys should be changed frequently. Changes should be made with consideration of cost, convenience, and security.
4. Records should be kept of users and their assigned keys.
5. Records should be kept of data resources assigned to keys.
6. Keys should not be available to persons other than those charged with generating, setting, and maintaining them.
7. The handling of keys should become a physical security problem of easily manageable proportions.

For small cryptographic systems key management can be readily accomplished. However, with larger communication systems, key management involves the problem of *key distribution*. The difficulty is essentially one of distributing keys to remote locations in a way that assures key secrecy. The suggested approach to solving this problem is the *master key concept*.

A *master key* is a key that generates other keys. In a system with several nodes, as shown in Fig. 9-3, each node would have a different master key. Each master key is stored permanently in the node's cryptographic device nonvolatile memory. For a communication session between two nodes the sending node master key generates a *session key*, which is distributed over the data path being used. This session key performs cryptographic operations along a single path, providing key security in that exposure is minimized. In addition, the chance that a key may be accidentally misrouted to the wrong node is eliminated if each node works from a master key.

Another key management problem that requires special attention involves *lost keys*. How are cryptographic keys lost? Briefly, keys become lost because of

1. A hardware malfunction
2. A software error
3. Human error in handling the key

What is the effect of a lost key? The effect of a lost key depends on the application area that made use of the key. In all applications where a key is needed for decryption, the result is permanently lost data.

Measures should be taken to minimize the effects of unknown or lost keys. This can be accomplished by maintaining backup copies of keys kept in physically secure locations. It is also wise to have backup copies of the protected data.

Summary

For communication security there are several ways to implement a Data Encryption Standard device. These approaches include link cryptography, session cryptography, and personal-key cryptography. Consideration must be given to key generation, key security, key distribution, and other key management problems.

Questions

1. Within a cryptographic security system, what is meant by
   (a) A *private application?*
   (b) A *system application?*
2. Describe each of the following:
   (a) *Link cryptography*
   (b) *Session cryptography*
   (c) *Personal-key cryptography*
3. Why is *key security* an important aspect of a cryptographic system?
4. Write a BASIC program that will produce a random 64-bit key for the DEA.
5. What is meant by the *key distribution problem?*
6. What is the *lost key problem?*

References

Ehrsam, W. F., et al. "A Cryptographic Key Management Scheme for Implementing the Data Encryption Standard." *IBM Systems Journal,* vol. 17, no. 2 (1978): 106–125.

Hsiao, D.; Kerr, D. S.; and Madnick, S. E. *Computer Security.* New York: Academic Press, 1979.

IBM. "Data Security through Cryptography." IBM Document GC 22-9062-0 (October 1977).

Lennon, Richard E. "Putting Data Encryption to Work—Part II." *Mini-Micro Systems,* vol. 11, no. 10 (December 1978): 85–88.

Matyas, S. M., and Meyer, C. H. "Generation, Distribution, and Installation of Cryptographic Keys." *IBM Systems Journal,* vol. 17, no. 2 (1978): 126–137.

Morris, Robert; and Thompson, Ken. "Password Security: A Case History." *Communications of the ACM,* vol. 22, no. 11 (November 1979): 594–597.

Nye, J. Michael. "A Primer on Security." *Mini-Micro Systems*, vol. 14, no. 7 (July 1981): 166–174.

Orceyre, Michel J., and Courtney, Robert H., Jr., "Considerations in the Selection of Security Measures for Automatic Data Processing Systems." National Bureau of Standards, Department of Commerce (June 1978).

Popek, Gerald J., and Kline, Charles S. "Encryption and Secure Computer Networks." *ACM Computing Surveys*, vol. 11, no. 4 (December 1979): 331–356.

Shamir, Adi. "How to Share a Secret." *Communications of the ACM*, vol. 22, no. 11 (November 1979): 612–613.

Appendix

Primer for the BASIC Programming Language

BASIC Program Structure

Sequence (Statement) Number

A program in BASIC consists of a series of lines or statements. Every statement must have a sequence number. The number can be from 1 to 9999.

BASIC Statement

There are four types of BASIC statements—operation statements, input/output statements, sequence and flow statements, and specification statements.

Statement Line

A statement line is composed of a BASIC statement prefaced by a sequence number. Each line has two or more parts. In addition to the line number, each line has a key word, which may be followed by an operand:

Line #	Key Word	Operand
10	LET	A = B + C

BASIC Program

A BASIC program is a group of statement lines arranged according to the following rules:

1. There can be no more than one statement per line.
2. Program statements are processed in the order numbered.
3. All types of statements may be mixed in a program.
4. Every numeric variable should start with an initial value set by the program before it is used in a computation or printing operation.

5. The statement with the highest line number should have the key word END (99 END, for example).

BASIC Character Set

The following character set can be used in programs written in BASIC.

Alphabet

ABCDEFGHIJKLMNOPQRSTUVWXYZ

Digits

1234567890

Special Characters

@	"At" sign	'	Apostrophe
#	Pound sign	"	Quote
$	Dollar sign	\	Left oblique
%	Percent	/	Right oblique
&	Ampersand	!	Exclamation
*	Asterisk	?	Question mark
(	Left parenthesis	,	Comma
)	Right parenthesis	.	Period
−	Minus sign	;	Semicolon
+	Plus sign	:	Colon
=	Equal to	[	Left bracket
<	Less than	]	Right bracket
>	Greater than	↑∧	Up arrow

BASIC Key Words*

Arithmetic Operation

LET
PRINT

Input/Output Operation

INPUT
READ
PRINT

---

* These key words should be part of the BASIC dialect found in most computers. They are also part of the word list found in the *American National Standard for Minimal BASIC*, X3.60-1978. Such a standard seeks to promote the interchangeability of BASIC programs from computer system to computer system.

Flow or Sequence Operation

IF/THEN	END
GOTO	STOP
NEXT	
GOSUB	
RETURN	
ON GOTO	

Specification or Information

DATA	REM
DIM	RESTORE
FOR	

Assignment Operation

LET
INPUT
READ

Numeric Constants

Numeric constants are used with LET, PRINT, INPUT, and DATA statements. They can contain decimal points. The plus sign is optional; a minus sign is used where required. Examples:

$$40 \quad 34.567$$
$$-6 \quad .00312$$

```
10    LET A = 56
20    PRINT -800
30    DATA 40, -6, 34.567, .00312
```

Variable Names

A variable name is a group of characters representing a data item whose value is assigned and/or modified by a BASIC statement. There are three types of BASIC variables:

1. Simple numeric
2. Array
3. String

Simple Numeric Variables

1. A simple numeric variable consists of one of the 26 letters of the alphabet (A to Z) or a combination of a letter followed by a single digit (0 to 9). This gives a total of 286 [(26 + (26 × 10)] simple numeric variables.

2. A simple numeric variable can only be assigned a numeric data value.
3. Before a simple variable can be used in a calculation or printing process, it must be set to a starting value by the program. Examples:

A	B2	C9	Z1

```
10    LET  A  =  94
20    PRINT  A
30    READ  X,  Y,  Z1
40    DATA  11.3,  4.5,  6.9
50    PRINT  X,  Y,  Z1
60    INPUT B2, C9
```

Array Numeric Variables

An array variable is any one of the 286 variable designations previously specified, followed by either one or two subscripts. Examples:

A(1)	C3(9)	W(23)	M5(7,23)
L(A)	X(I,J)	H1(X+Y)	A(B(I))

From these examples you can see that a subscript can be a number, a variable, or an expression. The array is an ordered set of data. The set can be in one dimension (as a list) or in two dimensions (as a table). It is also possible to have a subscripted variable within a subscripted variable, such as A(B(I)).

The following rules apply for array numeric variables:

1. An array is named by a letter or letter-number combination.
2. Arrays can have one or two dimensions—as in a list or table.
3. Array contents are only numeric when using numeric variable designations.
4. The beginning element of an array is 1 or 1,1.
5. Each member of a numeric array should be set (by the program) to a starting value before it is used in an operation or printed.
6. Subscripts are whole numbers (integers).
7. An array member can be referenced by a subscripted array name.

Given a list of five numeric data values to be stored as the array M, with subscripts going from 1 to 5, the array is illustrated as follows:

A	64	72	37	35	42
Subscript	1	2	3	4	5

The general reference for the array may be A(I), with I going from 1 to 5. A specific data value can be referenced by using A(4), for example. This would correspond to the value assigned to storage location A(4), 35.

Given a table of six numeric data values (two columns and three rows) to be stored as the array S, the array is illustrated by:

		Column Subscript	
		1	2
	1	86	56
Row Subscript	2	61	68
	3	32	11

The general reference for this table may be S(I,J), where I is the number of rows going from 1 to 3, and J is the number of columns going from 1 to 2. A specific data value can be referenced by using S(2,2), for example. This reference would correspond to the value assigned to storage location S(2,2) (that is, 68).

Array Declarations

An array sets up a storage area. If an array needs more than ten spaces (as a list or as a row or column in a table), such needs must be declared within the program. These declarations of space requirements can be made by using a specification statement called the dimension or DIM statement. For example, if a numeric data list contains 150 values and the name of the list is E, then we have

> 10   DIM E(150)

If a table of numeric data contains 200 values in 20 rows and 10 columns and the table name is B, then we have

> 10   DIM B(20,10)

An array declaration must be sufficient for the numeric data values being stored. Overdimensioning is permissible; underdimensioning will result in an error message and program termination.

String Variables

A group of characters is called a "string." A string variable has nonnumeric data assigned to it. A string may be up to 60 characters in length without a dimension specification. To have a larger string, the DIM statement can be used.

Simple String Variables

A total of 286 simple string variables can be defined using the same variable set as found for simple numeric variables. To form a string variable, a $ sign is appended to the variable name. Examples:

A$ B3$ L9$ Z$

Array String Variables

Subscripted string variables can be used for literal data in a single dimension. The form of the variable is the same as that of array numeric variables, but a $ is appended to the variable name. Examples:

A$(1)   C2$(25)   X5$(I)   Z$(X)

Strings may be used in the following types of statements:

CHANGE	IF	PRINT
INPUT	LET	READ

Examples:

```
10    READ  L$, M$, N$
20    PRINT  L$, M$, N$
30    DATA  A,  B,  C

10    INPUT  L$(1),  L$(2)

10    LET  A$(W)=A$(R(W))
20    LET  P$  ="PLAINTEXT"

10    IF  Y$  =  "NO"  THEN  130

10    IF  C$  =  C$(I)  THEN  100

50    CHANGE  B  TO  A$
60    PRINT  A$
70    CHANGE  A$  TO  X
```

Predefined Functions

The meaning of many functions has been incorporated as part of the BASIC language. These predefined functions include:

INT(X)   Integer part of X

RND(X)   Random number between 0 and 1 (the X has no meaning but is necessary)

SQR(X)   Positive square root of X

Examples:

```
30    LET  B  =  INT(B1)

40    LET  R  =  INT(26*RND(X)+1)

10    LET  P  =  SQR(M)
```

Arithmetic Operations

∧ ↑	Exponentiation:	X^2,	$X \uparrow 2$
*	Multiplication:	$A \times B$,	$A*B$
/	Division:	$A \div B$,	A/B
+	Addition:	$A + B$,	$A + B$
−	Subtraction:	$A - B$,	$A - B$

Relational Operators

<	Less than	>=	Greater than or equal to
< =	Less than or equal to	=	Equal to
>	Greater than	<>	Not equal to

Expressions

Evaluation of an expression follows the operations indicated in the usual algebraic order. Operations are performed from left to right observing the following rules:

1. Levels of operations (high to low):
   A. Operations within parentheses
   B. Exponentiation (↑)
   C. Multiplication (*) or division (/)
   D. Addition (+) or subtraction (−)
2. Operations within parentheses are performed before operations outside parentheses.
3. Operations on a higher level are performed before operations on a lower level.
4. Operations on the same level are performed in the order they appear in the expression (from left to right).

Examples:

$$X/(Y + Z)$$

② ①

$$A - B/(C * D) \uparrow 2 + 5$$

④ ③ ① ② ⑤

When an expression has parentheses within parentheses, the innermost operations are performed first, following the previously stated rules. Examples:

$$(X/(Y + Z)) \uparrow 2$$

$$\underbrace{\textcircled{1}} \quad \textcircled{3}$$

$$\textcircled{2}$$

This last expression corresponds to the following algebraic expression:

$$\left(\frac{X}{(X + Y)} \right)^2$$

Literal Strings

A group of characters surrounded by quotation marks is called a *literal string*. Such a string should not contain a quotation within the literal character group. Examples:

"CHARACTER STRING"
" XYZ CO. REPORT"
"123-45-6789"
"2.3 UNITS"

Data Files

DATA statement values are included as part of a program. Data may be stored as a file external to a program.* Such data files can be created and accessed by one or more programs to improve data handling and programming flexibility. The general format of a statement involving a file operation is

Line No. Key Word:File Name:Specification

Examples:

30 OPEN:CTF:100

creates a file named CTF with up to 100 characters.

60 INPUT:PTF:A$

reads into the program from the file PTF the string data A$.

100 PRINT:CTF:B(I);

writes data from a program to a file CTF as a subscripted numeric value B(I).

---

* Data file operations require an understanding of tape/disk storage concepts that are beyond the scope of this text. Refer to the system manual of your computer for the specifics of the statements to be used for file operations.

110   PRINT:CDBOOK:LNM(10);L$(W)

writes data to a file generating line numbers, starting with 10 and incrementing by one. The LNM(X) is a function for this process, where X is the starting line number for the file.

130   CLOSE:CTF:

aids in creating a permanent file by the name of CTF.

82   FILEND:GBA:190

tests to see if there is data for the INPUT:file:(GBA). If none is available, it transfers control to the line number specified (190).

System Commands

System commands direct the computer to perform various functions. Two functions that are common to most computer systems are RUN and LIST. RUN causes the program to be executed or processed. LIST causes the program or file to be listed out.

Input/Output Operations

Data Assignment

Data input or entry into the computer for processing can be carried out by the assignment of data values to variables with the READ/DATA, LET, or INPUT statements.

The READ statement assigns data values (found in the DATA statement) to the variables in the READ statement. Assignment is on a one-to-one basis until all the variables in the READ have been assigned a data value. There must always be sufficient values in the DATA statement to satisfy the variable list in the READ statement (see Lines 10 and 20 in Program A-1).

The LET statement assigns a data value to a variable on a one-to-one basis. The variable is placed to the left of the equal sign, and the data

```
10 READ A,B
20 DATA 5,10
30 LET C=-25
40 INPUT D
50 PRINT A,B,C,D
90 END

RUN

?10
5              10              -25              10
```

Program A-1. Data assignment and wide output spacing.

```
10 READ A,B
20 DATA 5,10
30 LET C=-25
40 INPUT D
50 PRINT A;B;C;D
90 END

RUN

?10
5   10  -25   10
```

Program A-2. Data assignment and narrow output spacing.

value is placed to the right of the equal sign, as shown in Line 30 of Program A-1.

The INPUT statement provides the user with an interactive assignment of data to a variable. When processed, the INPUT statement causes a prompting question mark (?) to appear. The user must respond to the question by typing sufficient data values to satisfy the variable list of the INPUT statement. Line 40 of Program A-1 and the first line of output illustrate this.

Wide Output Spacing

Data values assigned to variables can be outputted by using the PRINT statement. Commas between variables in the PRINT statement produce output results in wide fields. Many computer systems with printer output terminals provide 75 character spaces broken up into five print fields of 15 spaces each. The PRINT statement in Line 50 of Program A-1 follow this output spacing. Output on a cathode ray tube (CRT) screen may be limited to 64 character spaces broken up into four fields of 16 spaces each.

Narrow Output Spacing

Output on the printed page or CRT can be "packed" to take up less space. This is achieved by placing a semicolon between variables in the PRINT statement. Line 50 of Program A-2 contains semicolons in place of commas. Contrast the output of Program A-2 with that of A-1.

String Variables

Program A-1 illustrates the assignment of numeric data to variables with the READ/DATA, LET, or INPUT statements. Nonnumeric data can also be assigned to string variables using the same type of statements.*

---

* String items in DATA lines may also be in quotes. For example, 20 DATA "CODES", "CIPHERS". This use of quotes is optional for most dialects of BASIC but is necessary if leading/trailing blank spaces, special characters, and so on, are to be part of the string.

```
5 REM STRING VARIABLES
10 READ A$,B$
20 DATA CODES, CIPHERS
30 LET C$= "COMPUTERS"
40 INPUT D$
50 PRINT A$,B$,D$,C$
90 END

RUN

?AND
CODES          CIPHERS        AND            COMPUTERS
```

Program A-3. Data assignment and output of string variables.

```
10 READ A$,B$
20 DATA CODES, CIPHERS
30 LET C$= "COMPUTERS"
40 INPUT D$
50 PRINT A$;B$;D$;C$
90 END

READY

RUN

?AND
CODESCIPHERSANDCOMPUTERS
```

Program A-4. Packed output of string variables.

The PRINT statement can also output nonnumeric data assigned to string variables. Program A-3 illustrates the data assignment and output of string variables.

Note that Program A-3 contains Line 5, a remark or REM statement. Such statements do not generate output but provide the reader of a program with information or documentation about the program. REM statements are usually placed throughout larger programs to explain various segments and operations.

Program A-3 produces output in wide fields because of the comma in the PRINT statement of Line 50. When a semicolon is used between string variables in a PRINT statement, the output is packed without any spacing between data items. Program A-4 illustrates this point.

Flow and Sequence of Operations

The GOTO READ Loop

A process may be repeated by using the unconditional branching statement GOTO. Program A-5 shows the reading and assignment of data to C$ and the output of C$ as a process being repeated because of the presence of statement 40 GOTO 10 in the program. When all of the DATA in Line 20 has been processed, the program will terminate.

```
10 READ C$
20    DATA CODES, CIPHERS, AND , COMPUTERS
30    PRINT C$
40 GOTO 10
50 PRINT "PLAINTEXT"
60 END

RUN

CODES
CIPHERS
AND
COMPUTERS

OUT OF DATA- LN #   10
```

Program A-5. A GOTO READ loop.

```
10 READ C$
15    IF C$="ZZ" THEN 50
20    DATA CODES, CIPHERS, AND , COMPUTERS
25    DATA ZZ
30    PRINT C$
40 GOTO 10
50 PRINT "PLAINTEXT"
60 END

RUN

CODES
CIPHERS
AND
COMPUTERS
PLAINTEXT
```

Program A-6. An IF/THEN test for the end of data.

Line 50, the PRINT, is *not* processed because the READ statement has run out of data, as indicated by the *error message* "OUT OF DATA- LN # 10."

The repetitive process shown in Program A-5 is a GOTO loop. Such loops cause processing control to branch to the line number indicated in the GOTO statement. Note the use of *indentation* for Lines 20 and 30. Such indentation is often used to improve the readability of programs, as well as to identify the flow of the program.

Control with IF/THEN

Where the GOTO statement causes a process to transfer or branch without any conditions, the IF/THEN statement causes control to change based on a condition being found true. Program A-6 is a revision of A-5 with the addition of the IF/THEN statement in Line 15.

The IF/THEN in Line 15 examines each word of DATA as it is READ into the variable C$. If ZZ is found, then the program process will branch to Line 50, outside the GOTO loop. If ZZ is not found after Line

10 is processed, the GOTO loop continues. The process shown in Program A-6 includes a test to determine if the last DATA value has been reached. You will note that the DATA value ZZ is assigned and tested but not processed any further. ZZ represents the "dummy value" used to signal the computer via the IF/THEN to stop the process and go to Line 50.

Process Repetition with FOR/NEXT

Statements within a FOR and NEXT loop will be repeated based on the specification set out in the FOR statement. This statement provides the starting point, ending point, and optional increment (step) for the loop to follow. Upon reaching the upper limit specified in the FOR statement, the computer will continue to process the program beginning with the statement following the NEXT statement. Program A-7 illustrates this process repetition. A READ and PRINT sequence is repeated four times, followed by the processing of the PRINT statement in Line 50. Contrast this program with Programs A-5 and A-6.

By placing a comma or semicolon at the end of a PRINT statement within a loop, the output spacing can be changed. Program A-7 has been modified by the addition of a comma at the end of Line 30. This modification is shown in Program A-8, with the resulting output placed across a

```
5 FOR I= 1 TO 4
10     READ C$
20     DATA CODES, CIPHERS, AND , COMPUTERS
30     PRINT C$
40 NEXT I
50 PRINT "PLAINTEXT"
60 END

RUN

CODES
CIPHERS
AND
COMPUTERS
PLAINTEXT
```

Program A-7. A FOR/NEXT loop.

```
5 FOR I= 1 TO 4
10     READ C$
20     DATA CODES, CIPHERS, AND, COMPUTERS
30     PRINT C$,
40 NEXT I
50 PRINT "PLAINTEXT"
60 END

RUN
CODES          CIPHERS          AND          COMPUTERS          PLAINTEXT
```

Program A-8. PRINT and comma in a loop.

```
5 FOR I= 1 TO 4
10    READ C$
20    DATA CODES, CIPHERS, AND, COMPUTERS
30    PRINT C$;
40 NEXT I
50 PRINT "PLAINTEXT"
60 END

RUN

CODESCIPHERSANDCOMPUTERSPLAINTEXT
```

Program A-9. PRINT and semicolon in a loop.

```
5 LET C$="CODES, CIPHERS & COMPUTERS"
10 FOR A= 1 TO 3
15    PRINT" ",A
20    FOR I= 1 TO 4
30        PRINT C$
35    NEXT I
40 NEXT A
45 END

RUN

                  1
CODES, CIPHERS & COMPUTERS
CODES, CIPHERS & COMPUTERS
CODES, CIPHERS & COMPUTERS
CODES, CIPHERS & COMPUTERS
                  2
CODES, CIPHERS & COMPUTERS
CODES, CIPHERS & COMPUTERS
CODES, CIPHERS & COMPUTERS
CODES, CIPHERS & COMPUTERS
                  3
CODES, CIPHERS & COMPUTERS
CODES, CIPHERS & COMPUTERS
CODES, CIPHERS & COMPUTERS
CODES, CIPHERS & COMPUTERS
```

Program A-10. Nested FOR/NEXT loops.

single line in five fields. The comma serves to keep the output from advancing to the next output line as long as space on the current line is available. The next PRINT is also outputted on the same line as long as space is available for the output "PLAINTEXT."

Program A-9 is a modification of A-8, replacing the comma at the end of the PRINT statement in Line 30 with a semicolon. The resulting output is packed across the page and includes the output from the PRINT statement in Line 50.

Nested FOR/NEXT Loops

A FOR/NEXT loop can be placed within another FOR/NEXT loop. The inner loop will be processed as many times as specified by the outer loop. Program A-10 shows the nested FOR/NEXT loop structure. The inner loop, Lines 20 through 35, repeats the PRINT C$ in Line 30 four

```
10 FOR I= 1 TO 5
20      READ X,W$
40      DATA 2, TU, 3, XYZ, 1, B
50      DATA 3, ABC, 1, G
55      ON X GOTO 60,70,80
60          PRINT X;" CHARACTER ";W$
65      GOTO 85
70          PRINT X;" CHARACTERS ";W$
75      GOTO 85
80          PRINT X;" CHARACTERS ";W$
85 NEXT I
90 END

RUN

2   CHARACTERS TU
3   CHARACTERS XYZ
1   CHARACTER B
3   CHARACTERS ABC
1   CHARACTER G
```

Program A-11. The ON GOTO statement.

```
10 FOR L= 1 TO 5
20      PRINT L
30      GOSUB 60
40 NEXT L
50 STOP
60      FOR D= 1 TO 10
70          PRINT "-";
80      NEXT D
85      PRINT
90      RETURN
100 END

RUN

1
--------------------
2
--------------------
3
--------------------
4
--------------------
5
--------------------
```

Program A-12. A subroutine.

times. The outer loop, Lines 10 and 40, will process the inner loop three times. The result is that C\$ is printed 12 (3×4) times.

Control with ON GOTO

The IF/THEN statement provides a choice of one or two possible alternatives. The ON GOTO or computed GOTO statement, on the other hand, is useful for more than two possible alternatives. The program process will branch to the line number in the position indicated by the variable in the ON GOTO statement. Using Program A-11 as an example, when Line 55 has X=1, the program will branch to Line 60; when X=2, the program will branch to Line 70; and if X=3, the program will branch to Line 80.

Subroutines

A subroutine is usually a set of statements placed apart from a main program. Generally subroutines are found in larger programs when particular processes are going to be repeated. A subroutine can be constructed with the use of three BASIC statements—the GOSUB, which causes a transfer to occur to the subroutine; a RETURN, which causes a transfer back to the statement immediately following the GOSUB; and a STOP, which terminates processing and prevents an extra execution of the subroutine.

Program A-12 provides a simple subroutine example. The subroutine is found in Lines 60 through 90. Line 30 has the GOSUB 60 statement; Line 50 is the STOP; and Line 90 contains the RETURN that will transfer control back to Line 40 after the subroutine is completed.

Data in Arrays

Subscripted Variables

The assignment of many numeric or string data items to an array can be easily accomplished using a FOR/NEXT loop. Program A-13 illustrates such a process. The FOR statement will supply the subscript or index for each item as it is assigned to the array C$. The contents of the array can be outputted using a statement such as Line 30. A dimension (DIM) statement in Line 10 declares the storage requirements for each array in the program. Overdimensioning is permitted; underdimensioning is not.

String Manipulations

To convert a string of characters into ASCII code values, a CHANGE statement can be used.* Line 40 CHANGE A$ TO B in Program A-14 is an example of such a conversion. The character string A$ will be converted to ASCII code values, which are placed into an array B with the length of the array stored in location B(0). The array B must be dimensioned as in Line 10.

---

* Not every computer system has a BASIC dialect with the key word CHANGE. Other key words may be available to perform this conversion process. For example, CHR$(n) will return the single character represented by the ASCII code (n); ASC("A") will return the ASCII code value for the single string character "A"; and ASC(A$) will return the ASCII code value of the first character in the string A$.

```
10 DIM C$(15)
15 FOR I= 1 TO 4
20    READ C$(I)
25    DATA CODES, CIPHERS, AND, COMPUTERS
30    PRINT C$(I),
35 NEXT I
40 END

RUN

CODES         CIPHERS        AND          COMPUTERS
```

Program A-13. Assigning data to an array.

```
10 DIM B(50)
20 READ A$
30 DATA "CODES, CIPHERS & COMPUTERS"
40 CHANGE A$ TO B
50 FOR I= 1 TO B(0)
60    PRINT B(I);
70 NEXT I
90 END

RUN

67 79 68 69 83 44 32 67 73 80 72 69 82 83 32 38 32
67 79 77 80 85 84 69 82 83
```

Program A-14. Changing a string to ASCII values.

```
10 DIM C(20)
20 FOR I= 1 TO 4
30    READ C(I)
35 NEXT I
40 DATA 67,79,68,69
60 LET C(0)=4
70 CHANGE C TO E$
80 PRINT E$
90 END

RUN

CODE
```

Program A-15. Changing ASCII values to string characters.

To convert ASCII values into string characters requires the use of a CHANGE statement. Line 70 CHANGE C TO E$ in Program A-15 performs such a task. For Line 70 to work, the size of the array C must be specified as in Line 60 of the program. Contrast Program A-14 with A-15.

Data Manipulations

The RESTORE Statement

The contents of a DATA statement, once completely read and assigned to a variable or variables, can be restored for use by another

```
10 FOR I= 1 TO 3
20    READ A$
30    PRINT A$;" ";
40 NEXT I
50 DATA CODES, CIPHERS, COMPUTERS
60 PRINT
70 RESTORE
80 READ X$,Y$,Z$
90 PRINT Z$,Y$,X$
100 END

RUN

CODES CIPHERS COMPUTERS
COMPUTERS      CIPHERS           CODES
```

Program A-16. The RESTORE statement.

```
10 READ A$
40 DATA ABCDEF
50 FOR I= 1 TO 6
60    PRINT SUB$(A$,I)
70 NEXT I
90 END

RUN

A
B
C
D
E
F
```

Program A-17. The substring function.

READ statement. This restoring process is accomplished by using a RESTORE statement as shown in Line 70 of Program A-16. In this program, Line 20 READ A$ will assign each of the character strings in 50 DATA. Line 80 READ X$,Y$,Z$ cannot be processed unless it is preceded by the RESTORE in Line 70. The RESTORE makes it possible for the READ to have DATA starting from the beginning of the data list.

Manipulating Strings

When using data as character strings, it is possible to manipulate the string by breaking it up into separate characters. A substring function can be used to extract the Ith character from a data string. An example of the substring function can be found in Line 60 of Program A-17.* The data string ABCDEF is assigned to the variable A$. By using a

---

* Not every computer system will have a BASIC dialect with the substring function exactly as shown in Line 60 of Program A-17. For example, MID$(*string*,p,n) will return a substring of *string* with length n, starting at position p in *string*. Thus MID$(A$,4,1) refers to a one character substring beginning with the fourth character of A$.

```
10 FOR I= 1 TO 4
20 READ P
30     LET C= INT(P/2)
40     PRINT P;C
50 NEXT I
60 DATA 65,66,67,68
90 END

RUN

65    32
66    33
67    33
68    34
```

Program A-18.   The integer function.

```
10 PRINT "HOW MANY NUMBERS DO YOU NEED";
20 INPUT N
30 FOR I= 1 TO N
40     LET X=INT(1000*RND(X))
50     PRINT X
60 NEXT I
90 END

RUN

HOW MANY NUMBERS DO YOU NEED ?4
 499
 527
 670
 272
```

Program A-19.   Generating random numbers.

```
10 PRINT "HOW MANY NUMBERS DO YOU NEED";
20 INPUT N
25 RANDOMIZE
30 FOR I= 1 TO N
40     LET X=INT(1000*RND(X))
50     PRINT X
60 NEXT I
90 END

RUN

HOW MANY NUMBERS DO YOU NEED ?4
 431
 585
 636
 545

RUN

HOW MANY NUMBERS DO YOU NEED ?4
 602
 617
 277
 109
```

Program A-20.   Generating different sets of random numbers.

FOR/NEXT loop, Lines 50 and 70, A$ can be broken down into separate characters as seen in the resulting output.

Predefined Functions

The Integer Function

Sometimes it is necessary to produce computational results without the decimal part of the resulting answer. That is, only the integer part of a number is desired as output. To produce such integer values an INT function can be used. Such a function is shown in Line 30 of Program A-18. This program reads in four data values found in Line 60, divides each value in half, and outputs (Line 40) the original value and integer result.

You will note in this program that when the LET is used to perform a computation (Line 30), the computation takes place on the right side of the equal sign, and the result is assigned to the variable on the left side of the equal sign.

Random Numbers

Pseudorandom numbers are random numbers generated by a computer (as opposed to random numbers chosen from a random number table). The function RND(X), when appropriately placed in a BASIC program, will produce numbers between 0 and 1.* Since this range of decimal numbers may not be desired, it is possible to expand the range by multiplying RND(X) by some constant. For example, Program A-19 will generate pseudorandom numbers between 0 and 999. The random number function in Line 40 has been multiplied by 1000, with only the integer (INT) part being assigned to the variable X.

You will note that Program A-19 is a conversational program asking the user how many numbers he or she wants. The INPUT (Line 20) response is used in order to set the upper limit of the FOR statement in Line 30.

When a program containing a random number function is processed more than once, the random numbers generated are usually the same each time. Each computer system has a method available so that if *different* random numbers are needed each time the program is processed, they can be obtained. Program A-20 shows one such method. Line 25 RANDOMIZE has been added to the previous Program A-19. When processed each time, Program A-20 will generate completely different random numbers.

---

* Some dialects of BASIC permit the (X), a dummy term, to be dropped. Only the RND may be needed to produce the numbers.

```
10 LET X=0
20 FOR W = 1 TO 100
30    READ L$
40    IF L$ = "LAST ITEM" THEN 100
50        LET X=X+1
60        PRINT L$
70 NEXT W
80 DATA "CODES","CIPHERS","AND","COMPUTERS"
90 DATA "LAST ITEM"
100 PRINT "TOTAL NUMBER ITEMS READ IS";X
110 END

RUN

CODES
CIPHERS
AND
COMPUTERS
TOTAL NUMBER ITEMS READ IS 4
```

Program A-21. A counting process.

```
10 PRINT TAB(10);"CODE WORD"
12 PRINT TAB(9);"-------------"
20 FOR W= 1 TO 4
30    READ A$
40    PRINT TAB(11);A$
50 NEXT W
60 DATA CODES, CIPHERS, AND, COMPUTERS
90 END

RUN

        CODE WORD
        -----------
        CODES
        CIPHERS
        AND
        COMPUTERS
```

Program A-22. The TAB function.

Other BASIC Operations

Counting a Process

To count how many times a process has been repeated a statement such as 50   LET   X=X+1, shown in Program A-21, is utilized. Initialization of X in Line 10 provides a value for the variable X before Line 50 is processed.

Program A-21 contains an IF/THEN test for the end of the data list. Such a test was described previously and illustrated by Program A-6.

Control of Output Spacing

Programs A-1 and A-2 illustrated fixed output spacing based on the comma and semicolon. Flexible output spacing can be achieved by using the TAB(N) function within a PRINT statement, as shown in Lines 10, 12, and 40 of Program A-22. The value of N in the function specifies the number of spaces skipped, or tabbed, from the left margin.

Another approach to flexible output spacing found on many computer systems is the PRINT USING statement. This statement makes use of an image (or format) statement to indicate where the variables (or process results) are to be placed as output. Both statements might appear as

```
90      PRINT  USING  100,  A,  B
100     FMT        ###       ###
```

with the # symbols indicating the print positions for the variables A and B. An example of this type of output control can be found in the program in Fig. 6-3. In this program the PRINT USING statement is Line 250, and the format (FMT) statement is Line 260. Not every dialect of BASIC has these output control statements or presents them in exactly this way.

Flowcharts

A program flowchart is a useful device to aid in understanding the logic of a program. The flowchart is a pictorial diagram typically drawn

Symbol	Meaning
TERMINAL	Stop, start, or end the program
PROCESS	Calculations, assignments, or other operations
INPUT/ OUTPUT	Input/Output: reading or writing
DECISION	Compare, test, examine, and decide
PREPARATION	Initialize, set an index, perform an operation on the program for control
CONNECTOR	To go to, or come from, another part of the chart
FLOW LINES	Direction or flow or sequence of operations
ANNOTATION	Additional descriptive clarification, or comment

Fig. A-1. Flowchart symbols.

with conventional symbols that represent different events in the program sequence. The most commonly used flowcharting symbols and their meanings are shown in Fig. A-1.

Answers and Solutions

Chapter 1

1. *Signal intelligence* involves the gathering of information and intelligence by interception of someone else's cryptosignals. The U.S. *Pueblo* was a Navy electronic intelligence ship stationed off the coast of North Korea. On January 22, 1968, it was seized by North Korean military forces and the crew imprisoned as "spies."
2. A *code* may use symbols to represent words. Therefore, a traffic signal— red for STOP, yellow for CAUTION, green for GO—is a code system.
3. Common code systems in everyday use include those appearing in traffic signs, citizen band (CB) conversation, grades used in schools, and computer programming languages.
4. Data encryption is important in computer communications security because of the value and confidentiality of the information transmitted. Transmission of information via satellite presents a source of vulnerability that may require security techniques via encryption. Within computer communications networks where personnel records and other confidential information can be easily accessed, protection must be applied to ensure privacy.
5. *Cryptography* concerns itself with those methods used to prepare messages to ensure they cannot be readily understood. It is the science of secret communication. *Cryptanalysis* is the science of deciphering or decoding secret messages without knowing the key or methods used to develop the message.
6. *Cleartext*—the original message; also called a plaintext.
   Code—a method of putting messages into a secret form using words or symbols to represent the message words.
   Cipher—a method of putting messages into a secret form by using substitute characters for the original characters or by rearranging the characters of the original message.
   Cryptogram—a message in code or cipher.
7. *Cryptology* includes both cryptography and cryptanalysis.
8. See Fig. 1-3.

9. *Signal security* refers to the methods of protecting message signals from unauthorized interception. *Signal intelligence* concerns the methods used to gather message signals.

Chapter 2

1. A *one-part* code has both the plaintext words and code words in alphabetic sequence. A *two-part* code has the code words in a nonalphabetic sequence.
2. Code books should be distributed only to those persons needing them. Code books should not be left around; when not in use, they should be locked up. Periodically, an inventory should be taken to see if any are missing. Codes should be revised regularly.
3. $_6P_4 = 6!/(6 - 4)! = 6!/2! = 6 \times 5 \times 4 \times 3 = 360$ code words
4. Different letters should be used when creating code words. Otherwise, duplicate code words will result (see the next answer).
5. With duplicate letters in Line 110, the resulting code words can be seen:

```
110  DATA  M,B,B

RUN
HOW  MANY  LETTERS  DO  YOU  WISH  TO  USE   ?3
MBB
MBB
BMB
BBM
BMB
BBM
```

6. Here are the code words using a changed Line 110 in Fig. 2-1:

```
110  DATA  A,BC,DE

RUN
HOW  MANY  LETTERS  DO  YOU  WISH  TO  USE   ?3
ABCDE
ADEBC
BCADE
BCDEA
DEABC
DEBCA
```

7. Using the suggested letters AB, AC, AC, AD would result in two plaintext words having the *same* code word. This can be seen in the following output using the new data in the program of Fig. 2-4:

```
135  DATA  AB,AC,AC,AD

READY

RUN
HOW  MANY  LETTERS  DO  YOU  WISH  TO  USE   ?4
```

CODE WORD	PLAINTEXT WORD
ABACAC	AGREE
ABACAD	AMOUNT
ABACAC	BUY
ABACAD	CANCEL
ABADAC	DELAY
ABADAC	DISCOUNT
ACABAC	EXACT
ACABAD	FINAL
ACACAB	GET
ACACAD	GOOD
ACADAB	HURRY
ACADAC	INCLUDE
ACABAC	INVEST
ACABAD	LIKE
ACACAB	MONEY
ACACAD	MORE
ACADAB	NEED
ACADAC	OKAY
ADABAC	OPPORTUNITY
ADABAC	PLANS
ADACAB	RETHINK
ADACAC	START
ADACAB	STOP
ADACAC	TRANSMIT

8. (a) BDA   CDA   CBD   CBA   BCD   DAB
   (b) STOP   RETHINK   PLANS   GET   FINAL   AMOUNT
9. (a) 101112   111013   101113   121311
       131211   121113   121110
   (b) NEED   MORE   MONEY   DELAY   PLANS   RETHINK
10. On the left is the first part of the two-part code number dictionary. The
    code numbers are in a nonsystematic sequence. On the right is the sec-
    ond part of the dictionary by code number sequence.

121013	AGREE	101112	HURRY
121011	AMOUNT	101113	INCLUDE
121310	BUY	101213	EXACT
121311	CANCEL	101211	FINAL
121110	DELAY	101312	GET
121113	DISCOUNT	101311	GOOD
101213	EXACT	111012	RETHINK
101211	FINAL	111013	START
101312	GET	111210	OPPORTUNITY
101311	GOOD	111213	PLANS
101112	HURRY	111312	STOP
101113	INCLUDE	111310	TRANSMIT
131210	INVEST	121013	AGREE
131211	LIKE	121011	AMOUNT
131012	MONEY	121110	DELAY
131011	MORE	121113	DISCOUNT
131112	NEED	121310	BUY
131110	OKAY	121311	CANCEL

111210	OPPORTUNITY	131012	MONEY
111213	PLANS	131011	MORE
111012	RETHINK	131112	NEED
111013	START	131110	OKAY
111312	STOP	131210	INVEST
111310	TRANSMIT	131211	LIKE

11. On the left is the first part of the two-part code word dictionary. On the right is the second part of the dictionary with the code words in alphabetic sequence.

SRM	AGREE		BMR	TRANSMIT
SRB	AMOUNT		BMS	STOP
SMR	BUY		BRM	START
SMB	CANCEL		BRS	RETHINK
SBR	DELAY		BSM	PLANS
SBM	DISCOUNT		BSR	OPPORTUNITY
RSM	EXACT		MBR	OKAY
RSB	FINAL		MBS	NEED
RMS	GET		MRB	MORE
RMB	GOOD		MRS	MONEY
RBS	HURRY		MSB	LIKE
RBM	INCLUDE		MSR	INVEST
MSR	INVEST		RBM	INCLUDE
MSB	LIKE		RBS	HURRY
MRS	MONEY		RMB	GOOD
MRB	MORE		RMS	GET
MBS	NEED		RSB	FINAL
MBR	OKAY		RSM	EXACT
BSR	OPPORTUNITY		SBM	DISCOUNT
BSM	PLANS		SBR	DELAY
BRS	RETHINK		SMB	CANCEL
BRM	START		SMR	BUY
BMS	STOP		SRB	AMOUNT
BMR	TRANSMIT		SRM	AGREE

12.

```
10 RANDOMIZE
20 DIM A$(26),L$(30)
30 REM PROGRAM TO GENERATE
40 REM RANDOM CODENUMBER DICTIONARY
50 PRINT "HOW MANY NUMBERS DO YOU WISH TO USE";
60 INPUT N
70 FOR W= 1 TO 12
80    READ A$(W)
90 NEXT W
100 DATA "10","11","12","13","14","15"
110 DATA "16","17","18","19","20","21"
120 PRINT "RANDOM CODENUMBERS ARE:"
130 FOR W = 1 TO N
140    LET R(W)=INT(12*RND(B)+1)
150    PRINT A$(R(W));" ";
160    LET A$(W)=A$(R(W))
170    LET L$(W)=A$(W)
180 NEXT W
190 PRINT
200 PRINT "ARE ALL THE CODENUMBERS DIFFERENT(YES OR NO)";
```

```
210 INPUT Y$
220 IF Y$="NO" THEN 130
230 PRINT "CODENUMBER","PLAINTEXT WORD"
240 FOR W=1 TO N
250      FOR  I=1 TO N
260      IF W=I THEN 330
270         FOR J=1 TO N
280             IF W=J THEN 320
290             IF I=J THEN 320
300                READ P$
310                PRINT L$(W);L$(I);L$(J),P$
320         NEXT J
330      NEXT I
340 NEXT W
350 DATA FREEDOM,LAND,LET
360 DATA RING,THE,THROUGHOUT
370 END

RUN

HOW MANY NUMBERS DO YOU WISH TO USE ?3
RANDOM CODENUMBERS ARE:
10 12 20
ARE ALL THE CODENUMBERS DIFFERENT(YES OR NO) ?YES
CODENUMBER     PLAINTEXT WORD
101220         FREEDOM
102012         LAND
121020         LET
122010         RING
201012         THE
201210         THROUGHOUT
```

13. A code dictionary does not have to be physically present. It can be stored in the computer as a file or recorded (for instance, on magnetic tape).

14. The program in Fig. 2-13 contains Line 110, which outputs the results to a file named CDBOOK. This output is not printed to the terminal and can only be seen if a listing of the file is obtained. The program in Fig. 2-4 uses Lines 105 and 115 to output to the terminal a copy of the dictionary each time the program is run.

15. A computer code system needs an encoding program, a decoding program, and a code book program.

16. Leftover output or discarded materials often contain valuable information about the system and should be destroyed.

Chapter 3

1. Code systems transform plaintext *words* as a whole unit. Cipher systems transform *each character* of the plaintext.

2. (a) THE ENEMY HAS LANDED ON THE COAST
   (b) ATTACK ATTACK ATTACK

3. DO NOT ACCEPT ANYTHING LESS THAN THREE MILLION DOLLARS DRIVE A HARD BARGAIN

4. Six patterns can be formed: 2×12, 3×8, 4×6, 6×4, 8×3, 12×2

5.
```
W  E  W  I  L  L
N  O  T  A  C  C
E  P  T  L  A  T
E  S  T  O  F  F
E  R  S  S  T  O
P  T  A  L  K  S
```

6. (a) W W L N T C E T A E T F E S T P A K
   (b) E I L O A C P L T S O F R S O T L S

```
10 REM PROGRAM TO DO A TRANSPOSITION CIPHER
15 DIM L$(36)
20 PRINT "ORIGINAL MESSAGE IS:"
25 FOR I= 1 TO 36
30      READ L$(I)
35      PRINT L$(I);
40 NEXT I
45 PRINT
50 PRINT
55 PRINT"TRANSPOSED CIPHER MESSAGE IS:"
58 FOR J= 0 TO 1
60      FOR I= 1 TO 36 STEP 2
65          PRINT L$(I+J);
70      NEXT I
75      PRINT
80 NEXT J
85 DATA W,E,W,I,L,L,N,O,T,A,C,C,E,P,T
95 DATA L,A,T,E,S,T,O,F,F,E,R,S,S,T,O,P
98 DATA T,A,L,K,S
100 END

RUN

ORIGINAL MESSAGE IS:
WEWILLNOTACCEPTLATESTOFFERSSTOPTALKS

TRANSPOSED CIPHER MESSAGE IS:
WWLNTCETAETFESTPAK
EILOACPLTSOFRSOTLS
```

7. The ciphertext follows a vertical route with the message reversed.
8. (a) Vertical route, reversed.
   (b) Horizontal route, reversed.
   (c) Diagonal route.
   (d) Counterclockwise route.
9. A total of 720 transpositions are possible: $6 \times 5 \times 4 \times 3 \times 2 \times 1$
10. The key indicates the rectangle has six columns. Write the ciphertext as a six-column rectangle:

```
I  S  M  L  E  F
V  H  A  L  N  I
E  I  R  A  T  F
O  P  C  R  W  T
N  M  H  R  I  H
```

The key 728429 equals a transposition of columns 415326; when shifted back to 123456, the plaintext appears as

SHIPMENT WILL ARRIVE ON MARCH FIFTH

11. The key word BINARY becomes the columns 234156. Rearranging the ciphertext in six columns gives us the following:

$$
\begin{array}{llllll}
E & L I & S & MF \\
N & L V & H & A I \\
T & AE I & P & F \\
W & ROP & C & T \\
I & RNM & H & H
\end{array}
$$

When rewritten into column positions 123456, the plaintext is the same as that for question 10.

12. No solution provided.
13. No solution provided.
14. Ciphertext: USOFT IHFOO PIJUN MPURT EELTH NQYHE
15. Key word CANNONS and sequence ACNNNOS = 1234567 give

$$2\ 1\ 3\ 4\ 6\ 5\ 7 \text{ as column positions}$$

$$
\begin{array}{lllllll}
I & TRTEBS \\
MC I & I SYY \\
P & ONOECS \\
O & MF NCI & T \\
R & P OCUP & E \\
T & URARHM \\
A & TMNEES \\
N & E ABDRX
\end{array}
$$

In groups of four characters the ciphertext is

I TRT EBSM CIIS YYPO NOEC SOMF NCI T
RPOC UPET URAR HMAT MNEE SNE A BDRX

16. Revisions: 40   PRINT "MONTH", "NUMBER KEY"
           50   FOR M = 1 TO 12
           60   PRINT M,
         170   NEXT M

```
10 RANDOMIZE
20 PRINT "HOW MANY DIGITS IN THE KEY";
30 INPUT L
40 PRINT "MONTH","NUMBER KEY"
50 FOR M= 1 TO 12
60     PRINT M,
70     FOR I= 0 TO 9
80         LET A(I) = I
90     NEXT I
100    FOR N= 1 TO L
```

```
110              LET R= INT(10*RND(X))
120              IF A(R) = -999 THEN 110
130                 PRINT A(R);
140                 LET A(R)=-999
150      NEXT N
160      PRINT
170 NEXT M
180 END

RUN

HOW MANY DIGITS IN THE KEY ?4
MONTH               NUMBER KEY
1                   6  5  0  4
2                   1  6  4  9
3                   7  8  9  4
4                   9  2  8  1
5                   7  2  5  8
6                   1  8  7  9
7                   0  7  6  5
8                   7  6  9  0
9                   0  5  3  9
10                  1  6  8  5
11                  8  3  4  5
12                  7  5  2  6
```

Chapter 4

1. *Substitution cipher* systems involve the replacement or substitution of each character in the plaintext by some other character. *Transposition cipher* systems involve changes in the normal pattern of the plaintext characters.

2. Plaintext is THINK SECURITY AT ALL TIMES

3. (a) Plaintext is E PLURIBUS UNUM. This Latin phrase is on most U.S. coins; it is the motto of the United States: "Out of many, one."
   (b) Plaintext is SECURITY DEPENDS ON PEOPLE NOT COM-PUTERS.

4. 69 78 67 82 89 80 84 73 79 78

5. Plaintext is ENCIPHER SENSITIVE INFORMATION.

6. No solution provided.

7. The ASCII value 32 represents the space that occurs between words in the plaintext.

8. Plaintext is KEEPFIGHTINGHELPISONTHEWAY. Reciprocal ciphertext is PVVKURTSGRMTSVOKRHLMGSVDZB.

9. Plaintext is I BELIEVE IN DEMOCRACY BECAUSE IT RELEASES THE ENERGIES OF EVERY HUMAN BEING [a statement of Woodrow Wilson (1856–1924), 28th President of the United States].

10. (a) K = 8. The message to be enciphered is ADVANCEATDAWN. The Caesar ciphertext is ILDIVKMIBLIEV.
    (b) K = 27. The message to be enciphered is ADVANCEATDAWN. The Caesar ciphertext is BEWBODFBUEBXO.

11. Such a key as K = 30 will work since the Caesar cipher has a cycle from 1

to 26, and the real key is taken as K − 26 or 4 in this case. See the answer to question 10 (B) or run the program in Fig. 4-12 with K = 30.

12. (a) The plaintext is BEGIN OPERATION BARBAROSSA JUNE TWENTY TWO. Operation Barbarossa was the code name for the June 22, 1941 attack on the Soviet Union by Nazi Germany in World War II.

(b) The plaintext is START OPERATION OVERLORD JUNE SIXTH. Operation Overlord was the code name for the Allied invasion of Europe on D-Day, June 6, 1944.

13.
```
10 REM CAESAR CIPHER ENCRYPTION-DECRYPTION PROGRAM
20 DIM B(100),C(100)
30 LET C$(1)=P$(2)="CIPHERTEXT"
40 LET P$(1)=C$(2)="PLAINTEXT"
50 PRINT "WHAT IS YOUR KEY";
60 INPUT K
70 PRINT"WHAT IS YOUR MESSAGE";
80 INPUT A$
90 PRINT "TYPE'1' TO ENCIPHER, OR '2' TO DECIPHER"
100 PRINT "1 OR 2";
110 INPUT X
120 IF X=1 THEN 140
130    LET K= 26-K
140 PRINT P$(X)
150 PRINT A$
160 CHANGE A$ TO B
170 FOR I= 1 TO B(0)
180    IF B(I) > 90-K THEN 210
190            LET C(I) = B(I)+K
200            GO TO 220
210    LET C(I) = (B(I)+K-90) + 64
220 NEXT I
230 PRINT
240 LET C(0)=B(0)
250 CHANGE C TO E$
260 PRINT C$(X)
270 PRINT E$
280 END

RUN

WHAT IS YOUR KEY ?3
WHAT IS YOUR MESSAGE ?SECUREALLIMPORTANTMESSAGES
TYPE'1' TO ENCIPHER, OR '2' TO DECIPHER
1 OR 2 ?1
PLAINTEXT
SECUREALLIMPORTANTMESSAGES

CIPHERTEXT
VHFXUHDOOLPSRUWDQWPHVVDJHV


RUN

WHAT IS YOUR KEY ?3
WHAT IS YOUR MESSAGE ?VHFXUHDOOLPSRUWDQWPHVVDJHV
TYPE'1' TO ENCIPHER, OR '2' TO DECIPHER
1 OR 2 ?2
CIPHERTEXT
```

```
VHFXUHDOOLPSRUWDQWPHVVDJHV
```

```
PLAINTEXT
SECUREALLIMPORTANTMESSAGES
```

14. When spaces between words in the plaintext are converted to ASCII values, they have the value 32 assigned to them. If K = 3, as in Fig. 4-15, the Caesar cipher value for 32 becomes 35 (32 + 3). When 35 is changed back from ASCII, it becomes the character #. Thus with a key of K = 3, the plaintext space becomes a # character when ASCII code is used.

15. The character : results from the deciphering of the character #, which has an ASCII value of 35. In Fig. 4-15 the program sets K = 26−K, and with K = 3 Line 50 sets K = 26−3 = 23. When # is deciphered as a result of Line 130, C(I) = 35+23 = 58. If you look up 58 in the ASCII characters in Fig. 4-7, you will find it is the character :.

16. A *decimated alphabet* is preferred to a *Caesar alphabet* because decimation provides an alphabet without a specific sequence and shift, giving greater security than the Caesar alphabet.

17. The resulting decimated cipher alphabet for K = 29 is the same as for K = 3 found in the text.

18. (a) The ciphertext is RYYTETFSOYWREOVSWRVWVECY.
    (b) The plaintext is FOLLOW PLAN B RAISE THE BID.

19. The ciphertext is OXENVSKEXCIXCEVORQYSJVSOJI.

20.
S	P	T	T	T	Y	C	P	O
P	R	E	D	A	E	R	T	N
Y	O	C	A	B	N	Y	I	

S	H	L	L	L	Q	U	H	G
P	G	T	S	P	T	G	I	D
Y	M	A	Y	Z	L	W	G	

The ciphertext is HGMLTA   LSYLPZ   QTLUGW   HIGGD.

21.
B	Q	M	M	S	I	H	U	U	B	O	M	F	B	B	U	F
E	V	E	M	X	V	L	E	L	R	X	P	M	F	R	L	S
L	Z	T	M	J	Z	Z	W	P	O	Z	E	Y	T	E	P	Q
L	N	X	P	E	F	F	W	W	F	L	S	S	E	D	C	

B	P	L	L	R	H	G	T	T	A	N	L	E	A	A	T	E
E	R	A	I	T	R	H	A	H	N	T	L	I	B	N	H	O
L	O	I	B	Y	O	O	L	E	D	O	T	N	I	T	E	F
L	C	M	E	T	U	U	L	L	U	A	H	H	T	S	R	

The plaintext is   PROCLAIM   LIBERTY   THROUGHOUT   ALL THE   LAND   UNTO   ALL   THE   INHABITANTS   THEREOF [inscription on the Liberty Bell taken from the Old Testament, *Leviticus* 25:20].

22. The plaintext is CARRY OUT PLAN B WEDNESDAY. Your key word is END RUN AROUND THE BLOCK. The Vigenère table ciphertext is GNUISBUKDFNQUDIEYSUNEL.

23. (a) $_{26}P_4 = 26 \times 25 \times 24 \times 23 = 388,360$ keys

    (b) $_{26}P_5 = 26 \times 25 \times 24 \times 23 \times 22 = 7,893,600$ keys

24. The Vigenère table decryption program is shown here. Line 135 was added to Fig. 4-22 and Lines 50 and 60 were revised. The ciphertext is found in Line 40.

```
10 REM PROGRAM FOR VIGENERE TABLE DECRYPTION
20 DIM B(100),C(100),K(100)
30 READ A$
40 DATA GNUVLRYGSPNQFJHHAHWQDC
50 PRINT "CIPHERTEXT IS:"
60 PRINT A$
70 CHANGE A$ TO B
80 PRINT "YOUR KEYWORD IS";
90 INPUT K$
100 CHANGE K$ TO K
110 LET J=0
120 FOR I= 1 TO B(0)
130     GO SUB 250
135 LET K=26-K
140     IF B(I) > 90-K THEN 170
150         LET C(I) = B(I)+K
160           GO TO 180
170     LET C(I) = (B(I)+K-90) + 64
180 NEXT I
190 PRINT
200 LET C(0)=B(0)
210 CHANGE C TO E$
220 PRINT "PLAINTEXT IS:"
230 PRINT E$
240 STOP
250     LET J=J+1
260     IF J>K(0) THEN 290
270     LET K=K(J)-65
280     RETURN
290         LET J=1
300         LET K=K(J)-65
310         RETURN
320 END

RUN

CIPHERTEXT IS:
GNUVLRYGSPNQFJHHAHWQDC
YOUR KEYWORD IS ?END

PLAINTEXT IS:
CARRYOUTPLANBWEDNESDAY
```

25.
```
10 REM DECIMATED POLYALPHABETIC ENCRYPTION PROGRAM
20 DIM A(30),C(30),X(30)
30 PRINT "PICK A 3 DIGIT KEY FROM THESE VALUES:"
40 PRINT 1;3;5;7;9;11
50 PRINT"WHAT IS YOUR KEY";
60 INPUT K(1),K(2),K(3)
```

```
70 READ A$
80 DATA CLEARMESSAGE
90 PRINT "PLAINTEXT IS:"
100 PRINT A$
110 CHANGE A$ TO X
120 LET J=0
130 FOR I= 1 TO X(0)
140     GO SUB 260
150         LET A(I) =X(I)-64
160         LET B1 = (K*A(I))/26.1
170         LET B=INT(B1)
180         LET C(0) =26
190         LET C(I) =(K*A(I) - B*26) +64
200 NEXT I
210 PRINT
220 CHANGE C TO C$
230 PRINT "CIPHERTEXT IS:"
240 PRINT C$
250 STOP
260     LET J=J+1
270     IF J>3 THEN 300
280     LET K=K(J)
290     RETURN
300         LET J=1
310         LET K=K(J)
320         RETURN
330 END

RUN

PICK A 3 DIGIT KEY FROM THESE VALUES:
   1   3   5   7   9   11
WHAT IS YOUR KEY ?1,3,5
PLAINTEXT IS:
CLEARMESSAGE

CIPHERTEXT IS:
CJYABMEEQAUY
```

26.
```
10 DIM B(25),C(2),F(5,5),P(2)
15 READ A$
20 REM READ IN ALPHABET AND CHANGE TO ASCII VALUES
25 DATA ABCDEFGHIJKLMNOPQRSTUVWXY
30 CHANGE A$ TO B
35 REM SET UP A PLAYFAIR TABLE USING ASCII VALUES
40 LET C=0
45 FOR I=1 TO 5
50     FOR J= 1 TO 5
55         LET C=C+1
60         LET F(I,J)=B(C)
65     NEXT J
70 NEXT I
75 PRINT"PLAYFAIR CIPHER: ";
80 REM READ PLAINTEXT IN LINE 90 TWO CHARACTERS AT A TIME
85 READ P$
90 DATA PL,AY,FA,IR
95 IF P$= "END" THEN 330
100 DATA "END"
105 CHANGE P$ TO P
110 REM MATCH EACH CHARACTER IN PLAYFAIR TABLE
115 FOR M=1 TO 2
120     FOR I= 1 TO 5
```

```
125           FOR J= 1 TO 5
130               IF P(M)=F(I,J) THEN 145
135           NEXT J
140       NEXT I
145       LET I(M)=I
150       LET J(M)=J
155 NEXT M
160 REM TEST IF ROWS
165 IF I(1)=I(2) THEN 210
170 REM TEST IF COLUMNS
175 IF J(1)=J(2) THEN 260
180 REM THE DIAGONALS
185       LET X=J(2)
190       LET J(2)=J(1)
195       LET J(1)=X
200 GOTO 300
205 REM THE ROWS
210       IF J(1)=5 THEN 225
215       LET J(1)=J(1)+1
220 GOTO 230
225       LET J(1)=1
230       IF J(2)=5 THEN 245
235       LET J(2)=J(2)+1
240 GOTO 300
245       LET J(2)=1
250 GOTO 300
255 REM THE COLUMNS
260       IF I(1)=5 THEN 275
265       LET I(1)=I(1)+1
270 GOTO 280
275       LET I(1)=1
280       IF I(2)=5 THEN 295
285       LET I(2)=I(2)+1
290 GOTO 300
295       LET I(2)=1
297 REM CHANGE ASCII CIPHER VALUE TO STRING CHARACTER
300       LET C(0)=2
305       LET C(1)=F(I(1),J(1))
310       LET C(2)=F(I(2),J(2))
315       CHANGE C TO M$
320       PRINT M$;
325 GOTO 85
330 END

RUN

PLAYFAIR CIPHER: QKEUKFHS
```

27. (a) The Playfair cipher is QKEUKFHS.
    (b) The Playfair cipher is TDSIJCKQTNKO.
    (c) The Playfair cipher is EAKBXEATCPPYTC.
28. (a) ARRIVE NOON
    (b) DEPART AT ONCE
    (c) CODES CIPHERS AND COMPUTERS
29. (a) PLAYFAIR
    (b) USE CODES
    (c) SECURE DATA
    (d) DO YOU NEED MONEY

Chapter 5

1. Ciphertext: G Y A Y W   R A T P B   P U D P B
    Key: 8 2 9 4 1   8 2 9 4 2   8 2 9 4 2
    Plaintext: S E C U R   E V I T A   L D A T A

2.

23	E	A	I	E	E	E	B		N	K	Z	N	N	N	*	$
5	T	L	L	I	P	O	E		S	Q	Q	F	V	5	R	
11	E	V	A	S	R	F	R		V	X	2	I	F	+	F	
33	R	I	N	T	I	L	T		2	D	S	C	D	J	C	
1	N	G	C	H	C	I	Y		S	L	A	K	A	−	Q	

   Ciphertext: NSV2S   KQXDL   ZQ2SA   NFICK
                NVFDA   N5+J−   *RFCQ $

3. (a)

T	W	L	A	O	M	C	T	.		Q	W	?	I	.	O	U	4
E	I	L	V	N	A	H	2	M		F	Q	T	W	N	$	K	2
N	L	E	E	5	R	A	P	.		2	3	3	R	I	5	J	C

    The ciphertext is QF2WQ3   ?T3IWR   .NIO$5   UKJ42C
   (b) The plaintext is INVASION BEGINS 0800 JUNE 6

4.

```
RUN
WHAT IS YOUR PLAINTEXT:
  ?ETERNALVIGILANCEISTHEPRICEOFLIBERTY
WHAT IS YOUR KEY CONSTANT ?10

PLAINTEXT IS:
ETERNALVIGILANCEISTHEPRICEOFLIBERTY
CIPHERTEXT IS:
79   74   690  8.2  88   55   760  8.6  83   61   730  7.6  75   68   670
6.9  83   73   840  7.2  79   70   820  7.3  77   59   790  7    86   63   660
6.9  92   74   890  0
```

5.

```
RUN

WHAT IS THE KEY:A,B  ?15,−2

PLAINTEXT IS:
CHANGEKEYSTODAY

CIPHERTEXT IS:
−119 −129 −115 −141 −127 −123 −135 −123 −163 −151 −153 −143 −121 −115
−163
```

6. To decipher, use the transformation function $X(I) = ASCII$ value $= (N + 150 - I)/2$. The values derived yield the plaintext CHANGE KEYS TODAY.

7.
```
10 REM NON-LINEAR EXPRESSION ENCIPHERING PROGRAM
20 DIM X(100)
30 READ A$
40 DATA CHANGEKEYSTODAY
50 PRINT"WHAT IS THE KEY:A,B";
60 INPUT A,B
70 PRINT
80 PRINT "PLAINTEXT IS:"
90 PRINT A$
100 CHANGE A$ TO X
110 PRINT
120 PRINT "CIPHERTEXT IS:"
130 FOR I = 1 TO X(0)
140     LET N= A+B*(X(I)^2)
150     PRINT N;
160 NEXT I
170 END

RUN

WHAT IS THE KEY:A,B ?-15,2

PLAINTEXT IS:
CHANGEKEYSTODAY

CIPHERTEXT IS:
 8963   10353   8435   12153   10067   9507   11235   9507   15827   13763
 14097  12467   9233   8435   15827
```

8.
```
10 REM DECRYPTION PROGRAM FOR NON-LINEAR EXPRESSION
20 DIM B(100),X(100)
30 PRINT "WHAT IS THE KEY: A,B";
40 INPUT A,B
50 PRINT "CIPHERTEXT IS:"
60 FOR I= 1 TO 100
70     READ N
80     IF N=-999.99 THEN 150
90     PRINT N;
100    LET X(I)=INT(((N-A)/B)^.5 +.05)
110 NEXT I
120 DATA 8963,10353,8435,12153,10067,9507,11235,9507
130 DATA 15827,13763,14097,12467,9233,8435,15827
140 DATA -999.99
150 LET X(0)=I
160 PRINT
170 PRINT
180 PRINT "PLAINTEXT IS:"
190 CHANGE X TO A$
200 PRINT A$
210 END

RUN

WHAT IS THE KEY: A,B ?-15,2
CIPHERTEXT IS:
 8963   10353   8435   12153   10067   9507   11235   9507   15827   13763
 14097  12467   9233   8435   15827

PLAINTEXT IS:
CHANGEKEYSTODAY
```

9. The *one-time system* uses a different key each time a message is sent. Ciphertexts based on such a system cannot be broken and provide a high level of security.

10. The basic idea of the Vernam system is to add another *pulse* or value to each plaintext character to develop a ciphertext.

11. The following programs use the idea of a Vernam system: Figs. 6, 8, 10, 11, 14, and 16.

12. (a) DATA SECURITY

(b)
$$C = \begin{pmatrix} 34 & 32.5 & 42 & 32.5 \\ 41.5 & 34.5 & 33.5 & 42.5 \\ 41 & 36.5 & 42 & 44.5 \end{pmatrix}$$

(c)
$$C = \begin{matrix} 68 & 83 & 82 \\ 65 & 69 & 73 \\ 84 & 67 & 84 \\ 65 & 85 & 89 \end{matrix}$$

13.
```
10 REM ALGEBRAIC EXPRESSION ENCIPHERING PROGRAM
20 DIM X(100)
30 READ A$
40 DATA CHANGEKEYSTODAY
50 PRINT"WHAT IS THE KEY:A,B";
60 INPUT A,B
70 PRINT
80 PRINT "PLAINTEXT IS:"
90 PRINT A$
100 CHANGE A$ TO X
110 PRINT
120 PRINT "CIPHERTEXT IS:"
130 FOR I = 1 TO X(0)
140     LET N=A+B*X-INT(300*RND(X))
150         PRINT N;
160 NEXT I
170 END

RUN

WHAT IS THE KEY:A,B ?-20,5

PLAINTEXT IS:
CHANGEKEYSTODAY

CIPHERTEXT IS:
-169 -178 -221 -101 -200 -67 -177 -241 -228 -181 -311 -314 -67 -52
-90
```

14.
```
10 REM ASCII FILE DECRYPTION PROGRAM
20 LET C=0
25     LET B(0)=2
30     INPUT:CTF:B(1)
50         CHANGE B TO A$
60         PRINT A$;" ";
70         LET C=C+1
80     IF C<>31 THEN 30
```

```
90      PRINT
95      PRINT
100 GO TO 20
110 END
```

15. The program in Fig. 5-20 scrambles by using a random number function. Keys based on numbers and words have been used before. With a random number function, the key is the function and the "seed" or argument placed in it. For example, in RND(X), X is the "seed" or argument serving as a key.

16. Yes. A program can be treated as a file and scrambled by another program.

17.

```
E  PVCCITAMA  I  UESNIRMRROOIAL  EPRYNF  ELG    0(D  0IM)B1    :OOFPNC0T:E100
OO  O  F1T  R1=L  EEBLYEEFTLC  L  IINEAM  RR  I  LN  EERN      :PFUI:NPTAT$
DOIGLEP  REAESFH  N  O  VMC  ECATTA  SIUC    B  H$  EOATAN  GC  FB  T  O10=R  O(I)
P:TIB:I)RN(;CTF              EITNX           L  XNET              CELF:S:CTO
NED
```

Chapter 6

1. *Cryptanalysis* is the science of deciphering ciphertexts (through analysis and deduction) without the knowledge of the keys or methods used in the encryption process.

2. No solution provided.

3. From Fig. 6-2 the most frequent ten letters from left to right are:

   E   T   A   O   H   R   N   I   D   S

   Each has a relative frequency of 6 percent or more. This compares with the top ten letters from Fig. 6-1:

   E   T   N   R   O   A   I   S   H   D

   Although the frequencies do not exactly coincide, Lincoln's Gettyburg Address is fairly close to the letter frequency of Fig. 6-1.

4. The ciphertext is based on a Caesar cipher of key, K = 1.

5. The ciphertext is based on a reversed alphabet.

6. The frequency analysis of a polyalphabetic ciphertext produces results that do not conform with Fig. 6-1. The distribution of letters shows little if any concentration of a specific letter. In a single alphabet some of the letters would show a zero frequency. This is not the case with a polyalphabetic substitution. Note the letter frequencies in Fig. 6-7.

7.

```
CIPHERTEXT IS: ESTYVDJDEFXDFNFCTEJ

PLAINTEXT IS FOUND DOWN ONE COLUMN:

E: FGHIJKLMNOPQRSTUVWXYZABCD
```

```
S: TUVWXYZABCDEFGHIJKLMNOPQR
T: UVWXYZABCDEFGHIJKLMNOPQRS
Y: ZABCDEFGHIJKLMNOPQRSTUVWX
V: WXYZABCDEFGHIJKLMNOPQRSTU
D: EFGHIJKLMNOPQRSTUVWXYZABC
J: KLMNOPQRSTUVWXYZABCDEFGHI
D: EFGHIJKLMNOPQRSTUVWXYZABC
E: FGHIJKLMNOPQRSTUVWXYZABCD
P: QRSTUVWXYZABCDEFGHIJKLMNO
X: YZABCDEFGHIJKLMNOPQRSTUVW
D: EFGHIJKLMNOPQRSTUVWXYZABC
P: QRSTUVWXYZABCDEFGHIJKLMNO
N: OPQRSTUVWXYZABCDEFGHIJKLM
F: GHIJKLMNOPQRSTUVWXYZABCDE
C: DEFGHIJKLMNOPQRSTUVWXYZAB
T: UVWXYZABCDEFGHIJKLMNOPQRS
E: FGHIJKLMNOPQRSTUVWXYZABCD
J: KLMNOPQRSTUVWXYZABCDEFGHI
```

Chapter 7

1. *Data security* implies the protection of data and information so that it is not intentionally or accidentally modified, destroyed, disclosed, or compromised.
2. (a) *Communications security* involves protection against threats to electronic communications. Such threats include message interception and passive and active wiretapping.
   (b) *File security* involves protection against threats to data and information contained in storage media. Such threats include loss of material by accident or by theft.
3. The purpose of the DES is to provide cryptographic protection for computer data transmitted and stored in computer systems.
4. A *compound* cipher system uses both transposition and substitution operations for data encryption.

5.
```
            1  1  1
    7      A. 0  1  1  1      B.    0  1  1  1
  ⊕ 5         0  1  0  1        ⊕ 0  1  0  1
   12         1  1  0  0          0  0  1  0
```

6. (a) M 1 0 1 0 1 1 1   (b) C 0 0 1 0 0 1 1
     ⊕ K 1 0 0 0 1 0 0   ⊕ K 1 0 0 0 1 0 0
     = C 0 0 1 0 0 1 1   = M 1 0 1 0 1 1 1

7. 1 2 3 4 5 6 7 8
   S E C U R I T Y
   3 5 6 1 2 8 7 4
   C R I S E Y T U

8. A *product* cipher system or product transformation produces a ciphertext by making use of both transposition and substitution operations. It is also known as a compound cipher system.

9. (a) A P-box or permutation box provides the route for a transposition of characters.

(b) An S-box or substitution box provides replacement characters for message characters.

10. By *nonlinear* we mean that it is possible for a different number of 1's to result in a binary ciphertext than began with the binary plaintext. In the text example A, AB → 1 0 0 0   0 0 1   1   0 0 0   0   0 1 0 starts with four 1's; the ciphertext iA is 1   1 0 1   0 0 1   1   0 0 0   0 0 1, with six 1's.

11. The plaintext is ABLE. The ciphertext is 9i9M.

12. Three permutation tables and eight substitution tables.

13. See text for solution.

Chapter 8

1.

DES	*PKC*
Commercially available	Not commercially available
One key	Two keys
Key is secret	One key secret, the other "public"
Algorithm known to all	Algorithm a secret
No "signature"	Has a "signature" capability

2. 37, 41, 43, 47, 53

3. 71, 101, 313

4. (a) 2   (b) 3   (c) 4   (d) 6   (e) 17

5. (a) 1   (b) 7   (c) 32   (d) $32 \div 26 = 1, a = 6$

6.

```
10 READ N
20     DATA 57,71,101,313,903
30     FOR I= 2 TO N-1
40         LET X= N/I
50             IF N= INT(X)*I THEN 90
60         NEXT I
70         PRINT N;"IS PRIME"
80 GOTO 10
90     PRINT N;"IS NOT PRIME"
100 GOTO 10
190 END

RUN

57 IS NOT PRIME
71 IS PRIME
101 IS PRIME
313 IS PRIME
903 IS NOT PRIME

OUT OF DATA- LN # 10
```

7.

```
10 REM FINDING A= B(MOD M)
15 PRINT "B","M","A"
20 FOR D= 1 TO 4
25     READ B,M
30     DATA 12,11,87,10,8192,51,32,26
35     LET C1=INT(B/M)
40     LET A=B-C1*M
50     PRINT B,M,A
60 NEXT D
90 END

RUN
```

B	M	A
12	11	1
87	10	7
8192	51	32
32	26	6

8. Use $C = K \times a$ (mod 26) in each case. When remainder is 0, set $C = 26$.

9. (a) $d = 27$ (b) $d = 7$ (c) $d = 3$ (d) $d = 157$

10. The ciphertext using $C_i = M_i^5$ (mod 51) is

$$1,32,14 \qquad\qquad 4,14,1,4$$

11. Decipher using $M_i = C_i^{13}$ (mod 51). The plaintext is

$$M_i = 4,1,5,1 \qquad \text{or} \qquad \text{DATA}$$

12. The ciphertext using $C_i = M_i^3$ (mod 55) is

$$8,14,9 \qquad\qquad 17,14,13,17$$

13. Decipher using $M_i = C_i^5$ (mod 51). The plaintext is

$$M_i = 4,5,1,4 \qquad 5,14,4 \qquad \text{or} \qquad \text{DEAD} \quad \text{END}$$

14. $S_1 = 5^7$ (mod 39) = 8
$S_2 = 4^7$ (mod 39) = 4
$S = 8^5$ (mod 21) = 8
$S = 4^5$ (mod 21) = 16
Signature for ED is 8,16

15. $S_i = S^d$ modulo n
17^5 modulo 21 = 5 1^5 modulo 21 = 1
$M_i = S_i^e$ modulo n
5^5 modulo 51 = 14 1^5 modulo 51 = 1
14,1 = N,A

Chapter 9

1. (a) *Private application* is a cryptographic operation independent of the system.

(b) *System application* implies that cryptographic operations are all or in part under system control.

2. (a) *Link cryptography,* or link-by-link encryption, is typically used in electronic communications. It involves protection of data transmitted between two directly communicating nodes or devices.

(b) In *session cryptography,* or end-to-end encryption, the data is encrypted at a source. It remains unintelligible until it is reversed at the final destination. The system controls the session and key as well as the encryption devices at each end of a communication system.

(c) *Personal-key cryptography* involves cryptographic operations by an individual using an exclusive or personal key.

3. *Key security* is an important aspect of a cryptographic security system. The keys ensure that protected data will not be lost or compromised. Key security involves such activities as *key generation, key management,* and *key distribution.*

4.
```
 5      RANDOMIZE
10      FOR  I  =  1  TO  64
15      PRINT  INT(2*RND(0));
20      NEXT  I
30      END
```

5. The key distribution problem concerns the secure distribution of keys to outlying locations. A master key approach may be a solution to the problem.

6. What happens to encrypted data if the key is lost? In many situations a lost key can result in lost data. Backup keys are suggested.

Index